Code of the Suburb

FIELDWORK ENCOUNTERS AND DISCOVERIES

A series edited by Robert Emerson and Jack Katz

Code of the Suburb

Inside the World of Young Middle-Class Drug Dealers

SCOTT JACQUES
AND RICHARD WRIGHT

The University of Chicago Press
Chicago and London

Scott Jacques is assistant professor of criminal justice and criminology in the
Andrew Young School of Policy Studies at Georgia State University. **Richard
Wright** is professor in and chair of the Department of Criminal Justice at
Georgia State University and the author of five books.

The University of Chicago Press, Chicago 60637
The University of Chicago Press, Ltd., London
© 2015 by The University of Chicago
All rights reserved. Published 2015.
Printed in the United States of America

24 23 22 21 20 19 18 17 16 15   1 2 3 4 5

ISBN-13: 978-0-226-16408-3 (cloth)
ISBN-13: 978-0-226-16411-3 (paper)
ISBN-13: 978-0-226-16425-0 (e-book)
DOI: 10.7208/chicago/9780226164250.001.0001

Library of Congress Cataloging-in-Publication Data

Jacques, Scott (Scott Thomas), author.
    Code of the suburb : inside the world of young middle-class drug
  dealers / Scott Jacques and Richard Wright
        pages   cm
    Includes bibliographical references and index.
    ISBN 978-0-226-16408-3 (cloth : alkaline paper)
    ISBN 978-0-226-16411-3 (paperback : alkaline paper)
    ISBN 978-0-226-16425-0 (ebook)
    1. Drug dealers—Georgia—Atlanta Suburban Area.   2. Suburban
  crimes—Georgia—Atlanta.   I. Wright, Richard, 1951– author.   II. Title.
HV5833.A79J33 2015
363.4509758'231—dc23
                                                                  2014047608

♾ This paper meets the requirements of ANSI/NISO Z39.48-1992
(Permanence of Paper).

To Mark Cooney and the Department of Criminology and Criminal Justice at the University of Missouri–St. Louis

CONTENTS

ACKNOWLEDGMENTS

Sitting down to thank all those who have helped with this book it suddenly struck us that we should have thought to keep a list. To anyone we leave unmentioned: please forgive us; we owe you a drink. First and foremost, we are indebted to all of the dealers we interviewed, especially those who have continued to serve as a sounding board and who remain friends to this day. Indispensable financial support was provided by Lynn and Tom Jacques, Bill and Gerry Baxter, the University of Georgia's Center for Undergraduate Research Opportunities, and a Graduate School Dissertation Fellowship from the University of Missouri–St. Louis. Thanks to Mary Beth Walker for giving Scott a semester off from teaching, during which this book was completed. Colleagues who lent us an ear and encouraged the project include Frank Cullen, John Eck, Bonnie Fisher, Robbie Jacques, Janet Lauritsen, Marie Lindegaard, Jody Miller, Danielle Reynald, Rick Rosenfeld, Eric Stewart, Volkan Topalli, John Wooldredge, and others at the University of Missouri–St. Louis, the Netherlands Institute for the Study of Crime and Law Enforcement, the University of Cincinnati, and Georgia State University. Student assistants whom we hope to soon call colleagues include Liz Bonomo, Katie Busey, Mark Curtis, Tim Dickinson, Kate Elvey, Charles Hogan, Nicole Lasky, Leslie Lawson, Julia Mesler, and Clay Sabourin. Enough cannot be said about our acquiring editor, Doug Mitchell; series editors, Jack Katz and Robert Emerson; copy editor, Pam Bruton; editorial associate, Tim McGovern; promotions director, Levi Stahl; and the anonymous reviewers—we owe all of them a drink too. Last, but far from least, we thank Mark Cooney, who inspired and encouraged the research on which this book is based, and Andrea Allen Jacques, who critiqued drafts of the manuscript and provided moral support.

Studying Suburban Drug Dealers

This book explores the world of young, middle-class, suburban drug dealers as seen through the eyes of a group of dealers themselves. What leads
these adolescents to start selling? How do they conduct business? What
problems do they face? How do they handle those problems? Why do they
quit?

The dealers on which this book is based grew up in the commuter zone
of Atlanta, Georgia.[1] Most are from a town about thirty miles from the city's
center, although by car it could take an hour or more to get there, thanks
to the city's congested freeways.[2] This town, which we will call Peachville,
epitomizes what many Americans think of as the "suburbs": subdivision
after subdivision interspersed with a few shopping centers offering chain
retail outlets and restaurants. There is not much to see; everything—the
people, the stores—looks pretty much the same, no matter where you go.[3]
The place is "authentic" in its own way, but it is not heterogeneous.

Here, the inhabitants like to say that "everybody's somebody." That
might be because the citizenry and local government effectively have made
it impossible for "nobodies" to live there. Zoning regulations forbid apartment buildings and multifamily dwellings. Of the almost twenty thousand
people living in Peachville at the time of the study, 90 percent were White,
90 percent had at least a high school degree, and the median yearly household income was almost $70,000. Looking around, it actually appears to
be even more homogeneous and prosperous than those figures suggest.

The town is orderly and peaceful in a way that some outsiders might
consider boringly conventional. That is exactly how the natives like it. The
most obvious social problems are barking dogs and speeding teenagers.
Few of the adult residents are aware that an underground drug market
flourishes in their midst. That market is driven by their sons and daughters,

who supply both the demand for drugs and the drugs themselves. Peachville is peaceful, but like many suburban locales across the nation, it is not as crime free as it appears on the surface or as police reports suggest.

The accounts presented throughout this book are based on the lives of thirty young suburban drug dealers. The lead author, Scott Jacques, was a member of their peer group prior to becoming a card-carrying social scientist. He grew up in the town next door to Peachville, which we will refer to as Flynton. Flynton is less prosperous and homogeneous than Peachville but still solidly middle class and suburban. In 1999 Scott's family moved so that he and his younger brother could attend school in the Peachville system. From then until Scott graduated from the flagship state university—well known as a so-called party school less than an hour's drive away—he was surrounded by the same cast of characters. Some of these individuals, like Robert, Dave, Bruce, and Pete, among others, were Scott's friends, and he remains in close touch with many of them to this day.[4] In the course of these friendships, Scott had the opportunity to observe what these dealers did, to ask them questions, and to seek to understand their mind-set and behavior.

The initial inspiration for a formal study of young suburban drug dealers arose when Scott was offered an opportunity to do field-based research to earn the college credits he needed to graduate with honors. This opportunity required him to systematize his interest in the drug-dealing activities of his peers by moving beyond friendly interaction and undertaking semi-structured, open-ended, audio-recorded interviews with each of them, looking back on their days in high school. Those interviews, in turn, generated the quoted material that lies at the heart of this book.

The first eighteen drug dealers included in the study were Scott's friends and were formally recruited simply by being asked, "Will you do me the favor of letting me interview you about your drug dealing?" None of these individuals were paid for their cooperation, although a few received gifts of appreciation, such as a six-pack of beer or a batch of his mom's homemade chocolate chip cookies. The other twelve respondents were not Scott's friends but rather friends of his friends and were also from Peachville or, in a few cases, from another suburban, middle-class community such as Flynton. They were recruited with the help of three individuals, two of whom had been interviewed themselves. The first eight of these friends-of-friends were paid $20 for their participation; the last four agreed to take part as a favor and declined to be compensated.

The participants are homogeneous with respect to their demographic characteristics. In part, this absence of demographic variation is by design; to participate in the study, respondents had to be eighteen to twenty-three years of age and to have grown up in a middle-class suburban community. However, the sample also is homogeneous in ways that transcend explicit design and simply reflect the demographic makeup of Peachville's drug market. For example, all but two of the participants are male, and only one, who is mixed race (White and Asian), might be considered non-White. Every one of the dealers had graduated from high school, and almost all of them were in college at the time of the study. They sold mostly marijuana, but many of them sometimes sold other substances too, including ecstasy, cocaine, methamphetamine, LSD, and hallucinogenic mushrooms; none reported selling crack cocaine or heroin. Throughout the book please note that when we refer to "dealers" or other kinds of people, we are speaking only about the participants and the people with whom they interacted. That said, we believe that their experiences have general relevance; we will return to the issue of generalizability in the concluding chapter.

CHAPTER 1

The Pursuit of Coolness

At Peachville High, and other suburban high schools like it, illicit drug use leads to drug selling only in the sense that kissing leads to teen pregnancy. Many middle-class high school students use drugs, but few of them become drug dealers. How and why did the drug dealers make the transition from user to seller?

Coolness and Conventional Status

In time, most of the young suburban drug dealers featured in this book will adopt the lifestyle enjoyed by their parents. Day in and day out, they will wake up, travel to and from work, labor, eat, watch TV, and fall asleep. They will see their colleagues at work, and only there. They will walk or drive by their neighbors, waving hello or goodbye without stopping. They will spend time with their spouses and kids in the evening and on the weekends. Like their parents, they will come to appreciate and enjoy a steady, compartmentalized, isolated "social" existence.[1]

But as teenagers, the dealers' day-to-day lives are far more peer dominated and communal than those of their parents. This is due in large part to the disjuncture between what they perceive as conventional success and their present station. These suburban youth, for all their privilege, lack what they view as the foremost signs of social status: a professional career that generates enough money to buy what they need and want. They know achieving that status will take many years. As a result, their aspirations are bifurcated: the long-term self is concerned with graduating and staying out of trouble so as not to jeopardize their future life prospects; the short-term self is oriented toward obtaining and maintaining a more immediately achievable kind of status—coolness.[2] Many grown-ups could not care less about being cool, as teenagers will no doubt tell you. Adults with a well-paying job do not need to be cool to feel socially valuable or to be treated with respect.

The dealers see coolness as the opposite of lameness. Coolness and lameness derive from two traits: attractiveness and likableness. The first is a feature of physicality; the latter, of personality. Both can be inherited, learned, or purchased.[3] Attractiveness is how pleasant someone is to look at; while it is inherited to a degree, it is bolstered or diminished by things like working out or overeating and dressing well or poorly. Likableness is the extent to which someone's character makes them enjoyable to be around; they may be generous or greedy, fun or boring, interesting or dull, nice or mean, confident or apprehensive, and so on. People are perceived as cool to the extent that they are attractive and likable.

The benefits of coolness and the costs of lameness are both psychological and social. It feels good to be cool, humiliating to be lame. The dealers understood that their coolness, or lack thereof, reflected evaluations of their looks and characters. That weighed heavily on their minds because those appraisals affected how they were treated by peers on a daily basis.[4] Among the dealers and their peers, being seen as cool was the surest and safest path to feeling socially valuable. To be labeled as lame was to be a social failure.

Cool kids were respected, were befriended, and received numerous invitations to "hang out."[5] They were openly complimented by others, greeted with fist bumps or hugs, and asked to partake in recreational activities, including dates. The cooler someone was in others' eyes, the more those things happened to them. They had that "special something" that made people want to be around them and, therefore, treat them well. What these cool kids had—what in fact made them cool, respected, and socially desirable—were good looks, a particularly likable personality, or both.

On the other end of the continuum were the lame-os. They were stigmatized and disrespected: ridiculed and ostracized, forced to hang out with other lame-os or no one at all.[6] Some would eat lunch in the classroom rather than face the fact that no one wanted to talk, or even sit, with them. When cool kids and lame-os interacted, the lame-os often were treated as though they did not exist or, worse, made fun of for being fat, ugly, pimply, poorly dressed, a dork, or any number of other stigmatized traits. In an effort to avoid such treatment, many lame-os surrounded themselves with other individuals like them, creating a peer network of "losers" that—while making them look lamer still—nevertheless provided a support system and sense of self-worth.[7]

These two "social classes"—the cool kids and the lame-os—do not represent an inflexible caste system. Mobility is possible. Someone who was once widely regarded as being lame can become cool, and vice versa. The traits that make someone cool—attractiveness and likability—are not stable. Teenagers' looks and personality can change dramatically as they age. A high school freshman can appear to be a totally different person by his or her senior year, for better or worse. Changes for the better make someone more respected and desirable, while changes for the worse do the opposite.[8]

And of course not every student is regarded as being very cool or very lame. Whereas some people come to widely be seen and admired as good-looking and nice to be around ("upper-class"), and others as unequivocally ugly and annoying ("lower-class"), still others are viewed as falling somewhere between these two extremes. It is probably safe to say that Peachville High was mostly populated by individuals falling into this middle range of coolness.

In order to be perceived as cool, adolescents obviously first must demonstrate that they have the traits that make them so. High school offers them a perfect opportunity to do this; its compulsory nature brings hundreds or thousands of youngsters into close proximity with one another for hours on end, day after day, year after year.[9] Adolescents see and interact with each other in the classroom, hallways, lunchroom, auditorium, stadium, and parking lot. These in-school assessments affect who hangs out together and who is (dis)respected during and outside of school hours. With that said, school is not the only place to gain and lose cool points. There are other staging grounds and activities in which to win respect and make friends.[10]

The Allure of Drug Use

One way dealers and their peers sought to demonstrate coolness was by using and sharing drugs together. Drug use was not cool or lame in and of itself; in other words, there was nothing inherent in consuming a psychoactive substance that increased or decreased the user's status. But when a person used drugs and others got wind of it, the user sent a signal about who they were to their peers.[11] In the dealers' subculture, drug use signaled "I like to have fun" or "I do what I want, not what the law or my parents tell me to do." And sharing those drugs with others proclaimed "I'm generous." One of the dealers we spoke with, Bruce, explained drug use among his peers this way: "They want to be able to go out and do stuff. It's just like, 'Hell yeah man, I just bought this big ol' bag of weed man! Let's go smoke it!' And then whoever they're with—a bunch of their friends—are going to be like, 'Hell yeah dude!' They just go and get so fucking stoned." Doing drugs allowed students to exhibit traits that made them likable and desirable to be around.[12] Once adolescent suburbanites concluded that they would be perceived by their peers as cooler if they used drugs, they had taken the first step toward this deviant career.[13]

Presumably, almost all adolescents want to be cool to compensate for their lack of conventional status. The question of why some youths are drawn to drug use—and later to drug selling—as a way of achieving this while others are not is largely unanswerable at this point. Nor is it known why some students emphasize just one or draw on multiple coolness-generating activities. For instance, some of the sellers also played sports or music in a band, which were widely recognized as cool things to do. Certainly, choices as to how to be cool have to do with personal attributes such as attraction to and tolerance for risk and with social factors such as peer friendship networks. Suffice it to say, however, that a large body of research suggests that drugs and drug use are widely popular in US high schools, so it is only to be expected that some students will be drawn to supplying the demand for them.[14]

Whatever set it in motion, the suburban adolescents quickly developed a habit of illicit drug use to maintain and enhance their coolness quotient. After initiation, they rapidly learned a wide array of methods and motives for becoming intoxicated.[15] They learned, for instance, how and why to pack a bowl but not a bong; whether to snort or eat ecstasy pills; which kinds of weed or pills or other intoxicant were perceived as being the best.[16] At first, they were ignorant of these matters and appeared lame. But such knowledge was quickly cultivated, helping to confer status in the form of enhanced coolness.[17] And once individuals were confident about how to operate in the drug world, they became even more deeply embedded in it. Their drug use increased from a "monthly thing" to a "weekend thing" and, especially for marijuana, to an everyday occurrence—and not simply every day but every chance in the day: before school, during school, after school, up until bedtime. Drug use effectively became routine.

Not only did the adolescents' rate of consumption increase over time but so too did the quality of the drugs consumed. More experienced users knew how to distinguish between "grades" of a drug. Mark, for instance, described three different grades of marijuana:

> Shwag would be your normal, basic grass that's old, it's been bricked up, it's real seedy, it's not very quality weed, it's real cheap. But it tends to give you

a headache. Midgrade was dank at one time; obviously, it got pollinated by the male plant, which causes it to have seeds, and it's a little bit drier than dank, but it's better than shwag though. But then dank is the highest quality of weed, no seeds, it's fresh, it's moist, it's a different high, it makes you feel good, good aftertaste, good everything, all around great bud.

Like most products, drugs have telltale signs that attest to their quality: how they look, smell, taste, or feel. According to Phillip, with marijuana "you know by the smell, the color, by the shapes of the buds. You know by the looks of it in general, mainly color though." For any drug "there's a lot of things that tip you off; you just gotta get a feel for it" was how Jeff put it. The coolest users knew how to use clues to decipher whether a substance was good, bad, or just okay quality. That understanding is what set cool connoisseurs apart from uninformed lame-os.

With experience these individuals developed a preference for higher-quality and hence more expensive product, believing that it delivered more bang for the buck. For example, Phillip estimated that "shwag isn't gonna do much for you. Smoking mids will get you about three times higher than shwag, and same for dank—it'll be about six times higher than smoking some mids." And Dave noted that "mids is just old shit that has seeds in it, which take up some of your weight, because you're paying for those seeds, and they're just not as good. They're usually bricked up so they've lost all their crystals. If you know your shit, it's just not a good way to go if you're going to smoke."

There is more, however, to consuming the best drugs than merely getting the best high for your money. By using only the best drugs, these consumers signaled "I'm cool" to peers. The message was "Not only do I know which drugs are better than others, but I can also afford them and know where to get them. You should like me, treat me with respect, and make an effort to be around me."[18] The impact of this message was amplified when users shared with others because people tend to like those who are generous.

Unsurprisingly, as the quality of a drug increases, its price follows suit. At the time of the study, for instance, low-grade marijuana, or "shwag," sold for $25 a "quarter," which is seven grams; the price of midgrade, or "mids," was twice that; and the highest grade, known as "dank," sold at twice the cost of mids. For the dealers, a weed habit cost as much as $50 to $100 a week to support. Christian's experience is typical:

> I remember senior year: I'd been smoking pot all the time for like two years.
> I probably smoked a sixteenth to an eighth a week. Me and my friends try to

figure out how much money we spent on pot, and it's embarrassing, but god, we spent so much money, it's ridiculous. I mean, let's just go with the low end of how much I did: a sixteenth is 25 bucks and I'm smoking that a week, so a hundred a month, so 1,200 bucks in a year, and it's probably more than that. I'd definitely say that it's more because this is when I got my $75 a week allowance, so I'd take 50 bucks and buy an eighth. That would last a week, like smoking before school, after school, smoked all the time.

Why did these suburban teenagers devote so much money to getting high? Certainly one reason is that "they" could afford it owing to their parents' incomes, which provided them with a nice allowance. Dave, for example, pointed out, "We kinda live in a rich area around here. So there's a lot of people who just have the money to throw down $50 for a half-quarter like every couple days." Referring to why many people preferred to smoke dank, Trevor said, "There's lots of rich-ass kids with money to throw around like a motherfucker—people with daddy's cash in their pockets just ready to buy. That's what everyone smoked, and the reason is because they were all rich kids. You attain the best that your means can provide, and all these kids could provide for the best that there was."

Expensive drugs, of course, were only one avenue to coolness. The youths also wanted fashionable clothes, electronic gear, music, car accessories, sports equipment, and more. And whereas their parental allowance or part-time work might be sufficient to cover the cost of such items, it seldom was enough to sustain their heavy consumption of illicit drugs too. How was this problem resolved? One potential solution was simply to "slow down" or "back off" on their drug use, but that was widely viewed as lame by members of the dealers' circle. Another option was to ask parents for more money, but doing so, especially repeatedly, risked inviting a parental financial audit. Yet another possibility was to get a part-time job or, for those who already had one, to try to increase the number of hours worked. But the jobs realistically available to them, mostly in fast food and retail, paid poorly and could not generate enough cash to meet their perceived needs. The final possibility was the riskiest but also potentially the most rewarding: drug selling.

Drugs for Free

The most important reason that these young middle-class suburbanites turned to drug dealing was not to make money *per se* but rather to "smoke for free," "trip for free," "roll for free," "tweak for free," whatever the case may be.[19] For them, dealing was primarily a money-*saving* venture as op-posed to a money-*making* one. When asked why he sold ecstasy, Phillip answered, "Free pills. I mean you get a little bit of profit on the side too. But it wasn't for the money, just pretty much for the free pills. Dealing was a way to save money." Referring to his motive for dealing ecstasy, acid, and marijuana, Justin said simply, "To offset my own use." Responding to the same line of questioning, Bruce answered, "I wanted to be able to smoke for free. I never had any profit out of it." Andrea was motivated by "just the free pot." Katie told us, "I want to eat free pills," meaning Percocets. Frank and Trevor went so far as to say, respectively, "I couldn't care less about making money" and "I'll go through all the profit just happily smoking. Money really isn't an issue."

As these dealers sold mostly just to finance their own use, their business was restricted to drugs that they themselves consumed. When asked why he sold dank, Dave said, "That's what I smoked, so that's what I sold." Tom told us, "It's 'cause that's all I would smoke." And Mark explained, "'Cause you get high on your own supply, and that's what I wanted to get high on, so that's what I sold." These dealers viewed it as only logical to sell what they consumed, as Christian pointed out: "If you're getting into it to pay for your habit, then it makes sense to buy what you're doing anyways."

Dealers earned free drugs by purchasing a large quantity of the sub-stance below retail value and then selling most of it at a higher price to cover their own use. As an example, if an eighth of marijuana cost $50 but an ounce—which is equal to eight eighths—costs $350, then a person could buy an ounce, sell seven eighths for $50 each, and thereby be able to smoke $50 worth of weed (retail value) "for free." This is what Pete did ini-tially: "The first time I bought an ounce [of weed] I bought it for 350 bucks and sold all of it but an eighth, and I got an eighth for myself for free." Christian told us how it worked with ecstasy: "You buy like ten pills at a time for 180 and you sell those for 25 each, so you're making like 70 bucks. But you wouldn't use the 70 bucks; you eat the free pills. I completely got into it for the free pills; it had nothing to do with profit. You're gonna have no profit once you have the free pills." By buying in bulk and paying less per pill, mushroom, gram, or whatever, users could finance their consump-tion indefinitely. They might not generate a profit in the traditional sense, but for them, the upside was not spending any—or at least not as much—money to finance their own drug use.

For many of the dealers, the goal of selling transcended saving money; it also allowed them to use more drugs. It was common for dealers to in-crease their consumption by 50–100 percent over time. Individuals who were accustomed to using one or two ecstasy pills at a time would start to "eat" four or five at a time once they started selling. Adolescents who, pre-dealing, had smoked a sixteenth a day would start consuming an eighth a day; such as Brendan, who said, "I don't make any money. But I smoke a fucking ton now. I probably smoke an eighth every day." And Phillip told us, "I could smoke as much as I could possibly smoke; maybe like a half-quarter a day. It was unlimited." Dealers increased both the number of drug-using episodes and the amount consumed during those periods. Jason, for instance, told us, "I smoked so much, just smoke crazy, like smoking like for a fucking hour before school and then a fucking hour after school. I was smoking constantly. I boil it down to around like a half-quarter, maybe more, a day. I mean smoking the shit out of weed."

Selling drugs also facilitated the use of better-quality substances. Just as there were different grades of any given drug—high to mid to low—so too there were grades within any given grade: high-high to low-low. An analogy might be drawn to comparing a D to an F grade diamond, a K to an M, or an S to a Z. Only those who have trained their senses to appreciate the difference will know how to distinguish between grades within a grade. Such differences may not be important to individuals outside the subculture. But to those within it, the ability to recognize and afford the best among the best is part of what sets the coolest apart from the cool, as any wine connoisseur knows. For hard and soft drugs, recognizing quality distinctions comes down to color, taste, and feel. Because using and selling higher-quality product begets coolness, the dealers were motivated to find the best stuff available. Noting a perk of selling marijuana, Ed explained, "When I'm selling it, I'm like already ahead of other people, so that when there's good shit coming to town, I get to see that first. I get to get my pick through it."

Unlike other drugs, there is a specific characteristic of marijuana attributed to the buds, or "nugs," of the plant that subjectively distinguishes good, better, and best. Size plays a major part in this assessment. Some nugs are only a tenth of a gram, which is regarded as being pretty lame, whereas others are upward of three, five, seven grams, and beyond. Holding constant all other aspects of a nug (color, taste, feel), the bigger it is, the more it is worth in cool points. Accordingly, the marijuana dealers dug through each new bulk purchase to retrieve the best nugs for themselves. Doing so was immensely pleasurable, as Joseph told us: "Having a giant bag of weed was really fun. Always having a bag, like picking out the best buds, knowing you were going to smoke that one this time—that was awesome." It is worth pointing out that bigger and smaller buds are pharmacologically indistinguishable; the only meaningful difference between them is the subjective subcultural perception that one is more prestigious than the other. Christian explained it this way:

> It's awesome to have a quarter pound of weed, especially when you've been a stoner for like two years. Being a dealer is so cool—if you're a stoner. If you don't care about weed and you're just selling weed, I think it would be a complete pain in the ass. I had a quarter pound, so I had all different kinds of nugs to choose from; I had like seven-, eight-gram nugs that were like as big as four fingers put together. I'd take that out for my personal stash because you were smoking all day, every day. I'd always have my own nugs to smoke, and that's like part of dealing: you just get the best nugs and you deserve it. Weed is weed—like, really, when it comes down to it, one nug being bigger than another doesn't matter when it comes to getting high—but it's status, or a symbol. It's like, "I got a seven-gram nug." You got the best nugs, and they're just gorgeous. It's like getting the best driver for your golf club set or something like that.

Extra Money

Although every dealer was motivated to sell by their desire for free drugs, for some there was a second motive too: namely, to make a profit. Typically, the money they hoped to acquire was modest. They did not intend to make a career out of drug selling. All they wanted was a little bit of extra spending money. Robert, for example, told us that he sold for "free drug use and a little money on the side." Another dealer, Joe, "sold weed and Xanax" because "I smoked a lot of weed, and if I sold the weed, then I would get a lot of weed for free; and also because I wouldn't make that much money, but I would make enough money to be comfortable." For Ron, selling provided "mostly just weed, and it's just extra cash. I smoke for free like a half-quarter a day, and make some money off it." Mike's summary of his dealing history emphasizes similar themes:

> I feel like my story of just start using, and you get contacts, and next thing you know it's not like you're a big-time dealer, you're just somebody who can get drugs. I feel like that's common among my middle-class sort of upbringing. Like Blake is a good example: he got into coke, suddenly he could get a lot of coke, suddenly he was dealing coke. Low-income drug dealers do it to make money, like, "I can sell rocks. I'm not going to be able to get another job. This is what you do to make money." For us it was more of a you start smoking weed, you start getting X, you get more, you can use more, you can sell

more, you can make money off it now that you have a contact. I understood that I was a criminal by law standards, but never really thought of myself as a criminal. See, with me, it was more than anything else that people would just call me for whatever they want. The biggest things, I'd say, were weed and ecstasy, and then coke. Buying coke was more of a couple friends go in—you know it's high school—like five people. And if people wanted acid, I'd be like, "I can get you acid." I'd buy twenty, thirty hits, keep five or six of them, and sell the rest. I'd say the closest I came to only really buying something to make money was probably ecstasy. I think at this point I was probably doing coke twice a week and ecstasy two or three times a week. There was a guy who was getting something like a hundred pills, or something like that, and so he'd sell me maybe ten at the time for maybe $15 each, and then I could be selling them for 25 each, something like that, so it was easy money. Plus I was using; I pretty much made some profit and got some free pills. It was never like a moneymaking venture. It was more just providing for people who I liked and making a little extra money on the side. If I needed to make extra money, I probably could and I did sometimes, I think, but more than anything, it was just for use, and it was some extra money.

These dealers clearly thought of their drug profits as "extra" cash rather than as essential money, which is hardly surprising given that their parents provided for their basic needs and most, if not all, of their reasonable wants. They did not worry about helping to put food on the table or to pay the electricity bill or the rent. Their parents had that covered, and more. Allowances of $20 to $100 a week were common and were given by parents to kids for the sole purpose of nonessential expenses. Many of the dealers had been given credit cards to use for such things as gas and restaurant bills; the parents figured it was easier to track and pay expenses that way than to give them cash. Some parents were less generous than others, either because they could not afford to be or because they wanted to instill a work ethic and sense of independence in their children. Those teenagers had to work a part-time job to pay for luxuries that their parents deemed nonessential, such as concert tickets or a new car stereo system.[20] But even these young workers had everything they needed and most of what they wanted; the only reasons they worked, it seems, was to keep up with the richer cool kids, to get out of school on a work-study program, to be around friends while getting paid, or to have an excuse for having so much money.[21] For these reasons, the dealers described their drug profits as "extra cash" or "spending money," implying that they did not really need it, though it was nice to have.

Another reason the dealers viewed the monetary profit as a bonus rather than a wage is that they did not always seek it out. Even when the adolescent sellers took no active interest in expanding their business, word that they were dealing almost invariably spread quickly through their peer network. Such gossip was functional for everyone. From the users' perspective, this information was useful because it helped them get drugs to consume and knowledge that they could share with others. From the dealers' perspective, being the subject of this gossip was beneficial too, as it generated more customers. The financial upside of having more customers was that more sales equated to more free drugs for the dealers. But the dealers inevitably reached a point of maximum consumption. Few of them had any interest in smoking more than an eighth or a quarter of marijuana a day, for example. Upon reaching that point, some sellers simply refrained from taking on more customers. Other sellers, however, capitalized on the fact that they could make "extra" cash without much additional work. All they had to do was buy more product and meet a few more people on a few more occasions; four extra sales of quarter-sized marijuana bags, for instance, could net a dealer an extra $100 in pure profit. The money was so easy it was "ridiculous," they would say.

Once the dealers realized how much profit they could earn by expending just a little extra effort, it was difficult for some of them not to capitalize on that opportunity. That is exactly what happened to Dave: "I got into it to support my habit at first, and then I realized how much money I could make and that kinda drove me from there." Pete started by buying an ounce of marijuana for personal use but quickly escalated to dealing to finance his habit and, ultimately, for monetary gain:

> I started trying to make profit, and profit, and profit. I'd buy an ounce, try to make a little more money, buy an ounce, try to make a little more money, and then eventually when I had enough money, I started buying two ounces, and then more and more, gradually and gradually. When I started, it was for free drugs, and then as I went along it was like, "Wow, the more I buy, the cheaper I get it, and the more I sell, the more money I can make, and the more I can smoke." I started selling it more and more, and people found out I had it regularly and it started going faster. As soon as I started buying QPs [i.e., quarter pounds], I was making at least $300 per quap [i.e., quarter pound] that I bought, which took about two to three days to sell, so about a $1,000 a week. By the end I made about $10,000, smoked probably $25,000. Toward the end I was smoking an ounce out of every QP, me and all my friends; if I had sold that ounce, that's $400 right there that could

have been profit. But I just smoked it. Toward the beginning and middle I smoked like an eighth to a quarter of every ounce that I bought. If I bought an ounce, I'd smoke an eighth of it; if I bought a QP, I might smoke like a half ounce of it. I probably smoked an eighth to a quarter a day.

Whereas dealers like Dave and Pete became motivated by profit only after they started selling, others got into the game with money already on their minds. Although these individuals dealt primarily to make money, they also did it to earn free drugs, even though this cut into their profit. Asked why he started dealing, William told us, "Money and being able to have fun with my friends without having to worry about the money aspect of it. Plus we took a lot of pills back then. I mean I was past the point when I could take fifteen Valiums and that not being a big deal, or ten rolls [ecstasy] and it not being a big deal. I mean it was just the money and the getting fucked up for free." Another seller, Jared, said something similar:

> I sold weed, a little acid, and mushrooms. I use drugs and dealing seemed like an easy way to make money—not have to keep spending money from buying overpriced drugs. Say Xanax, I would buy about a hundred at a time and they'd probably be about $2.50, and I'd sell them for about 5 apiece; and the acid, buy like ten or twenty and make a little money off that; and weed, buy a couple ounces, no more than a quarter pound at a time. For a bit I was working with another person, and we had a system where we'd try to get a quarter pound every week. We'd get those for $1,100 and split it fifty-fifty, and if we sold all that, that would be 1,600 street price, but obviously, we'd be smoking some and hooking some people up, so we wouldn't make that much. We'd probably make about 200 a week.

Some of the dealers saved a portion of their profits, but all of them spent at least some of the cash on coolness-enhancing items. They purchased, in their own words, "shit": luxury items that did little more than satisfy their immediate wants in an attempt to score cool points.[22] The social value of so-called shit should not be discounted. Although these luxury items had little long-term fiscal worth or—for the more expensive items—quickly depreciated, they did have a daily impact on youngsters' communal life. Buying and possessing "good shit" made people cooler, whereas purchasing "bad shit" was lame. With almost every purchase, big or small, adolescents demonstrated to their peers whether or not they were cool. They revealed the extent to which they were in tune with subcultural understandings of what to buy, how to consume it, and to what end. In this way, conspicuous displays of shit made people more or less attractive and likable.[23] Drug dealing was a way to afford what it took to be perceived as cool by peers.

At the low end, "shit" referred to everyday goods like food, drinks, and other drugs. As Tom put it, "I spent [the cash I got from selling drugs] on other drugs or random stuff, maybe gas, food, munchies, random accessories, maybe tickets to a concert; nothing I really saved it for. Mostly concerts, alcohol, food, and shit." Mark described what he did with his profits:

> Bought lots of other drugs with it and got really fucked up. I blew all of my money, bought pointless shit. I didn't ever care about it. The money I made from selling, I put it back into the party fund for drugs pretty much. A lot of it goes to gas, cigarettes, food, all that sort of stuff, drinks at the gas station, or whatever. But for the most part marijuana, alcohol, and whatnot.

At the high end, though, shit could be expensive. Josh bought what he described as "stupid shit, random stuff: my jeep, stereo system in my jeep, stuff for my jeep, just whatever. Just spending money really." Dave purchased what he perceived to be a really cool glass bong and a variety of other entertainment products:

> Pretty much just spent it on stuff that I needed—not really needed—just wanted. Bought a PlayStation with it, a bunch of games, movies, DVD player, just stuff that I'd like to have. My favorite things that I bought were for my car: my surround sound and DVD player, and my TV for my car. I bought a bong for $500, well 470, but I like to call it 500.

Phillip spent money on "electronics, car stuff," and "vacations," including "senior spring break—the best spring break I ever experienced." Ron poured money into musical instruments, both conventional and modern: "When there's a little bit of excess after I've gotten some weight a couple times and have a bunch of money, I'll go and buy something. I play drums and guitar and the chord, so I'll just go buy a microphone, a cymbal, like I bought my own drum set, four guitars, mixers, computers, all that kind of shit, all from selling. I probably wouldn't have it otherwise." All of these dealers' purchases may have had direct sensual benefits—pleasing the ears, eyes, or taste buds—but the selection of particular products was oriented by the buyers' subcultural desire for coolness.

A Place among Peers

The young suburban dealers did not spend their profits exclusively on themselves. They were more or less expected to use a portion of that cash to finance partying with their friends and intimate partners. Everyone, including the dealers, reasoned that they could afford to do so. William, for instance, described what he liked about selling:

> The party life; everybody having a good time all the time. And of course the money. You go out partying and you're the guy with $1,000 in your pocket. You're paying for everybody's beers, you're paying for drinks, and of course girls are going to think, "Oh, money." A lot of girls weren't the girls from high school; they were the girls that were twenty and see a little kid with all this money, and girls are attracted by money, it's a sad fact. Partying, taking drugs, girls, all my friends always having a good time, that's what I really enjoyed about it.

Like William, Pete used the profits from his dealing to treat his friends to meals out and other forms of entertainment. He also "smoked them out," meaning that he provided marijuana for communal consumption at no cost to them:[24]

> I went out to eat a lot. I took people out to eat; when I went with my friends, I'd buy them everything—it didn't matter, I had money. If we went through the drive-through or something to pick up some burgers or something, I'd just cover it all. When I had made plenty of money, I started being generous as hell, smoking with all my friends for free—and then it was like an ounce every two or three days, but that's just not me.

Pete spent much of the time smoking out his friends in his best friend's basement. His best friend's parents reserved the basement for their son's use so that he and his buddies could have a space to call their own. It was not uncommon for parents to treat particular rooms in their houses as the property of their children.[25] This was a perfect environment for smoking and dealing; it afforded a comfortable environment for consumption and trade, and it was safer—legally speaking—than driving around. Pete and his friends would smoke for hours on end, gaining a sense of belonging—even while hurling friendly insults at one another.

As we noted earlier, selling served to increase the dealers' level of drug consumption. A major reason for this increase was that in the natural course of dealing, they found themselves constantly surrounded by other people who were consuming their favorite products. There was a mentality in which sellers were expected to share a bit of their stock with their customers and vice versa. As Jeff told us, "I got to like selling a lot to my friends, and I got to where I had weed around me all the time and just smoked way, way too much. I was pretty worthless. Every time I sold something to someone, I'd smoke a couple bowls with them, so by the end of the day I had smoked like more than an eighth, sometimes more." And Robert recounted an incident in which he and his friends pushed their drug consumption to the limit:

> I'm a sociable person, a people person. It was fun hanging out with buddies because you know we'd always get high, and you meet a lot of new people as far as hooking people up. Marijuana is a social drug. Most people don't smoke pot by themselves, so it's a social thing. We smoked a shitload of weed. That was an extreme amount of consumption. I remember one time we sat down and we got high and we fucking smoked an ounce in one sitting. It was ridiculous. I was stoned out of my mind. We were doing wombats— upside-down bong hits—like all kinds of shit. We sat down with an ounce and smoked it all, between like six people.

Robert's out-of-school activities were similar to Pete's in that both had a comfortable and safe place from which to use and deal. But unlike Pete's situation, Robert smoked with his friends at his own house. Robert's house was typical of those found in Peachville's subdivisions, but it had a pool and stood on a larger plot than most.[26] After school he, his friends, and some of their friends would hang out poolside or on the porch. They would smoke a "ridiculous" amount of marijuana and, in doing so, show how cool they were.

In addition to giving away drugs and picking up tabs, dealers "hooked up" some buyers by giving them more than the current market rate dictated or by providing them with higher-quality product. Christian, like many dealers, hooked up his friends in addition to smoking them out:

> It's fun to hook your friends up all the time. You can just hook up your friends, you can smoke them out, you can let them have the best nugs. Like one friend, he'd buy a sixteenth from me, and he loved—and I loved letting him do it—picking up the QP and searching through it for the perfect bag. He would take out like six nugs and weigh them—'cause you've got to have a certain weight—I'd be like, "You can weigh it out at 1.9 today," and it's sup-

posed to be 1.75. So you like compare and contrast nugs and stuff, 'cause if you're a stoner, there's just something about having the best-looking nugs: the ones that are a good density, have nice crystals, a nice tip to them, a nice base at the end, there's a lot to it. If you smoke a lot, you'll really appreciate somebody letting you pick your own bag. I only had like three or four people that I'd let do that—my best friends. It was enjoyable for me to be able to give back to them because I've known these kids. We grew up together.

Mike mentioned engaging in the same sorts of altruistic behavior:

My good friends really didn't buy weed as much as they'd just want to smoke. All of my friends' first experience with drugs was smoking with me. Even the guys that don't do drugs, they'd be at a party and they'd be like, "God, I've never got high before." And I'd be like, "We can avenge that, not a problem." So I think my friends just wanted to smoke more than they did buy any weed. But if they did want something like an eighth, I'd just give it to them for cheap.

Trevor explained that he got immense pleasure from hooking up his buddies:

Mostly just centers around smoking, playing with the herb, providing my buddies with some good herb that they wouldn't have gotten otherwise. Most of the time I was either providing them with a better price or better herb than they could ever find. Nowadays, people call me and are like, "Dude, do you know where any herb is?" and I'm like, "Come over here and chill," and then just watch their face light up, you know, and be like "Yeah." It's like a provider thing, hooking my boys up.

The dealers' altruism inevitably cost them potential profits, but they nevertheless enjoyed being generous. A good question to ask, then, is what was in it for them? If only subconsciously, the sellers understood that they were rewarded for their gifts with extra cool points.[27] Generous individuals tend to be popular. And givers are all the more popular when the gift is something of high social value. The more often the dealers gave away free drugs and the greater the size of each gift, the cooler they were perceived to be and the better they were treated by their like-minded peers, even if only in the pursuit of additional drugs.

By this point it should be clear that adolescent drug use in and around Peachville was largely a group activity. "You're like a part of a community that's always sociable" is how Jeff explained it. To be an accepted and valued part of a community made people feel and look cool. For that reason, when people consumed drugs together, they all were certified to a greater or lesser degree as being socially desired in each other's eyes. At the same time, that interaction gave all of the participating parties an opportunity to demonstrate their likability.

Recall that one reason young suburbanites started to use drugs in the first place was to be liked and thereby to gain respect and social desirability. The question might reasonably be raised: why use drugs as opposed to doing something else together? One factor is that Peachville offered little in the way of recreational outlets. Residents could get a bite to eat, shop, or see a movie; and that was about it.[28] The dealers believed that there was little "to do"—or at least little that they wanted to do—other than engage in drug-related activity. According to Christian:

> I spent a lot of money in high school on drugs, but there was nothing else to do. I could have gone to a movie every single night, or I could have gone out to eat every single night, but getting stoned is just something to do. That's why it's so popular. There's a lot more to it than getting high. It's not even about getting high. I personally don't even get high anymore if I smoke pot. It's a very social thing. I guess when you're a weed dealer, you're at the top of that social ladder because that really is what everybody I knew, which is like one hundred to two hundred people, would do: just drive around and smoke all day. That's what we did. I don't know what else you would do. We don't go to the arcade; we don't do any of that shit. We don't go to the ice cream parlor. We drive around in our vehicles and smoke.

Christian makes an important point: dealers were cool—"at the top of that social ladder"—at least in part because they distributed what their peers wanted. Drugs were the glue that bonded these adolescents' social lives. Drugs gave them something to do, a reason to be together. This provided them with an opportunity to interact with their peers and demonstrate their social desirability in the process, which in turn served to increase their perceived subcultural social status. With no professional career and little else to show for their time on earth, being regarded as cool by their peers took on enormous importance in the minds of many of these adolescents; without it they had little to hang their hats on.

Part of what attracted these high school students to dealing was that it made them the focus of attention and inclusion among people who wanted drugs, thereby making them feel valued and valuable within their

own subcultural community of interest, which was a reward in and of itself. Mike put it this way, "It's something really good to have something
people want. If somebody needed something, they would call me and
I'd give it them. There was a certain amount of power and self-respect in
that." Joseph explained, "I like having people always coming over to get the
weed. It was kind of fun and a bit of a head trip to be the dealer, there's no
question about that. It was definitely part of it." Phillip felt the same way:

> There's fame to it in a sense. If everyone wants to talk to you, that's a good
> thing, even if it's just for like a bag or just to chill out for ten minutes. It's
> cool just to see a bunch of people. I'm always a big fan of making new
> friends too, so that's a plus. I met a lot of interesting people; I met a lot of
> people I probably would have never met if I hadn't been doing that. I made
> some good friendships. I felt good about it. And there's perks like getting
> invited to a party when no one's got bud and you show up and everyone is
> like, "Hell yeah! Hell yeah! Let's smoke! C'mon, weed man is here!" Things
> like that. I was on cloud nine, seriously.

We already noted that communal drug taking offered users the opportunity to demonstrate their coolness. Drug dealing did the same. As Mike,
Joseph, and Phillip pointed out, dealers were sought after by their peers.
Beyond that, though, the interaction inherent in any drug transaction afforded dealers plenty of opportunities to meet people and forge friendships, which in turn paved the way to more social interaction. As Mark
explained:

> I really just met so many people through it. A lot of them are acquaintances
> or whatever, but a lot of them became friends out of it. And you're always
> having something to do; you're never bored. There's always somebody to at
> least go around with and cruise neighborhoods and smoke some pot. Always
> had something to do because you're always talking to everybody. And you al-
> ways have money to go do something if you wanted to, but I mean we really
> never spent money on doing something, we just spent money on drugs all
> the time—it was fun. Besides the fact you know a lot of people from it, you
> always have something to do, and you got money.

Tom echoed his sentiments:

> I really met a lot of people through selling drugs, and some of them have ac-
> tually become really good friends. Selling drugs has made me a lot of really

good connections as far as good friends go that you can trust, and I had fun and got high while I was doing it. Obviously, when you're in high school, you get popularity, you kinda feed off of that. Obviously, a lot of people like to go and party, and a lot of people like to party with marijuana, so when you got it, you're like their best friend. When you hook them up, everybody's happy, and you're on a good level with everybody.

Similarly, Ed told us that one of the major advantages of drug dealing was that it kept you in close touch with your peer network:

Dealing has people coming over all the time. Like I have girls coming over telling me about parties and shit they're going to. It makes it like I'm completely 100 percent in touch with everything that's going around all the time since I am not in a single clique and I get to see twenty different kinds of people every day. I get to know what the hell is going on. I get to do whatever the fuck I want. I always know what's out there.

And Pete described the effect that dealing had on his social life:

Most of my customers were my friends. Some of them were just acquaintances, but I mean a lot of people wanted to hang out with me more. Everybody wants to hang out with a drug dealer. I started hanging out with a lot of people. I mean I know a lot of people that weren't the closest friends became closer friends with me during my dealing period. They wanted to come over and drop out [i.e., play a game described below] with us and get high. I was hanging out with them, and yeah, they were my friends. They became my friends, and after I stopped dealing, they were still good friends. I mean I consider a bunch of people my friends; even if I don't hang out with them that much, they're still my friends.

These dealers and their peers spent a lot of time engaged in what they called "being stupid." This is recreational activity with no explicit purpose other than to be part of a group.[29] The dealer quoted above, Pete, provided an example of this behavior and what motivated its occurrence:

We used to have this game that we played in my friend's basement. We'd get high as hell and just throw a ball around in his basement. It was a stupid, pointless game that had no purpose, but it was fun as hell, and I was just with my best friends every day getting high and playing this stupid game every day. It's called drop out: you throw this ball around and you have to catch it, and you get three outs and you're out. It's a stupid game, but for some reason we played it every day after we got high, and we got high the whole time we played, and we played for like four hours a day, just being stupid.

According to this seller, their game was "stupid" and "pointless" and "had no purpose." But when viewed through a sociological lens, the goal of the game is evident. The reason they played it every day is that doing so provided them with a reason to be together. It gave them an activity in which to be relaxed and competitive at the same time, having fun in the process. To use the words of another dealer, Jeff, they liked to "vegetate" because—consciously or not—it gave them a feeling of self-worth and social desirability:

> When I sold weed heavily, I was living the kinda lifestyle where I could basically vegetate all day long and not have to worry about it. I have a pool in my backyard, so my friends would be over at my house all day, every day. My mom was out of town or not home most of the time, so we would just set the bong up outside and just smoke all day and chill at the pool. I'd have in between five to twenty people over at my house swimming and buying weed from me. I laid out at the pool every day. It was just like that type of thing where I could basically not ever move a muscle and get by and have everybody happy.

Through being stupid, then, the dealers demonstrated to each other that they were cool. The reward was better treatment by their peers, which led to even more invitations to be stupid, which gave them yet more opportunities to demonstrate their coolness and thereby enhance their perceived status.

CHAPTER 2

Securing a Supply

Anyone who aspires to become a drug dealer first must have access to a supply of drugs. To gain that access, dealers have to overcome two major obstacles. They have to establish a connection to a supplier and get their hands on enough cash to make a bulk purchase.[1] How do they go about doing this?

Locating Suppliers

Not every young drug user in Peachville had access to a "supplier"—meaning someone who sold drugs in bulk or "weight." As noted in the previous chapter, many high school students use drugs, but few of them deal, and fewer still supply dealers. Being a supplier is more profitable than being just a low-level dealer, who sells directly to consumers, but it requires substantial upfront outlays of investment capital and entails greater legal and extralegal risks.[2] Some young suburban drug dealers become suppliers or do both at the same time, that is, sell to users as dealers and to dealers as suppliers. Most, however, are concerned to minimize their risk and sell drugs simply to smoke for free or to make a bit of extra cash, showing little interest in the more lucrative—and dangerous—business of supplying.

The fact that few young suburban dealers are willing to become suppliers serves to limit opportunities for others to start selling drugs simply because they cannot get the necessary stock. Recognizing this, users who have good connections to suppliers often are motivated to exploit their deviant ties to support their own drug use, make a small profit, and, relatedly, to "help" their friends.[3] One of the dealers we interviewed, Jason, explained how and why he started dealing drugs:

It was my freshman year in high school. I knew a lot of people who liked to smoke weed, and I knew a lot of people who I could get it from, and I knew that a lot of people that I knew that liked smoking pot didn't know where to get it, or couldn't find it, and I happened to be one of the only ones who knew where to find it. So I just started helping all my friends out. Basically, it was just so I could smoke for free and not have to spend my own money on it. I could just sell it to people that I knew and then I would have some left over and I could use it.

But how did dealers like Jason initially get to know their suppliers? Probably the most common way in which the young suburban dealers were connected to their suppliers was via a preexisting relationship as pals. In answering a question about how he knew his supplier, Josh explained, "I played T-ball with him. I knew him real well." Similarly, Bruce said of his suppliers, "They were just friends that I have that were already involved in doing it. They were all my close friends. I didn't deal with anybody who I didn't know real well." Josh said this about his supplier, "He's just an old friend of mine." Jeff detailed how his connection to a group of drug supplier friends facilitated his own dealing:

There was a big group of friends that all sold weed; I guess you might say one level above me in the whole thing. They would get quarter pounds from somebody else, sell me an ounce at a time for anywhere from $300 to like $325. Then I could turn around and sell that for about $400. The guys were my friends, so that made it easier because they would always weigh it out for me and make sure that I knew that they were giving me a fair deal, and they were always real straightforward with me. They didn't always give the best prices, but they always came through and were always accountable. You could count on if you had $325, you could go and get an ounce from the guys. It wasn't ever hard or anything. They always had it. They were real fair and everything.

Often the dealers forged their friendships with suppliers in school. Students learn more there than reading, writing, and arithmetic; they also develop peer group relationships that determine everything from who and what is cool to who has access to illicit goods. The dealers clearly understood that getting a good education was vital to ensuring their adult success; and they would not argue that it should be any other way. They were attached to and involved in school. But as part and parcel of that involvement, they inevitably encountered numerous opportunities to commit delinquent acts.[4] Of course, there was nothing about formal education *per se* that caused crime. What made schools conducive to lawbreaking was the way in which these institutions shaped networks among youngsters, creating overlapping social ties—some strong, many weak.[5]

Classes at Peachville High begin a little after seven o'clock in the morning and end at about two o'clock, Monday through Friday, from August to May. The school is in many ways similar to a prison. Students are allowed twenty minutes to eat and little or no time to exercise; they are told when to wake up (by the first bell), where to go and when (one classroom or another at an appointed hour), and what to do while there (learn math, history, or something else), and—importantly for understanding crime among them—they are forced to interact with other students for long stretches of time. In class they sit together, learn together, laugh together, and suffer together through lectures. In the process, they develop a shared culture centered on figuring out what is cool or lame, who exhibits those traits, and who therefore warrants being respected or dissed and incorporated or omitted from recreational activities.

Because young people are required—day after day, year after year—to be around other youngsters with whom they might not naturally intermingle, their social networks are far broader and stronger than those that will characterize postschool life for most of them.[6] At school, there are many people to judge, and many people by whom to be judged.[7] Peachville High, with an enrollment near three thousand teenagers, cannot help but be a hotbed of public acclamation ("He's cool") and ridicule ("He's lame"). Students are constantly crossing paths and intermingling, walking by and sitting next to one person after another. And at each such encounter they reevaluate that individual's likability and attractiveness. These judgments carry great weight not only because they directly affect how one person treats another but also because evaluations are shared among peers and thereby have indirect effects on social interaction. One person will hear that another kid is cool or lame and, in turn, will treat that individual better or worse and spread the assessment further. Overlapping ties ensure that word will spread; and the word of a strong tie is taken seriously.

What happens at school plays a powerful part in what happens before classes begin and after they end. The degree to which individuals are viewed as being cool by their classmates determines their centrality in peer networks that transcend school walls. Those who demonstrate that they are attractive and likable will be invited by others to hang out at the pool or to smoke before class; and their own invitations to others are more likely to be accepted in return. Such extracurricular activities provide youngsters with opportunities to prove—or undermine—their coolness. The outcome of these performances is likely to be discussed among peers, thereby enhancing or damaging their reputation.

For many high school students, trying to be cool is hard, emotionally draining work. They must discern what to look like, what to say, what to do, and whether to conform—or not conform if that is cooler—to a seemingly infinite number of other aspects of youth and suburban culture.[8] Plus, they need to surround themselves with the coolest people possible and steer clear of the lame-os.[9] They become anxious over the smallest acts; saying or doing the wrong thing can be humiliating in the extreme.[10] On one occasion, for instance, an inexperienced drug buyer showed up at a young Peachville dealer's home to purchase a quarter of weed. The dealer said, "That'll be a bill," and then the buyer—looking confused—said, "What's that?" The seller turned from the buyer to his friend, who was sitting nearby, with a look of disbelief and derision, before they jointly laughed. The dealer looked to the buyer and said, "$100." The buyer's face left no doubt that he was embarrassed by his failure to understand the latest drug lingo.

Had everyone in Peachville been homeschooled, adolescent lawbreaking would almost surely have been lower there. School brought drug-involved youths into contact with like-minded others, which served to encourage crime. While drugs could be consumed alone, they usually were taken in the company of others. What is more, obtaining them required interaction with a dealer. If we reason by analogy, it is easy to grasp how the characteristics of high school peer networks increase drug market activity. Imagine a contagious virus spread through communication over the phone, Internet, or in person. The virus would spread more quickly in populations with greater interaction between more of their members. School-based gossip behaves like a virus in that it spreads from person to person. Because students have overlapping ties to one another, it is easier for them than it would be for more isolated individuals (e.g., their parents) to find out where to buy drugs. Some students received and sent signals that drug use was cool, that dealing was even cooler, and about where and how to obtain the product. In highly contagious environments like Peachville High, these ideas spread faster and more extensively, reaching people who would have been uninfected in less-connected networks. Moreover, due to their perceived coolness and other variables, some individuals became what the public health officials might call "supercarriers": people who hold and transmit multiple and/or more complex pieces of information about why and, more importantly, how to participate in the drug underworld.

Frank's story illustrates how school-based interaction facilitated and intensified drug use and sales: "I met some kid in class one day, and I said, 'I can't wait to smoke a blunt when I get out of school.' He sold pot and we just hung out that day and since then been hanging out every day smoking over at his house. I went to see him about selling, and he decided to front me out with some stuff." Similarly, Ron's drug dealing was made possible by a classmate who worked part-time at a local pharmacy:

> I was probably fifteen. Probably around tenth or eleventh grade. I was selling mainly pharmaceutical pills because I knew someone that worked at a pharmacy store, and she would just give me a bunch and I'd give her money for them. Valiums and just stuff like that, just generic stuff, like Lortab and pain pills and just stuff like that. They were cheap, maybe a dollar apiece. I made like 100 bucks every two or three days. The girl who got me those pills was just a friend from school that I had classes with. She worked at a local pharmacy, and she just put them in her apron. Like there was millions, so she could just take like two and put them in her apron every couple hours so that they added up.

After-school and weekend jobs also brought dealers and would-be dealers into contact with like-minded peers. Not all of the dealers had jobs, but those who did held menial positions far below those to which they aspired upon completing their education. Most of these individuals worked in the fast-food industry as chefs, cashiers, or delivery persons; at least one was a bagger and stocker at a grocery store; a few of them did construction, landscape, or warehouse work on behalf of their parents' companies. Whatever the job, they all made about $10 an hour and worked ten to twenty hours a week during the school year, maybe more during the summer.

The general perception among these young middle-class suburbanites was that performing menial labor is not cool. Many of them regarded it as borderline embarrassing. The simplest reason for this is that they felt as though lower-class work was beneath them; by definition, it is the kind of labor that middle-class people do not do. Relatedly, they were inclined to perceive the tasks associated with such jobs as demeaning; cleaning up after others, for example, was hard for them to swallow, especially because they seldom cleaned up after themselves at home. Another reason that these jobs were seen as humiliating is that some of them required employees to wear unbecoming attire. Young people forced to wear outfits that their peers define as lame cannot help but feel self-conscious about their image.[11]

And yet, to be cool, these kids "needed" money to spend while out and about with their friends, whether for movies, food, or drugs. They needed a vehicle, which required gas and insurance. They needed a cell phone with plenty of call minutes and text messaging. They needed a wardrobe that allowed them to fit in with their chosen clique, be it hippy (tie-dyed shirts, ripped jeans, and Birkenstock sandals or clogs), preppy (polo shirts, khaki pants, and boat shoes), or athletic (workout shirts, basketball shorts, and sneakers). Although working a lower-class job could be embarrassing for these adolescents, it would have been lamer in their eyes not to have what they needed to be regarded as cool by their peers. Thus, adolescents whose parents were unwilling or unable to pay for fashionable clothing and other items that conferred subcultural status often set off to shopping malls or fast-food restaurants to fill out applications, asked their friends to hook them up with a job, or worked for their parents.

While at work, some of these individuals made a connection that offered them the possibility of doing what they perceived to be a much cooler job: drug dealing. This typically began with idle conversation between coworkers in which both confessed that they liked to consume a particular drug, which led to a discussion about where they obtained it, at what price, and evaluations of its quality. These conversations also sometimes culminated in the coworkers joining one another in drug use, typically of marijuana, while on the job or during their lunch break. In some cases, one party found out that the other was a supplier, or knew of one, and this opened up the door to becoming a dealer. In this way, a so-called pro-social part of communities—namely, legitimate labor—increased the opportunity for and the prevalence of illicit drug trade.[12] By working and, in turn, making more connections, users who otherwise might have been unable to make bulk purchases suddenly found themselves able to do so.

Jason, for instance, met his supplier at the restaurant where he was employed: "He was a guy who worked at a restaurant where I worked at. He was a lot older than me. At that point I was seventeen, eighteen; he was twenty-five. I started talking to him and then I realized, 'Hey man, this guy can get weed. He can hook me up for a fair price.'" Likewise, Trevor described his suppliers as "people you work with, usually older kids, 'cause at the time we were pretty young. I guess we were around sixteen or something; these kids were older and out of high school and stuff."

Typically, these supplier-colleagues were at least a few years older than the dealers. Most of the older suppliers had failed to achieve the role of a successful adult or even to make significant progress toward that social position. In their community, recall, status is earned by becoming a well-paid professional or a successful businessperson. In well-to-do places like Peachville, individuals who fail to achieve conventional success or are not perceived as well on their way to doing so by their midtwenties are often-times dismissed as losers by almost everyone—including their own parents. In discussing how he knew his supplier, Brendan inadvertently revealed how little he and the rest of the middle-class dealers understood about the world of working-class labor:

> He was just this hippy dude that worked at the grocery store. I'd say he's twenty-eight, twenty-nine. He didn't have an education or anything like that. He was a baker, and he was coming up in the world of baking, I guess you'd say, if you can do that. I don't know if you can come up in the baking world, but if you could, he was. I started buying from him, and I noticed everybody liked the herb. When I first started getting weed from him, I wasn't selling weed, and then I started noticing everybody liked the weed that I was getting, and then I started getting it, and then I started selling it.

Dealers preferred to obtain their drug supplies from friends or, to a lesser extent, from coworkers largely because such individuals were perceived as being less risky than others. But as already noted, there are few suppliers available to these high school dealers, and even the most reliable suppliers sometimes run out of stock. In order to obtain product, then, the dealers occasionally had to branch out beyond their own personal network.

How did dealers connect with suppliers who were not already known to them? By far the most common way was via friends they knew through school. Jared, for instance, characterized his suppliers as follows: "Most of them were friends, people I already knew. If it was someone I didn't know, then it was a friend-of-a-friend who introduced me." Phillip and his supplier were introduced to each other through mutual friends: "When I started dealing, I bought it from just the guy who was some of my friends' friend. I didn't know him too well. We weren't like in the same social group or anything. We just knew each other through other people. He needed to get rid of stuff and I needed to get stuff so that was our relationship." Pete's best friend put him in touch with his sister's boyfriend, who happened to be a supplier:

> I met him through one of my best friends. He lived kind of far away, further away than the first dealer I had. So, basically, if I called one of them and he didn't have anything, I'd call the other one and he'd for sure have it. It was my best friend's sister's boyfriend. My friend told me he could get me better

prices for the amount I was buying at the time. I was buying a QP [quarter pound] for like $1,200 at the time, and he was like, "You know, my sister's boyfriend can get it to you for $1,150." I was like, "Really?" I went out there, got it, met him, chilled out at his house for like two hours with my friend, rode around on some dirt bikes and four-wheelers, chilled out with him.

Christian too met his supplier through a mutual friend:

I had a friend who had two friends that were like really big dealers, like really big, like way above us, like buying pounds and pounds grown in middle Georgia, so they were getting it from the actual grower and bringing it back here and selling it. I would deal with him. His name was Bubba. As soon as I found out this guy's name, I was like, "Who the fuck is this guy? Who the fuck names their kid Bubba?" It's like the worst redneck name I've ever heard. But he was always straight.

Mike recalls how he met a college-based ecstasy dealer through a mutual friend and suddenly realized that he could extend that operation to his high school: "The main ecstasy guy, he was in college. He was in a fraternity. I think I just met him through a friend. It dawned on me the fact that he was in college and had access to college kids, but I knew all the high school kids." Ed described the process through which he connected with a supplier: "My friend was friendly with this guy. He told me that this guy was trying to move up and that I should talk to him. So I talked to him and he was a cool guy." And something similar happened to Stephen: "I met him through a friend, a good friend of mine. I sort of met him at the party with the friend of mine and we just hung out that night, and that was really the first and only night we knew each other before this all started."

That dealers were connected to their suppliers through mutual friends should come as no surprise; we observed earlier that the school-based network—through which most people acquire their friends—is characterized by overlapping ties. Users who wanted to be dealers, or dealers who wanted to expand their networks, would use their friends as intermediaries to reach suppliers. This benefited all drug market participants—suppliers, dealers, and users alike.

As there were far fewer suppliers than there were retail dealers in Peachville, it is unsurprising that most of the sellers obtained their contraband from just one or two individuals. Over the course of their careers they might buy from others occasionally, but only to avoid becoming overly dependent on their regular suppliers. Phillip's experience is representative of this group: "Eventually I needed it more and more often, but he [the regular supplier] couldn't always come through, so I had to go through different people; maybe just like three or four tops."

The suppliers that the dealers dealt with were demographically homogeneous; practically all of them were White males. The dealers did not get their drugs from Black, Asian, or Hispanic suppliers. At least two factors explain the dearth of racial and ethnic heterogeneity in dealer-supplier relations. First, the dealers did not trust Blacks and so steered clear of them; this fear will be addressed in chapter 5. Second, the community in which the dealers operated was overwhelmingly White; for instance, at the time of the study, nine out of ten Peachville residents classified themselves as being White (non-Hispanic).[13] This meant that the dealers hardly knew any minorities to draw on.

In discussions about our research, several criminologists have asked us whether these dealers were getting their drugs from suppliers located in the inner city. The answer is no. With rare exceptions, those who supplied the dealers also lived and plied their trade in or near Peachville. These suppliers, after all, were the dealers' friends, coworkers, and friends-of-friends who lived, went to school, and worked in the same community that the dealers did. Thus, we should not be shocked to discover that, by and large, they too were middle-class suburbanites.[14]

The dealers described their suppliers as belonging to everything from the upper to the lower class, though their classifications do not wholly match those of social scientists. It is unlikely that many of the sellers had ever visited a "ghetto"; there certainly were not any such areas anywhere near where they lived. When Dave, for instance, said of his suppliers, "Some of them were in the lower class," what he probably really meant is something akin to lower-middle class. And it is similarly unlikely that many of the dealers had encountered true wealth; their families did not have vacation cottages in the Hamptons, although a few had lake houses located a short drive from home. When someone like Mark, Jason, or Mike described his supplier as being, respectively, "high upper class," "higher social class," and "rich," he most likely was exaggerating, though he would not recognize that he was doing so unless pressed for a definition.

By and large, and as most of the dealers realized, their suppliers were middle class, both perceptually and empirically, just like themselves. Brendan's description of his supplier characterizes the lot: "I guess you'd call him a middle-class White guy." At the extremes, these suppliers resided between the lower-middle class and the upper-middle class. No one was confirming the dealers' impressions with pay stubs or income tax forms; so, in practice, these perceptions of class were based on where the suppliers resided and the kinds of material wealth they displayed. Jeff described the area where he and his suppliers lived as follows, "We were all upper-middle-class White kids, living in a majorly White town. All their parents probably make around like a $100,000 a year, plus or minus $25,000." In estimating his main supplier's social class, Phillip told us, "I'd say lower-middle class, based on just his house and the way his family was set up; it was just him and his dad in a house." Pete had two suppliers, one of whom was at the lower end of the middle-class continuum, while the other resided at the upper end of that continuum:

> One of my guys, he was I guess like twenty-four, a big guy, like six four, two hundred and forty pounds, White guy, had a shaved head. He's a White guy that thinks he's Black: had the Ecko wear on, the straight bill cap cocked to the side, had one of those fucking do-rag things on his head. I could tell he was into dealing for the money. He lived in a bad part of town. He paid for his house—he lived with his mom and his sister—and he was paying for a lot of their bills with the money he made from selling weed; that was his job. He had a nice car. He had a nice stereo system in his car. I guess they were low-middle class, like a lower-middle class. They weren't slumming it, but they weren't living where I was used to living. In his house, the carpet was missing in a couple rooms; the floor smelled. He had like three or four pit bulls running through the house; it was nasty, like dog hair everywhere. The whole house was pretty trashy, except for his room was like a friggin' five-star hotel suite. It was bad. He had marble floor in his room upstairs. It didn't even look like it belonged in the house, let's put it that way. The other dude was twenty-six, and I guess he was upper-middle class. He lived with another guy. It was a nice house, as nice as my house that I was living in with my parents. They had nice cars; they had four-wheelers, dirt bikes, motorcycles. They were living nice.

In theory, the dealers could have ventured beyond their existing social network to find suppliers. For example, they could have sought suppliers in Atlanta's disadvantaged inner-city neighborhoods, many of which were characterized by flourishing street drug markets. In practice, however, these suburban dealers did not seriously consider this option; they perceived the inner city as being too dangerous, too unfamiliar, and too far away.[15] They had little choice, therefore, but to buy their contraband from suppliers who were demographically and geographically similar to themselves.

Buying from Suppliers

Even if would-be dealers had a supplier lined up, they still had to acquire the financial capital required to make a bulk purchase. While the young suburban dealers were objectively well-off, they were not independently wealthy, with much of their wealth being provided by their parents. Some parents, as already noted, were more generous than others, and some kids were needier than their peers. To be cool in a place like Peachville, adolescents needed a vehicle, stylish clothes, a cell phone, and spending money for miscellaneous items like fast food. Parents varied in the extent to which they provided their children with these things; some kids got them all, and some got none. Even kids whose parents paid for all of these "needs" sometimes could find themselves short of cash. By definition, an allowance is not unlimited.

Suburban adolescents typically received their parental allowance in daily or weekly increments. That money was quickly burned on drugs and other coolness-enhancing items or activities. Practically speaking, it was difficult for these youngsters to save money. In turn, this meant that they could not afford to buy drugs in bulk, despite it being cheaper in the long run to do so. For instance, rather than saving up to buy $300 worth of weed, they instead spent their allowance of $25, $50, or $100 as soon as they received it. This short-term orientation made it difficult for them to build up enough capital to enter the drug-dealing business. Some users never became dealers simply because they failed to squirrel away enough money to get started.

How, then, did these young suburban would-be drug sellers accumulate enough cash to buy their first supply of drugs? A few dealers sidestepped this problem by obtaining drugs on credit. "Fronting," as it was known, could work to the advantage of suppliers in that it allowed transactions to proceed even when their customers—the would-be dealers—were unable to afford what they wanted to buy.[16] Getting fronted was good for dealers too because it facilitated revenue generation without an initial outlay of capital. Jim, for example, was hesitant to enter the drug trade until a supplier offered to front him the drugs he needed to get started:

I have an interesting little story. Some friends of mine, they were potheads, and they'd be like, "Hey, we're smoking," and I'd smoke with them. Then I was smoking with these guys all the time; I took to their habits. I turned into a pothead and—like any other pothead—we got a bunch of phone numbers to call of people we could get pot from. While we were doing that, this guy who was a friend-of-a-friend was like, "Hey, call this guy. He knows his stuff. He does good shit." I called him up pretty often, and then at one point he approaches me about dealing—if I'd like to do it. I was a little on the defense about it. There was capital in this, you were going to get money for it, but you've got to spend all your money on the stuff so that you can buy a family-sized economy cheaper bargain, and then you sell it at retail in small amounts and then make money, but I didn't have any money to do this. The guy was kind of like, "Well, I'll take care of that." The way he worked it for a long time was he would give me the product, give me the marijuana, and I would then distribute it and then come back to him and pay him back his money.

This example notwithstanding, obtaining drugs on credit was not particularly common among this group of sellers and suppliers, both of whom were averse to fronting and being fronted, which was seen as risky business. The major concern was that the debt would not be repaid for one or another reason: fraud or theft by the debtor; poor salesmanship; or confiscation by law enforcement officials or parents. If any of these problems occurred, it meant that the creditor was out of pocket. And if the creditor was out of pocket, the debtor might feel threatened and, depending on the circumstances, be forced to pay off the debt with personal funds and absorb the financial loss. For these reasons, most suppliers and dealers chose to steer clear of credit whenever possible.

More often, then, the funds needed to make that first bulk purchase were inadvertently provided by the sellers' parents in the form of a windfall. Pete launched his drug-dealing career with money his parents gave him as a birthday present:

The first time I bought an ounce was with birthday money that I got. I got the birthday money and I had a bunch of money, and I was offered an ounce just randomly, and I bought it. It was just a guy in a car; like, one of my acquaintances—not a friend, just a guy I went to school with—was with one of his friends from another school. He just pulled into a parking lot that I was at, and he knew that I smoked, and I asked him, "I'm looking for some weed, blah-blah-blah-blah." And was like, "My buddy is in the car. He's got plenty. You want to buy an ounce?" And I was like, "Yeah, yeah, I'll buy an ounce." After I got it from him that one time, I found out who he was getting it from. A girl at school, I told her that I got an ounce from this guy, and she was like, "I know him; he gets weed from my boyfriend." I was like, "Oh really, well can I meet your boyfriend? I want to get into a little business." She was like, "Yeah, sure. Not a problem, come with me tomorrow after school." So we went over to his house after school, and that's how that got started. She introduced me to her boyfriend, and then I started getting an ounce, two ounces from him, and then eventually I was buying like half pounds. That's how it all started.

In a similar vein, Christian bought his first supply of drugs with cash his parents had given to him as a high school graduation present:

So senior year I started talking to this kid on my soccer team, and we decided that we'd go in together with our graduation money and buy some quantity and we'd start selling right when we graduated from high school. We'd put our graduation money in—like that was the thing, getting the graduation money—because we didn't have enough money to put up otherwise. We graduated from high school and we had it planned out where what we did is we went and bought a scale, bought an ounce for like 325, maybe we bought two ounces, and I let the other guy keep the scale, but the deal was—because the scale is 100 bucks—the first 50 bucks that he makes comes to me so I can get my own scale so we could each have our own scales. The idea was to work together until we could separate. We kinda had like different groups of friends, and although they overlapped each other, it was more of distinct groups of where I could have one group and he could have one group. We worked together and it went well.

Parents were not the only source of start-up funds for these young suburban dealers. Some of them worked to acquire the money they needed to make a bulk buy. None of the dealers had taken a job with the explicit aim of earning enough money to move into drug dealing; rather, they simply wanted to be able to afford the various trappings of coolness, of which drugs were a part. Unlike allowances, paychecks typically were issued every two weeks, thereby allowing accumulated wages to build substantially. Many of these young workers probably would have preferred to be compensated—and to spend their money—daily, but this was beyond their control. The upside of delayed compensation, however, was that by the time payday rolled around, an employee who had logged, say, forty hours over the course of the previous two weeks had earned enough income to buy a supply of drugs in bulk. As Ed's story illustrates, the fact that most of their legitimate expenses were met by their parents meant that these adolescents were able to redirect their licit income into the illicit drug business:

> The first time was eleventh grade. Somebody just came to me; I think it was when I started working with college kids. I had the cash 'cause I was working and I was at high school, so I wasn't paying for my car or anything at that point, so it worked out. I bought an eight ball [of cocaine] for like 140 bucks or whatever, just to get a free gram, and it was just available. It was an opportunity that fell in my lap. I wasn't looking for it, but somebody was like "Hey" and I had the cash. I knew there were two or three people I knew who would definitely take it, so I thought, "Fucking hell, I'll do it."

To supplement his income through drug dealing, another seller, Mike, invested the money he earned from refereeing youth soccer: "I had money from refereeing and shit like that, so it was like, 'Okay, I got six people that want a half ounce of weed or whatever; I go get it, get a discount, give them the regular price, make a little money off of it.'"

Of course, many suburban teenagers worked fewer than twenty hours a week and had paychecks to match, which made it difficult for them to save enough money to purchase drugs in bulk. But precisely because they earned so little, once a year these individuals received a sizable income tax refund check from the government. As Jeff observes, these checks offered youngsters an opportunity to enter the drug business:

> I started smoking weed in like high school, eleventh, twelfth grade maybe, maybe tenth grade, something like that, and just got into the habit. And when I got to college, I smoked a lot. I got my income tax return, which was like $600 or something like that. So I had a lot of money to invest. I figured it would be a lot cheaper if I would buy an ounce and just kinda distribute it to friends and people I trusted.

Once would-be dealers had enough capital to invest, they were in a position to solicit a supplier; in a few cases, the supplier initially solicited the potential buyer. When dealers solicited a supplier or vice versa, in effect they were negotiating trade terms, including not only price but also when, where, and how the transaction would take place. When it came to buying stock for trade, it was usual for dealers to call the supplier, arrange a place to meet, and make the trade. Mike's experience was typical: "I would go meet him at the fraternity house. I'd call up; obviously, no words. I think

Securing a Supply / 39

a lot of time he'd ask about how many I want and shit like that, but more than anything just 'Come over.' So I'd go over there; we go into a room downstairs in his fraternity house. 'How many do you need?'" Likewise, Katie told us, "I'd call him when I had the money and go over to his house." Robert did the same: "I'd call, go over to their house."

Arranging a place to meet was not always easy. It depended on the parties' preferences—some favored residences, others neighborhoods, and others public parking lots—as well as on how well the two parties knew each other and Peachville, with greater intimacy facilitating an easier agreement.[17] Some meetings were quick, while others lasted for hours as the traders "chilled" together before or after making the transaction. Chilling is somewhat analogous to acting stupid—which, as discussed in the previous chapter, is a communal recreational activity that includes things like consuming drugs, watching television, or playing video games together—except that it need not necessarily involve others. As Dave explained, "I'd go over to his place or he'd come over to mine, either way, hang out with them and talk to them and smoke a bowl with the guy and just chill and talk about how we can do." Because many dealers and suppliers were friends before they started doing business together, chilling often flowed naturally out of their preexisting friendship. In that sense, making a drug trade was little more than an excuse to hang out. Consider how Jeff typically set up buys with his supplier:

> I would page him, he would give me a call back and tell me to come over to his house. I'd say hi to his mom, and we'd go down into the basement, and he would weigh me out an ounce on the scale and put it in the bag, so I'd give him the money. We hung out a lot too. I remember we used to play Frisbee golf a lot, or he'd come over to my house and chill.

Chill sessions varied in length. Pete and his supplier, for instance, typically chilled for only a short time before making a trade: "If I ever needed something, just give him a call. When I'd go pick stuff up, we'd chill, smoke a bowl, and talk for about ten minutes." Brendan, conversely, typically had to chill with his supplier for a substantial period before the transaction took place:

> Man, he was a fucking procrastinator. We'd go to his house sometimes, and he knew why you were there, but he wouldn't mention weed for like forty-five minutes. You'd just be sitting there waiting, and then he'll break out the sack later. Sometimes people be calling and I'd be like, "Dude, I'm going in

his house but that doesn't mean I'll be coming out for the next hour and a half." He would just talk and talk and chill. When you got there, he'd be cooking and he'd be like, "Come in," and he wouldn't say shit; he would just cook and eat and make you smoke one—he always made you smoke one, always. If you told him you couldn't smoke one, he'd tell you to leave.

Brendan's account suggests that hanging out is not necessarily a mutually desired activity. He might have enjoyed chilling with his supplier, but whether or not that was the case did not seem to matter; he had little choice but to hang out lest he lose the opportunity to make a purchase. In the social world of these dealers, whoever held the drugs was in a position of power—the power to make others treat them as socially desirable, at least until the transaction was completed. Some inclusion was better than none, especially for individuals, like Brendan's supplier, who were old enough to have attained a well-paying job and the respect that comes with it and yet had failed to do so.

Instead of meeting at one of their residences, sometimes the dealers and suppliers arranged to make the exchange of money and drugs in a public setting. In the case of suburban drug markets, such transactions are best described, not as street dealing, but rather as parking lot dealing. Josh often met his supplier at one of their homes, but sometimes they relied on parking lots instead:

Well, the guy that I barely knew, I would just come over and pick it up and he would have it in like a brown bag, just like a paper bag, in individual zip-up bags, like maybe ounces broken up. And then with my friend, we would just switch book bags. Maybe I'd have one book bag, I'd show up with it, I'd drop it off. If his parents weren't home or something, then we'd do it at his house. If my dad wasn't home, then we'd do it at my house. Also at parking lots. I'd have one book bag, give it to him, and then he'd have the money and he'd give me the pot. We'd just do it like that. Or he would just come over and weigh everything out and then put it in a zip-up bag and give it to me. Or I'd drop off the money to him and he would run it back over to me.

Likewise, Christian made purchases from his supplier at a local strip mall: "We'd decide on a time and place to meet. A lot of time we'd meet at [a Mexican restaurant]: we show up, he gets in the truck, shows me the weight, I hand over the money, and then we kick it."

Parking lots are a prominent feature of the Peachville landscape, reflecting the fact that car ownership is crucial to life there. Distances between residential areas and commercial districts are pronounced, making walking or biking impractical for many and impossible for some, and public transportation is nonexistent.[18] Most everyone who is old enough to do so drives, and virtually every business, strip mall, gym, church, school, park, or public pool has its own parking lot. As coming chapters will make clear, those lots play a central role in teenage suburban drug markets. This notorious feature of America's suburbs serves not only as a place to park your vehicle while conducting legitimate business but also as a simultaneously perilous and protective environment for local drug traders.

CHAPTER 3

Selling to Customers

Once the would-be dealers successfully had acquired a supply of drugs, they were in a position to put their intentions into practice. With quantity in hand, they could initiate the process of converting their investment into free drugs, extra money for various coolness-enhancing items, and a more central place within their peer network. To net these benefits, however, the dealers first had to find or be found by customers, set up exchanges, and carry them out.[1] Each of these steps is bathed in legal and reputational risk and must be negotiated accordingly. How did the dealers establish a customer base? How did they set up and carry out transactions? Did they charge everyone the same price? If not, why did one customer get a better or worse bargain than someone else?

Acquiring Customers

When asked how they obtained their customers, almost all of the dealers indicated that these individuals were friends.[2] Jeff, for example, reported, "An average buyer was a friend that was over at my house that would hang out with me every day at my pool. They were people I had known for years and years, so they would just come over and I was the guy who had the weed. It was simple." And Andrea explained, "I only sold to my friends—someone I've known for a really long time, that I've been through school with."

Not every dealer sold exclusively to friends, but all of them saw their customer base as being populated largely by buddies. The most obvious reason that the bulk of the dealers' customer base consisted of friends is that they were using drugs with these individuals already and so had a preexisting population of known and trusted potential buyers. Moreover, most of the dealers had meager financial goals and were anxious to reduce risk, which served to minimize any desire to expand their operation beyond their immediate social circle. For a majority of these sellers, the sole objective was to offset the cost of their own drug use. But even among the dealers who were motivated by the prospect of extra cash, the goal typically was to earn only enough to buy fast food and small items for themselves, their friends, or their intimate partners; it is not as though they used their drug proceeds to make house payments or to save for retirement. Justin's experience is illustrative; he described his customer base thusly: "It was friends usually. I probably had ten people, tops."

Up to this point, we have left the concepts "friend" and "friendship" undefined.[3] In one respect, these concepts have to do with actions. For young people, friendship consists of doing things "together"; they may watch television, listen to music, play sports, or do drugs, for instance. Another way of conceptualizing friendship is as a feeling of mutual regard preceded by personal interaction. Friends are people who are personally known to one another and who deem one another to be cool. The dealers subscribed to both of these notions of friends and friendship. They wanted to be labeled as a friend by people they regarded as cool, which made them feel socially desired and affected evaluations of their coolness by others. Having friends, especially cool friends, implied that they were likable or attractive. A perceptual rule of thumb is that more friends equated to more coolness. The reason that this rule of thumb is not a law is that some friendships were detrimental to coolness. The cooler or lamer other people perceived a person to be, the cooler or lamer it was to be seen as their friend.[4] Because some friendships could undermine perceived coolness, the dealers and their peers were selective about those whom they claimed as friends. They were reluctant to hang out with or call someone their buddy who was perceived by others to be unattractive or unlikable, especially when that assessment was shared by people whom they regarded as being cool.

If a person met a minimal level of likability and attractiveness, it was advantageous for the dealers to interact with that individual in a friendly way and to embrace the friend label. That is true because their own perceived coolness increased as they acquired more cool friends. And for that reason, and also to make additional profit, most dealers were willing to sell to "friends-of-friends." Jared said of his customers, "Most of them were friends, people I already knew. I didn't deal with people I didn't know. If it was someone I didn't know, then it was a friend-of-a-friend." Stephen explained that his clients were "primarily friends and it quickly became friends-of-friends." Joseph described the loose tie—knotted by shared friends—that held him and some of his customers together: "I had a lot of friends who smoked and they all bought from me. They would tell their friends, 'Come and buy from this guy.'" Nathaniel characterized his clients as "all acquaintances at the very least. I never sold to anybody I didn't know personally or wasn't introduced to previously before by one of my friends. Friends would be like, 'I got this buddy, blah blah blah, this and that,' and you know I'd go meet them."

Selling drugs facilitated coolness in another way: by providing opportunities to display and win cool points above and beyond those directly tied to selling. Making a trade almost invariably required the seller and buyer to engage in face-to-face interaction. That interaction allowed them to demonstrate how cool they were, thereby facilitating an expansion of their friendship network. Recall that Mark said of his customers that a "lot of them are acquaintances or whatever, but a lot of them became friends out of it." Tom told us, "I really met a lot of people through selling, and some of them have actually become really good friends." And Pete explained that many of his friend-of-a-friend customers "became my friends, and after I stopped dealing, they were still good friends." Not only did dealing help turn friends-of-friends into friends, but it also opened doors to other sorts of social opportunities. Dealers—if they were deemed to be cool enough—were invited to various gatherings by their customers. Such encounters allowed dealers to acquire even more friends in the process.

Besides friends and friends-of-friends, some of the dealers also sold drugs to workplace colleagues. Josh explained, "I ended up selling a lot to people that I worked with. I had people that I worked with buying stuff off me every week or a few times a week. I sold to people at work as long as I knew them somewhat." Frank described how the people he worked with started buying drugs from him: "I was working at a real upscale restaurant. After I'd worked there for a while and people got comfortable with me, they'd be like, 'Hey, aren't you?' and I'd say, 'Yeah,' and you know word of mouth. People would just come out to my car after work or something. I'd weigh it out and give it to them."

Seldom, however, did coworkers account for more than a small proportion of the dealers' customer base. For one thing, not all of the dealers had jobs. For another, the vast majority of them had very modest financial goals and plenty of customers who were friends or friends-of-friends. Lastly, these dealers did not much care whether their coworkers, who tended to be older than they were, perceived them to be cool. In their eyes, older colleagues were usually "losers" trapped in dead-end "kids' jobs" that required few skills and garnered little in the way of conventional status and respect.

The only reasons to sell to such persons, then, were to subsidize their own drug use or to make some extra cash with which to impress their peers.

Given that dealers did business mostly with friends and friends-of-friends and occasionally with coworkers, it is unsurprising that the demographic characteristics of their customers reflected those of the sellers themselves. Indeed, the demographic makeup of the entire market was largely the same from top to bottom. Almost all of the dealers were White, male, and middle class, as were their suppliers and customers. Brendan summed up the average buyer when he described them as "all middle-class White kids."

The dealers universally defined their customers as being middle class and as residing at the upper end of the spectrum. Justin, Christian, and Robert, for instance, respectively described their customers as "all middle class, maybe some upper-middle class"; "pretty much all middle and upper-middle class"; and "middle class, upper middle." Such assessments were based in part on the outward trappings of middle-class success. Andrea said that the youngsters she sold drugs to were "mostly upper and the middle classes, based on their house and the way they live and their parents, what car they drive, and clothes they wear." Similarly, Pete told us, "They were all higher middle class. I base that on the success of their parents. I mean most of the people I sold weed to I knew their parents too, I knew where they lived, and I knew what kind of cars they drove. All these kids had cars that their parents bought for them. You know, they had money. All of them had money."

Beyond social class, Whites dominated the dealers' customer base. Some of them consciously avoided selling to Blacks, but truth be told, Peachville's racial homogeneity ensured that this typically required little effort on their part. Christian neatly summed up this idea when he said, "I'd sell to Black people, but there aren't any."

The homogeneity of two other demographic factors—age and gender— cannot be explained simply in terms of community makeup. Peachville had an almost equal number of males and females, and people there varied in age from young to old. Yet the dealers' customers, like themselves, were mostly male and young. The majority of their customers were, in Jared's words, "same age or younger or older by a few years." When asked how old his customers were, Tom told us, "Anywhere from three years older to three years younger, mostly my age, mostly to my peers I would sell it to." Likewise, Justin said, "All around the same as me." The fact that the dealers were close in age to their customers obviously reflects the fact that they sold mostly to their schoolmates.

The only exception involved coworker customers, whose age could stretch upward of thirty. Ed, for instance, told us, "My customers are my friends. And I've got thirty-year-olds that I work with." Brendan, who found his supplier through work, also sold to his coworkers: "Most of the people were my friends before I started selling weed, or I know them from work. I know a couple of older folks and they're all White. We used to work at a grocery store together. They're probably like thirty, thirty-five years old." Bruce was one of the dealers who had access to a more mature customer base:

> They were lots of different ages because there were so many employees who were older than me that were off living on their own, trying to make as much money as they could, and then some of them were just teenagers that were just working, trying to make money so they could go out and spend it on pot. I'd say probably fifteen through probably twenty-seven.

The dealers were willing to sell to these individuals simply because it was financially profitable, which is to say that they showed little interest in befriending their older customers.

Adolescent males represented the bulk of the dealers' clientele. For any given dealer, the percentage of female customers ranged from nil up to about 30 percent. On the low end were dealers like Jason, who reported: "They were all guys. I didn't sell to any girls." Christian had a few female buyers: "My customers, they were probably 5 percent girls." And Bruce said, "Like 90 percent guys." Mark offered a more refined estimate of "83 percent guys, 17 percent females." When we asked Brendan about the male-to-female ratio of his customers, his answer was "four to one." It is noteworthy that the two female dealers we interviewed, Katie and Andrea, were no different from their male counterparts in terms of the gender distribution of their clientele. Katie figured that her customers were "80 percent male," whereas Andrea's buyers reportedly were "all dudes."

Only one of the dealers claimed that he dealt with as many female customers as male ones. Asked about the gender composition of his customer base, Ed said, "Fifty-fifty." He went on to add, however, "The girls won't get it as often, but I just have more girls than guys. I'd say there are more guys regular wise." Thus, the exception proves the rule: even though this dealer had more female than male clients, members of the latter group were more frequent buyers. Frank explains that the females he sold drugs to were not regular customers: "I never had any regular girls. The times I'd sell to girls mostly would be like at parties or something. They'd find out I had some bud and buy something then."

In short, males made up a greater percentage of unique customers and also were more likely than females to buy on a regular basis.[5] We know from observation that a fair number of females used drugs frequently. We also know that many of the females who used drugs did not pay for the product but instead received it for free from boyfriends or male acquaintances. Without further research, why this is the case remains a mystery.[6]

The bottom line is that the retail-level drug market that the dealers participated in was strikingly homogeneous, both relationally and demographically.[7] Dealers and customers alike were predominantly young, White, male adolescents with a middle-class suburban upbringing. In part, these similarities result from the fact that the dealers knew their customers as or through friends and colleagues, most of whom they met at school or a part-time job grounded in their own homogeneous local community.

Dealing with Customers

The dealers most commonly set up their drug transactions over the phone. Virtually everyone in their peer network owned a cell phone, which was paid for either by their parents or with money earned through a part-time job. Cell phones offer a degree of privacy that perhaps no adolescent should enjoy, at least not if keeping them out of trouble is the goal. It would be harder for young suburban drug dealers to disguise their lawbreaking if they had to rely on their family's home phones. What makes cell phones well suited to adolescent crime commission is that they are singlehandedly controlled by the lawbreaker. That control reduces the ability of parents to detect deviance. As the dealers did not share their cell phones with family members, parents had little reason to answer them when they rang. Indeed, they might not even know that someone was calling, given that such phones can be put on "silent" or "vibrate" for greater privacy. For these reasons, the dealers' parents had limited knowledge regarding how often their children made or received calls, what times they did so, to whom they talked, or what they discussed. Any one of these elements—such as too many calls, at odd times, with known troublemakers—could hint at wrongdoing and prompt further investigation. And whereas a call on a home landline could be spied on simply by quietly lifting the receiver and listening on another phone located elsewhere in the house, cell phones were not vulnerable to this form of eavesdropping and therefore less penetrable by parents.

By the time these individuals became drug dealers, they were well versed in the motives and mechanics of cell phone use. Without much thought, then, they used their cell phones to solicit, be solicited, and arrange sales with customers. Brendan described how it worked with his clients: "Most of the time maybe two or like three people will call a day, and then they just come over. They just call and I'm like, 'Yeah, come on over.' We don't really say anything on the phone. They come over, buy a sack." Another dealer, Christian, told us, "The typical deal would just happen in terms of somebody would just call me up, and I'd be like, 'What's up, man?' I'd see what they need, and then we'd meet here or there." Josh simply said, "People would call me and I'd be like, 'Just meet me here.' I'd drive somewhere and meet them and would make the deal and then go back to wherever I was." And Katie explained that arrangements were made "just over the phone. 'Yeah okay, that's cool, meet me up.' We'd just compromise. I'll come to you, you come to me; it didn't matter."

These arrangements were easily negotiated when the dealers had done business with the customer before, but they could be tinged with anxiety and suspicion when the potential buyer was not personally known to them. When dealing with strangers, the dealers often would first seek to confirm that the supposed customer was not actually a predator or an undercover cop. They would attempt to do this by asking questions such as "How did you get my number?" and "What are you looking for?" In doing this, the dealers were seeking verbal cues to determine whether the potential buyer was "sketchy"—meaning up to no good. As Jim explained:

You're gonna get random people calling you saying, "Oh, you know so-and-so, I'm his buddy. He said you can help me out," and there you go. It's just a matter of do I want to deal with this person or do I not want to deal with this person. A lot of it tends to be judgment. I'm good at reading people. I can sniff people out. I mean, granted it's not like I'm a magician or something, but I can tell. Lots of times I'll have friends of mine who I do trust and who are customers of mine and they'll call me and they'll be like, "Hey this is my friend, blah blah blah." I ask lots of questions. I do this now because I have learned. How do you know this person? What does this person do? Are they in school? Do they have a job? Then you tend to use your judgment. I'll sniff out a shady person.

If the caller passed muster, the dealer would arrange a time and place to make the exchange, which was not always easy. Peachville is not an especially big town, but it is large enough that not every resident there shares the same cognitive map, which means that they have different zones of consciousness. A person from the west side of Peachville, for instance, may be more comfortable doing a trade at the strip malls on that side of town rather than those located on the east side. Such preferences could complicate the process of negotiating a place to meet, especially when the exchange partners were strangers to one another and already somewhat apprehensive about their safety.

Dealers were not always willing or able to fill a buyer's order immediately. Sometimes they were busy with other activities, such as work or school. Adam mentioned the conflicts he faced: "I worked in a warehouse on the weekend. I'd take phone calls every now and then, but it never really affected it. I would meet people on my lunch break at work. School and work came first. I never skipped work."

While the dealers sometimes refrained from making sales to avoid disrupting another activity, they did not always let other obligations stand in the way of business. Instead, they would fulfill multiple social roles at once. A few sellers described how they conducted legitimate and illegitimate labor simultaneously. Jason, for example, said:

> I was out cooking at a restaurant every night during the weekdays. I was selling it out of the bar, and the management there turned their backs to it. People would call me—I could keep like an ounce in the fridge, like in the back of the restaurant—and then whenever someone needed some to buy, I'd just take it out of the fridge, just drop it off at the back door. It was just so easy.

Another dealer, Phillip, explained how he balanced the demands of drug dealing with his job at a fast-food restaurant:

> I did have a job. I only worked like one day a week for like five or six hours. Just a food service job, just so I could have some kind of income, some kind of legitimate income coming in. I was dealing out of that job too at times. While I was working, I would have people call me up, and I'd run to the bathroom, answer the phone, see what they needed, run out to my car, weigh it out, leave it like tucked in the seat, and leave the door open; people would come by and just leave the money in the car and grab the bag.

Pete worked at a similar establishment, where he took advantage of his position at the drive-thru window to further his illegal business:

> Sometimes, since I worked at a fast-food restaurant, I'd just keep the weed on me and just sell out of there; I had it preweighed out before work. I'd have two quarters, three eighths, and five sixteenths. They would call me and tell

me what they wanted; I'd tell them to come through the drive-thru, order something and a drink, and I would take an empty cup, put a lid on it, hand it to them when they came through the drive-thru; they'd open the lid, put cash in there, hand it back to me, and tell me that it was the wrong drink. I would say, "Oh, I'm sorry." I would open up the cup, put the weed in it, take out the money, give it back to them, and say, "Here's your drink."

Similarly, Bruce's work as a food delivery driver allowed him to sell drugs while making his deliveries:

They'd call me and say, "Hey, do you have a sixteenth, eighth, quarter?" Where we'd meet depended on where I was at the time. As I got older, I would deliver food, and people would just call me and I could meet them while I was on delivery. Like if I was delivering to a specific neighborhood, I could tell the person to meet me in that neighborhood and lose like ten seconds off the delivery.

School, studying, and homework, like legitimate work, could interfere with drug dealing. As Peachville residents see it, students must—or at least should—attend class and, outside school hours, complete assignments and prepare for quizzes and tests. Still, it was not uncommon for the dealers to suspend homework or studying in favor of making a sale. Far less common, although it happened, was for dealers to make sales at school. These transactions took place, not in public spaces such as classes or hallways, but rather in more private locations on the campus. One such place was the restroom. Tom, for instance, recalled, "I dealt a couple times in school. We did it in the bathroom during classes when nobody was in the hallways." Another private place was the gym locker room; Jared sold there and in one of the school bathrooms: "At school I remember selling a couple things. Did it in the bathroom, in the locker room." Christian set up a deal in which his customer left money in her locker, which he then took and replaced with ecstasy:

One girl in my world history class, sophomore year, knew what I was into. She asked me where she could get it, and I told her she could get it through me. So the way we did the deal is that I talked to her on the phone, and she wanted like six or seven or something 'cause it was for her and her friends, and I told her the price and that was fine. She just gave me her locker number, I brought the stuff in a CD case, and just put it in her locker and got the money.

By and large, the dealers were committed to school and the labor market, which is to say that they had strong social bonds to conventional society and a stake in conformity.[8] Clearly, participation in conventional activities like work and school did not entirely preclude their involvement in crime.[9] The dealers were able to be good and bad at the same time. Their conventional social bonds did not keep them out of drug dealing at least in part because their subcultural ones—that is, their bonds to their peers—called for the pursuit of cool.

Potential customers typically were anxious to get their drugs as quickly as possible. When they could not get what they wanted right away, many would resort to calling the same dealer—or multiple dealers—every few hours to ask when they could get their drugs. This put pressure on the dealers to fulfill orders immediately, lest the sale be lost to another seller. That said, shoppers also worried about how much they were paying for their drugs and whether they were getting their money's worth. Buyers with access to multiple dealers differentiated between them according to their availability, reliability, trade terms, and perceived honesty. Dealers who were accessible, consistently had stock, offered better deals, and were viewed as trustworthy were better positioned than others to attract and hold onto customers. And the dealers were well aware of these user preferences.

All of the dealers were reluctant to admit that they did not have any drugs to sell, which was seen as bad for future business. Instead, many of them endeavored to create an illusion of busyness. The trick was to persuade customers that they had the drugs on hand but were too busy to make an exchange at the present time. The illusion of busyness could be signaled explicitly or implicitly. Explicitly, the signal involved an outright claim to be in stock but otherwise engaged; this technique was useful insofar as it gave dealers breathing room to "re-up" their supply of drugs. For example, when we asked Christian how he handled customers who called him while he was out of stock, he answered:

> It would basically consist of a lot of bullshitting: either me not picking up my phone or I'd pick up and say that "I've got to do this" or "I've got to do that," 'cause you don't want to act like you just don't have any, 'cause they'll go to someone else. You want to give the perception that you're always in stock, they can always come to you and get it, 'cause otherwise they'll start calling somebody else. Every drug buyer has a chain: person one first; person two second; so on and so on. You want to get as far up on everybody's chain as possible, but if you're constantly out, then that doesn't look good.

Dealers also conveyed the illusion of busyness implicitly by not answering calls or replying to text messages. Consider how Jared handled solicitations when he was dry: "If somebody was calling me and I knew it was for weed and I didn't have any, then I wouldn't answer, because it's better just not to answer, because they'll think something is going on, that you're doing something, 'cause you want them to constantly think that you have it. Otherwise, they'll just think you're unreliable and call somebody else."

A problem with the illusion of busyness, however, is that it highlighted the dealers' unreliability. To counter this problem, some dealers opted to employ another delaying tactic instead: the illusion of impending stock. They sent an explicit verbal or written signal to potential customers that although they did not have any drugs to sell in hand, more would be arriving very shortly. Pete, for example, explained, "Sometimes I'd run out and go like, 'Well okay, I'm meeting up with my dude in an hour. Call me then.' I always wanted the sale. I'd say I hadn't got any but I was meeting up with him later." Sometimes, of course, restocking really was imminent. But whether a dealer was actually going to obtain stock was never truly known until it happened, because their suppliers, too, tried to create similar illusions to hide the fact that *they* didn't have any drugs to sell either. When the dealers promised potential customers that restocking was imminent, therefore, they were counting on their suppliers not to let them down even while knowing that this could, and sometimes did, happen.

When the dealers did have drugs in their possession, it was common for them to conduct transactions in public places, especially parking lots, and in private residences reached by car, truck, or jeep. Pete, who already has described how he sold drugs at the drive-thru window at work, went on to discuss how he met clients at various places in and around Peachville, including his friend's house:

A lot of it was out of my car. I'd meet at different places. If I have it, I ask them where they're at and I'll tell them where I'm at and then we'll both decide and pick a good place to meet that's a safe spot where nothing is going to look scandalous or anything like that. And then I gave them their weed and they gave me their money, and I went on to where I was going or went to a new spot to meet somebody else. Or I'd be at my friend's house chilling in his basement. Both of his parents worked, so we'd go there after school and people would come by.

Phillip used essentially the same delivery strategy:

For the most part people could call me. I had a period from about twelve to twelve, like twelve a.m. to twelve in the afternoon that I wouldn't sell; I'd be sleeping or something and just wouldn't feel like doing it. But other than that, it was fair game. You could call me during any time of the week. I'd tell you I'll meet you in about fifteen minutes somewhere, basically just halfway in between our locations. Or if you can't really find a happy medium, I'd just go to someone's house whose parents are out of town or it's cool there, somewhere where you could smoke maybe.

Tom said the same thing in fewer words: "I'd just give them my cell phone number and we'd meet up anywhere. I just pretty much dealt it anywhere: people would come to my house; I would meet them at their house; anywhere in between." These "in-between" places were most often the parking lots of restaurants, grocery stores, malls, neighborhood pools, and the like. Trevor made note of this in describing his sale spots as "anywhere from someone coming to your house to going to their house to meeting them in a parking lot, just sitting and waiting in some parking lot for somebody, them jumping in your car, you're weighing out bags in the parking lot and stuff." Christian described the way he went about deciding where to make exchanges:

> I think dealers try to get their few favorite spots but have enough where they wouldn't be in the same place all the time. Like it was good for me to stay near my neighborhood 'cause I could run in and out real quick, and it was low profile because people just mind their own business basically. Other times we'd meet up in neighborhood pools, but we met a lot of times in a grocery store parking lot, like Burger King or something like that.

Mark detailed what were, for him at least, the most important factors to consider in deciding where to make a drug transaction:

> You'd always either talk to them in person and find out what they wanted, or they would call you and ask for what they wanted and then you could take care of it. Once you get the arrangement done, you have to meet somewhere, and if that's by car, if you're both meeting by car, I'd usually do that in a neighborhood—one going one way and one going the other way, it's window to window, very quick, get out of there. But if you're going to meet them at somebody's house or something, you can do that too. I'd say most of the time I met people in neighborhoods in cars. I usually chose neighborhoods

that people are the most familiar with or public places that people are the most familiar with, just easy spots to get to that everybody knows where they are so there's no confusion about it and so that it can get done as quickly as possible without it being a hassle.

The prices that the dealers charged their customers varied from one person to the next, which is to say that some individuals got better deals than others. Exchange rates varied, in part, for purely economic reasons. Whether dealers offered any given customer a poor, fair, or good deal depended on their perception of how this would affect their short- and long-term drug profits. But there is another reason that dealers treated some customers better than others. In the course of completing a sale, traders transferred more than just drugs and money. They also exchanged signals about coolness. By over-, fairly, or undercharging a customer, dealers implicitly communicated to the buyer (and to third parties who learned of the trade terms) whether they—meaning the seller and the shopper alike—were cool.

First, let us consider dealers' preferential treatment of customers. Preferential treatment refers to cases in which a seller gives a buyer a better than fair deal in relation to the going market rate; the dealers referred to this as a "hookup." One way the dealers gave preferential treatment to customers involved offering them a "price break," that is, charging them less than the going rate for a given quantity of drugs. Take Phillip's action as an example:

> For old friends, good friends that I'd been smoking with since the beginning, that I hang out with every day, go to school with, have to see in class every day, I'd just hook them up in price, I'd give them 3.5 [grams] and bring it down to like 40 bucks—something I'm not necessarily making money off them, but keep the business going without having to lose any money.

For his friends, Adam would "make it weigh and charge them 20 bucks," meaning he would sell 1.75 grams of marijuana for $5 less than customary. Referring to his buddies, Mike told us, "I'd just give it to them for 45 or whatever" instead of $50, which was the prevailing market price for an eighth of marijuana.

The dealers also gave certain customers more product than they had paid for. Robert, for instance, told us, "I would always hook up my friends more. Maybe give them the same price but more weight. It depends on the quantity; if they were buying a quarter, maybe a gram more, for a half-quarter maybe a half gram or something like that." Frank said, "I'd give my friends like two gram sixteenths [that are supposed to weigh 1.75]." In the suburban market, these preferential bargains were often referred to as hooking someone up "fat." In Christian's words:

> I had those primo customers who were my best friends—the people I'll talk to for the rest of my life—I would hook them up pretty fucking fat. I'd weigh them out at 4 for 3.5; a sixteenth, I'd weigh them out at 2 [instead of 1.75]. It actually came to the point where I was tired of making it different every time, so I was like, "Look dude, when you buy a sixteenth from me it's 2, when you buy an eighth it's 4, and when you buy a quarter I'll weigh you out at 7.5." So I just told them straight up, and this was like four or five people, "Look, don't hassle me or anything, that's what you get." That's fucking an awesome deal for them, like 0.5 is like 10 bucks depending on how you look at it.

In general, the dealers hooked up three kinds of customers: friends, good clients (frequent buyers or those who purchased large quantities), and trade facilitators (those who helped the dealers complete sales, such as by selling on their behalf, storing their supply, driving them around, or connecting the dealer to new clients). These three groups, of course, were not necessarily mutually exclusive. For example, a friend could also be a regular buyer who helps in dealing.

When dealers hooked up good customers or trade facilitators, their behavior was motivated largely by self-interest. Sellers reasoned that by rewarding such individuals they would remain loyal to them. As Mark put it: "Good customers, I'd always give them extra treatment, made them feel more special: went to them right away, didn't make them have to wait, would always come to them, give them better bags. I took care of my consistent customers because they help me out." Likewise, Christian offered some customers better-than-fair deals to keep them coming back for more:

> Some people I'd just hook up like a tenth of a gram; if it was an eighth, I'd weigh them out at 3.6 instead of 3.5. There's no reason other than just that people really like that; they love getting a little extra; they love to feel special. It was a complete business thing. It felt good to hook my friends up, but anybody else I would hook up would be a business strategy. If you weigh somebody out fat every time, they'll come to you every time, and that's just how it is, even if they have to wait an hour for you, which is kinda ridiculous when you're talking about 0.1 or 0.2.

Phillip explained that he rewarded not only his regulars but also those who brought him especially lucrative new clients: "Steady customers that are coming to me two or three times a week, especially with their friends too—start bringing friends who need like quarters, half ounces—I'm definitely hooking them up."

Fiscal concerns also motivated sellers to give their friends the hookup. For drugs that can be easily shared while being consumed, like marijuana and cocaine, the dealers figured that they might as well be altruistic toward their friends, who then would turn around and share their purchase with them. Tom, for instance, said, "I'd hook up my friends with a little bit more than what they paid for. Obviously, I'm going to give them a better deal because I'm smoking with them. If I'm going to be smoking with my better friends, I'm going to hook them up."

The dealers also gave their friends better deals because they had received preferential treatment from them in the past or had reason to expect it in the future. When we asked Dave whether he had ever hooked up anyone, he responded, "If it was a really good friend, of course. I expect them to do the same thing for me if I need something. But I only hooked up people who were going to hook me up later on. I'd just throw a little bit extra in there for them." Trevor talked at length about how his friendships shaped his pricing policies:

> If there's a buddy of mine and say he's getting an eighth and was like, "I got $40. What can I get for that?" I'd be like here's an eighth. Then next time they'd give me 50, and I'd be like, "Naw, it's cool, give me 45," and they'd just be like, "Ah, keep the 50 for the last time." Seems like things sort of even out. But just in general, I'd say just kids that are real close to me I would charge them not necessarily the price that I get it for because they wouldn't expect me to because it's not like I just go out of my way to provide them a sack every time they need it, but it's like I'll make half the profit that I usually would, whatever that is. Instead of making $20 off a quarter I make 10, something like that, or 5. It's just kids I like a lot, kids that have been good to me, that we have a nice relationship, giving and taking, because basically for me herb is a really communal thing. Dope smokers need their herb, everybody gots to get high; sometimes people got money, sometimes people don't; they always need to smoke. Like me, sometimes I'm fucking out of weed forever, sometimes I got a shitload all the time, but I always need to smoke. I always got my buddies to get me high, so the same kids that I could just walk up to them and if they had a big sack I could be like, "Yo, I need a

bowl. I don't have any money, can you give some weed—straight up," they'd be like, "No problem, dude"—the same kids of course I'm gonna kick back to them any way that I can.

Reciprocity notwithstanding, most of the dealers felt that their friends deserved better deals than their other customers simply because they shared a close social bond with them.[10] Pete said it best:

> Because they were better friends, I'd known longer, I might give them 3.6 or 3.7. I wouldn't give them the 3.5. Most of the people who were close friends when I was out selling never bought weed from me. They just smoked it with me. A lot of my close friends would buy like a sixteenth a week, and I'd smoke with them the rest of the time. That was just like a sixteenth if they wanted to buy a little bit if they were planning on doing something [without me]. Like a couple of them would split a sixteenth or an eighth, you know if they had a baseball game. I'd give them a sixteenth for two grams, or I'd just give them a regular sixteenth but cheaper. It would be whatever I felt like, or them standing over my shoulder saying, "Come on dude, give us some more." Just because they're my friends, they deserve a better deal. They were there before I started selling, and they'd be there when I'm done.

As the account above illustrates, sellers and buyers alike believed that friends should receive preferential treatment. Justin described his business relationship with his longtime friend:

> I've been friends with him since fucking ever. He was real good about making me feel like shit for getting money off of him, without really being aggressive and calling me a dick or anything like that. I'd be open with him about the prices like I was getting it for, and so he'd be like, "You're selling me this, so you're making this much money off me," and I was like, "Fine," and sell it to him for maybe even 85, 80, sometimes [instead of $100].

Some dealers calculated that the price of hooking up their friends reduced their profits. Jared said exactly that: "Friends you would definitely give more. I was a little too generous sometimes and not make as much money as I could, a lot of times. Per eighth for a friend would be like 3.7. Going back to acid or Xanax, maybe if they bought a few, I'd give them a free one or something, a free hit or a free pill." Such statements indicate that hooking up customers was not always viewed by the dealers as the most financially lucrative line of action. But they persisted in doing so. Why? One reason is that they emphasized the benefits of selling over its risks and yet, paradoxically, thought of profit as something to which they were not always entitled. As Jeff said, "I wasn't ever stingy with it because I was getting it more or less for free." And Ron reported, "Sometimes I would give my friends free ones, shit like that. Like my good friends, I would charge them like what I paid. I was making money either way." What these dealers failed to acknowledge is that by buying in bulk they were exposing themselves to increased legal risks, whereas their friends were not.

Dealers perceived giving their friends the hookup to be as much a social obligation as a business arrangement. The reason that the sellers were obliged to give their friends preferential treatment was that individuals who were friends by definition were seen as cool, and cool people—according to the prevailing social code among suburban kids in Peachville—deserved better treatment than others. Were a dealer to give a friend only a fair bargain without justification, such as being low on stock, this action would send the customer a signal that he or she was, in fact, not a friend and not cool. This was a major reason, perhaps *the* major reason, why customers cared about being hooked up.

Dealers choosing not to abide by the prevailing social code would put their own reputations for coolness in jeopardy. In the first chapter, we explained that sellers benefited from being altruistic; the more individuals gave, usually the more they were liked, which equated to more perceived coolness, which led to better treatment by peers. By treating people preferentially, then, the dealers themselves came to be treated preferentially. For this reason, giving gifts had social benefits, whereas not giving them carried social costs. A slighted customer, for instance, could feel offended and take back their friendship, which in turn could make the dealer appear less cool. Moreover, the customer might tell others that the dealer was not a giver, which could further reduce the dealer's coolness. If sellers did not give their friends what they thought they were owed, even if the amount provided was objectively fair by market standards, they risked being treated less well by others.

Although the drug dealers could be generous by hooking up certain buyers, especially their friends, they also made fair trades with other customers at the going market rate. Fair trades are sales in which the seller and buyer each turn over what they agree to—nothing more, nothing less. Dealers offered this exchange rate to customers whom they perceived to be neither particularly cool nor lame. Usually these clients were not close friends, but they were known to the dealer, who did not actively dislike them.

Some customers had to pay even more than the going market rate; this was called a "price hike." Individuals unknown to the dealer, such as friends-of-friends, were often charged more than "normal." As Ron told us, "If it's somebody I don't know, it's automatically a lot higher." Another factor that helped to shape the price of any given exchange is the customer's knowledge of the going market rate. Individuals who were ignorant of that rate often were asked to pay more. Katie, for example, charged customers as follows:

> Depending on the person, 4.50 to $6 a pill. Close friends—4.50. Someone who knew something about it—5 bucks. Someone who's a dumbass—6. It just depended on the person's ability to know what they were buying. Everyone was 5, unless you were a close friend and you had hooked me up in the past; then you got 4.50. And if you were just a complete dumbass who's like, "Yeah, I'll take four," you get 6.

When Tom was asked if he gave anyone a worse price, he responded in the affirmative, describing such customers as "people I didn't necessarily like so much, people I didn't know, younger people who didn't know any better, because they were willing to. I'd probably give them what they paid for, except I'd make them pay for it $10 or $15 more."

Whether they admitted it or not, at one time or another most of the dealers had defrauded at least a few of their customers by giving them less than they had paid for. The fact that cons were widespread does not mean that the dealers or their peers generally approved of such behavior. Not surprisingly, customers who discovered that they had been swindled invariably became angry, or "pissed off." But customers' reputations were not the only thing potentially on the line in these fraudulent exchanges. By ripping off a client, the dealers opened themselves up to the possibility of being labeled a "dick" by their peers. A few of them steadfastly refused to rip off their customers to avoid this label. Pete, for instance, said, "I wouldn't want that kind of stuff done to me. I just don't want to short anybody anyway. I'm not that type of person. I don't like being a dick." Phillip offered a similar explanation for why he didn't cheat buyers: "No, really, honestly, I really wouldn't do it. I really wouldn't do that because I hated all the times when that happened to me and I got so pissed off." Although Pete and

Phillip explained their unwillingness to defraud customers with reference to the golden rule, it is clear that they also were anxious to protect their own reputations. They knew that dealers who were reputed to scam their customers were less popular among their peers.

Why, then, would sellers ever risk defrauding clients? Remember that the dealers engaged in three different forms of trade: predatory, fair, and altruistic. At the simplest level, the motive for predation comes down to math: the smaller the quantity of drugs a dealer provides to a customer for a given price, or the higher the price charged for a given quantity, then the more profitable the sale. As already noted, typically the dealers were not too concerned about making a profit. But because friends often were given *more* drugs than dictated by the going market rate, the dealers' margin—whether counted in drugs or in money—could quickly dissipate. Giving to friends, then, produced a quandary: how to maintain a sufficient level of profitability and yet still hook up their buddies? Christian adopted the following strategy to do so:

> I have a plush life and it's not required that I fuck people over. The only reason that I even slacked people—it wasn't that I enjoyed it, I didn't get anything out of it—is to hold my $100 profit for selling an ounce. I need to slack somebody 0.1 if I'm going to hook someone else up 0.1. So it was like some of my customers, I had to give them 3.4 or I'm really starting to cut into my profit at that point. You need to do what you can to even everything out at the end.

For some of the dealers, predation was seen as a necessary evil: the only way to hook up friends and still make a sufficient return on investment. While they might feel badly about cheating some of their customers, they were able to neutralize their guilt by appealing to higher loyalties.[11] As in many facets of social and economic life, the dark side of giving preferential treatment to some customers was that, by definition, it required discriminating against others. The question, then, essentially came down to which customers to prey on?

Many of the dealers viewed everyone except their close friends as acceptable targets for predation. Joseph, for one, said, "I'd often weigh a bag under what it was supposed to be. It's like if somebody asked me for 3.5, I'd go for like 3.4 or 3.3 to save that little bit, unless they were a friend of mine. So it was definitely short on occasions." Frank echoed that sentiment: "Somebody that I know, not like a good friend, just somebody I know, they get 1.5″ instead of 1.75. Another dealer, Dave, explained how he decided whom to rip off:

> Most of the time I really don't slack people. I usually just give them what they deserve. But people I didn't know, people who probably wouldn't buy from me ever again, or just somebody that I don't even know, like know me as a person, they treat you like you're a drug dealer that they're getting something from, I would slack them. If you're at a party or something and somebody is drunk as hell and they just want weed, and they don't ever see you, you don't ever see them, and you're just like, "Cool, whatever. I'll weigh them a couple grams," and be like, "Here you go, 50 bucks."

Nonfriends—with the exception of good customers and trade facilitators—were the group most likely to be defrauded. This was not necessarily because they were regarded as lame but rather simply because their coolness was unknown. The dealers reasoned that their own coolness could hardly be affected, for better or worse, by defrauding people who—likable or not—had little or no influence within their immediate social network. If the dealer lost out on a potentially cool friend by cheating him, then that was simply the unfortunate consequence of satisfying a more immediate concern: hooking up friends while maintaining a sufficient level of free drugs or extra cash.

Dealers were especially likely to defraud customers they disliked, neutralizing their predatory behavior by recasting it as a form of payback or punishment.[12] Joe, for instance, told us that he ripped off not only strangers but also those he looked upon unfavorably: "If I didn't know them and for some reason they did something to give me a bad impression of them or to make me not like them, that was really a majority of [the reason I cheated them]: kids doing something to piss me off that I really flat out didn't like." Robert said the same thing more succinctly: "Just people who were assholes, or who I didn't like. If you don't like them, you can fuck with them." Ed described the factors that led him to defraud a particular customer: "I short-bagged someone like a little kid or someone I don't like or some little douche bag, because there's a lot of kids who think they're hot shit when they're younger and are buying drugs, so I like to keep them in check." When we asked Tom about defrauding customers, he initially denied doing so; when pressed, he admitted: "I did slack a few people, but that's only because I despised them."

The dealers also were prone to defraud nonfriends who were ignorant about how much a given drug typically cost. Unsurprisingly, it was easier for them to rip off people who did not know what they were owed in the first place. Jared put it this way, "If you knew they didn't know what was going on, a lot of people just like that would get slacked." Josh explained that he repeatedly defrauded one of his customers who appeared to be oblivious to prevailing market exchange rates:

> There were a few people I would slack. I remember this one guy kept calling. I met him through my cousin and he kept calling. He called me up and he'd want like a twenty bag, like a sixteenth or something, and I would give him maybe like half a gram or something for 25 bucks, and I did that every time and he never complained, you know. I gave him a little bit more or a little bit less. I was just waiting for him to say something, but he never did, so I figured he didn't know. He just wasn't, like, when it came to drugs and stuff, he wasn't that smart. He didn't know how each thing was broken down: like a quarter, seven grams and eighths, like three and halves and stuff like that. He just didn't know how much you would pay to get what, basically, and so I sort of took advantage of that. That was probably the only guy that I ever really slacked.

It is one thing not to know the going market rate for a drug but quite another to be misinformed about what a specific quantity of that substance, such as a sixteenth or an eighth, should weigh. Without accurate knowledge of this sort, buyers became prime targets for predation. Christian, for instance, told us about a customer who "knew that an eighth weighs 3.5 grams, but for some reason thought that a sixteenth weighs 1.5 grams. I could rip this customer off without any deception." In truth, this is barely predation at all, but it goes to show that uninformed buyers essentially ask to be swindled.

Customers who were both ignorant *and* disliked by the dealers were especially vulnerable to predation. Consider the following account by Robert:

> I fucked people. I sold a kid a bag of oregano that one time. He called me up, and he was kind of a douche, and he was wanting pot. So we put like half a joint—it was a roach from one of our joints, and there was real marijuana in that—but the rest of it was just oregano, and he was a fucking idiot anyway, so I sold it to him for $25. I'd usually try to be on the up-and-up, but that kid was a fucking idiot, so whatever. We thought it was funny. He just didn't know anything about that line; he didn't know anything about drugs at all;

he didn't know what marijuana looked like or anything. I don't even know why he wanted to buy it. He probably was doing it just to be cool. I sold him a bag of oregano and we laughed forever.

To be clear, whether or not the dealers believed that their customers were cognizant of going market rates was not the only factor that determined whether they attempted to swindle them. More important was the dealers' perception of the buyer's coolness. While knowledgeable customers generally were perceived as cooler than others, and therefore more likely to be sought after and accepted as friends, this was not the only variable that determined social desirability and respect. Because of other positive traits like good looks or a nice personality, some uninformed buyers were regarded as cool and befriended by the dealers despite their ignorance. The dealers did not con their customer friends, even if they were uninformed about what they were owed. While these customers might have been even more popular had they been more knowledgeable, they were seen as friends nonetheless and deserving of at least a fair bargain, and usually more.

Figure 1. This strip mall and grocery store parking lot served as a trade locale for some of the young suburban drug dealers. It allowed sellers and buyers to come and go without attracting undue attention because, for one thing, it was legitimate for persons of all ages to be there. For another, the high volume of traffic meant that it was ordinary to see vehicles come and go on a regular basis.

Figure 2. Some of the dealers would make purchases and sales at this movie theater adjacent to a larger strip mall. Because going to the movies is one of the few recreational activities available to young persons in Peachville, they had a legitimate reason to be here, which served as cover for their deviant trade activity.

Figure 3. This self-service car wash was used by dealers to avoid apprehension; seller and buyer would arrive in separate vehicles and go about vacuuming their upholstery, which served to legitimize their presence. They then would feign surprise at seeing one another and pretend to be showing off their vehicles, during which the drugs and money changed hands.

Figure 4. Dealers sometimes sold drugs at the side of this gas station, which is out of view of employees and most patrons (although visible from the road). As with fast-food restaurants, the dealers chose to make trades at gas stations because the nature of the business is such that people are expected to arrive and leave quickly.

CHAPTER 4

Police and Parents

.

Whatever its perceived benefits, drug dealing clearly entails the assumption of considerable risk. For the dealers, the "big three"—meaning the most common and serious—risks were punishment by the law, trouble with parents, and victimization.[1] This chapter focuses on the first two of those risks. How did the dealers feel about the possibility of suffering legal or parental sanctions? What steps did they take to avoid these sanctions? And how did these preventive actions shape their drug-dealing activities?[2]

Trouble with the Law

The fact that dealing drugs such as marijuana, ecstasy, and cocaine is against the law in Georgia obviously did not absolutely deter the dealers.[3] This was true, in small part, because they had little clue about the penalty they might suffer if caught red-handed by the cops. The formal sanctioning of drug dealing was extremely rare in their community, so they had little experience to draw on.[4]

In Peachville, people seldom went to prison.[5] Although citizens there rarely committed serious street crimes like robbery or burglary, that cannot be the whole explanation; the felony distribution of drugs was far more widespread than the imprisonment rate would suggest. For whatever reason, the Peachville Police Department did not appear to be interested in finding and punishing drug dealers. Policing was almost entirely reactive; proactive measures, like undercover investigations, were almost unheard of. The most visible task undertaken by the police involved directing traffic in and out of parking lots at Peachville High sporting events and church gatherings. In this community, adults and youngsters alike did not worry about being hassled by the cops.

This is not to say that adolescent dealers in Peachville were wholly immune from police action. Occasionally, one of them got caught as the result of a routine traffic stop. And despite the rarity of such events, the dealers clearly worried about the possibility of getting busted. When asked to describe the most stressful parts of dealing, Ron said, "Riding with weight, that's stressful. 'Cause I know that if I get pulled over and searched, I'm pretty much going to jail." Asked the same question, Joseph responded, "Every day knowing we do something pretty huge and illegal; something we could go to jail for." Jim put it this way: "I get scared. I get really scared. If I get busted, I'm fucked. I feel paranoia and fear on a heavy daily basis." Bruce recounted, "I knew I was selling weed, and it could put me away for a while, and get extreme penalties from it." And another dealer, Christian, explained:

> It is stressful because you're dealing with a lot of weight. The most stressful part for me was worrying about getting caught by the cops. Like if I had gotten caught by the cops, that would have sucked. If they had caught me at a roadblock or whatever—I was always smoking too and that was a problem—I had my stash right behind me in my truck. I had it in a fanny pack because it was perfect for holding everything: it had a spot for my bags, a spot for my scale, a spot for my weed. But I knew if I ever got pulled over, I was done pretty much.

Driving around with large quantities of drugs was especially stressful for the dealers. Almost anything could instigate a traffic stop: a broken taillight, failure to yield, a roadblock. Dealers were well aware of this fact, and the sight of a patrol car in their rearview mirror made their hearts race. They would see a police car parked at the side of the road, watch it out of the corner of their eye as they drove past, and then keep glancing into the rearview mirror, praying that it did not pursue them.

Besides traffic stops, the other major way in which the dealers imagined getting arrested involved being "ratted out" by a customer whom the police had incentivized to snitch on them. This was very far from commonplace in Peachville, but by chance, we observed one such occurrence. After buying some weed, four friends went to the home of one of their parents. They proceeded to take bong hits from underneath a raised porch adjacent to the backyard. About thirty minutes later one of them saw two police officers walking up the path and alerted the resident to this fact. The resident raced upstairs with the bong, hid it in a cubbyhole in his brother's closet, ran downstairs, and exited through the garage, where the police were questioning his friends. The police told them that there had been multiple reports of marijuana smoking at the house, with the friends denying everything. After several minutes of verbal jousting, the police offered the youths a deal: give up the name and phone number of the dealer and they would be left alone. After obtaining further assurances from the police, one of the youths pulled out his cell phone and gave them the requested information. The police then left as promised. When the resident was asked why he had snitched rather than take the heat, he said, "I don't really know the kid."

Worry notwithstanding, the dealers continued to sell drugs, at least in part because they were able mentally to discount the chances of getting caught by the cops. As Phillip explained, "No one wants to get caught with an ounce and go to jail, obviously. But I wasn't all that concerned. I should have been because I was driving around town five or six hours a day and I would have pot on me. I should have been more worried than I was." When asked whether he considered the chances of being arrested for dealing, Clay said, "I think about it sometimes. I mean, it's always in the back of your mind. But I don't usually worry about it too much." Phillip, Clay, and others were able to carry on dealing in the face of threatened legal sanctions, recognizing that the likelihood of legal punishment was extremely low. Jeff put it bluntly, "It's not very risky. I know people who've done it for years and not had any kinds of run-ins. As far as something serious like a run-in with the cops or anything is really few and far between, especially if you exercise some sort of caution."

Preventing Legal Trouble

Jeff made an important point when he noted that illicit drug dealing is not unduly risky if you exercise caution. The sellers actively took steps to minimize the risk of apprehension.[6] These steps included customer filtering, communicating in code, and—when it came to transporting drugs in a vehicle—hiding the contraband, following the rules of the road, selling at inconspicuous places, limiting the amount of drugs carried, and minimizing the number of trips taken.

Customer filtering is the process whereby dealers sell to some people but not to others.[7] A major impetus to customer filtering is a desire to avoid formal punishment by not doing business with snitch-prone buyers or undercover officers attempting to infiltrate the drug trade network. Although the dealers perceived such risks as extremely remote, their meager financial goals, coupled with their desire not to jeopardize their long-term futures, led them to be safe rather than sorry.

The type of potential customer most likely to be filtered out by the dealers consisted of unknown persons. A rule of thumb among the dealers was "Don't deal with people you don't know," as Mark put it. Bruce, for example, would sell only to people in his own social circle: "I wouldn't sell to people I didn't know. I didn't want to have to trust anybody with like anything I didn't want to trust them with." Robert explained the role that perceived coolness plays in determining who is safe to deal with and who should be avoided: "I would have to know someone is cool before I would sell to them. If they came over here and ripped the bong with us a bunch, you just knew they weren't a nark. Then I'd hook them up."[8]

Not all strangers were regarded as being unknown; a person's reputation could precede them. As discussed in the previous chapter, some of the dealers did business with friends-of-friends. One reason they did so was to obtain the benefits of dealing—free drugs, extra money, and a more central and high-ranking place in the peer network. The other reason was that they were far more comfortable trading with friends-of-friends than with individuals who had not been referred by someone they trusted. Trevor, for example, recounted, "If someone called me asking for herb, I'd tell them I didn't know who they were and hang up the phone. There were some people who were just friends-of-friends, but I never sold to random people that would just be like, 'Hey man, you got some weed?'" Nathaniel said of his customer base, "They were all associates, like they were all acquaintances at the very least. I never sold to anybody I didn't know personally or wasn't introduced to previously before by one of my friends."

That said, other dealers steadfastly refused to sell to friends-of-friends. Dave, for instance, said, "I didn't deal with people I don't know. If somebody is like, 'Hey, I know this guy, he's a pretty good friend of mine,' I'm just like, 'Nope, I don't really want to deal with him. I'll give it to you and you can give it to him." Even sellers who generally were open to friends-of-friends as customers would occasionally get a "bad feeling" about someone and therefore refrain from making the exchange. According to Joe:

> I got to know who it is that I'm selling to. If someone called me and said, "My friend gave me your number," I would tell his friend to tell me exactly who it was that he gave my number to and his name. There were a few times where I just didn't feel comfortable really with the situation. If the kid sounded really young, I wouldn't; I just wouldn't sell anything to them because I'd be worried their parents would catch me and like rat me out [to the cops]. I really knew everyone I was selling to.

Customer filtering is interesting because it demonstrates how the threat of legal punishment can fail to preclude dealing but nonetheless constrain its frequency or magnitude.[9] By its very nature, this preventive measure necessitates restricting sales. As seen above, dealers were most likely to screen out complete strangers. Total unknowns were perceived as risks who could be undercover agents or, far more likely, vulnerable to being turned by the police if apprehended. It is probably no coincidence that the one case of snitching we observed involved a customer who was unfamiliar with the dealer, having been connected to him via a mutual friend.

Not all arrest avoidance techniques required the dealers to limit their sales. Communicating in code, especially over the phone, is perhaps the best-known method employed by members of the underworld to avoid formal sanction.[10] While one way of doing so is to assign special meanings to words or come up with new ones altogether, more popular among the dealers was simply to leave things unsaid. The shared culture of these drug market participants ensured that conspirators' intentions could be implicitly understood without the need for either of them to make those intentions explicit. Dave detailed how he communicated his desire to re-up to his would-be supplier: "I'd call the person and be like, 'You want to hang out?' If I was getting it from somebody, I would definitely be like, 'You just want to hang out, man? Let's just chill.' There's no reason to blab about it all over the phone. They knew what I was talking about."

As already noted, driving with drugs was risky business; "bad luck" or a simple mistake could result in a police stop. To limit the damage that could result from such a stop, dealers typically hid their contraband and other potentially incriminating evidence. Both the interior and the exterior of their vehicles offered ways to conceal drugs and paraphernalia.

Some of the dealers, for example, capitalized on the fact that their cars were littered with everything from Frisbees to fast-food wrappers and empty soda cans to disguise their wrongdoing. As Jared told us, "I always used to have a bunch of junk in my car, so I'd just wrap it up in something and put it in a pile." Adam took a similar approach: "I'd usually just have it in a McDonald's bag, or something really obvious, a bag or something, like sitting out in the open. I try not to hide it." Ironically, then, we see that one technique of concealing drugs was to hide them in plain sight, covering them with something unlikely to arouse suspicion.[11] The dealers believed that the disorder of their vehicles protected them from the law rather than inviting its wrath.[12]

But this preventive technique was effective with marijuana only to the extent that the dealer minimized any telltale odor that it might emit. Phillip described one technique he used to do this: "When you got an ounce of pot, it smells. You can roll down your window, and a cop could definitely smell it. So I would have it in the tennis ball holders that keep tennis balls fresh. I would stick an ounce in there, wrap it up or tighten it up; 'cause it's airtight, you can't really smell it." Of course, not all of the dealers kept their contraband out in the open. Many concealed it in the car's glove box or trunk. Such spaces served as especially useful places to hide drugs because police officers had to have probable cause to search them.

Some dealers exploited their vehicle's unique design features to stash their drugs safely. Dave, for instance, hid his weed in "a space that's under the dashboard." Robert "had a jeep so the carpet comes up, and you could just put it underneath the carpet." Ed told us, "I have hiding places in my car, like where the gear shifter is and stuff. I have little hiding places all in my car. If I have Valium, there's a little place where I can put pills, like where my mirror attaches to the roof of my window. I can pop that off and put shit in there. I can whip out my intercom from the console, shit like that." Fred believed, "I have really good spots where I can hide things where it's almost impossible for a cop to find." And Josh explained, "If I was coming back from my supplier's place, if I had a lot of weight—like a half pound or a QP [quarter pound] or something—I would always put it under the backseat just so I could cover it out of sight."

Most of the dealers did not actually know whether their hiding spots were effective because they had not yet been stopped by the police. Tom, however, described a case where the efficacy of his secret place actually was put to the test:

> I wasn't necessarily concerned about getting busted from people, because I had a really nice little space to hide my weed. I had a place in my car, a little secret spot. The little console has a little opening in it. You can't really see the opening unless you look down below the steering wheel where the gas pedals are. If you got a really fat hand, you can't really fit your hand in that hole, and I have pretty skinny hands, so I can fit it in there. Then you have to reach and pull open a flap and then pull it open yourself. It was pretty secure. I just hid it in that spot in the car. One time we were in the middle of smoking in a neighborhood and a cop pulls up, pulls right into the neighborhood. I remember pulling out, and he flashed his lights and told me that my headlights aren't on. I think that was bullshit because he probably got a complaint in the neighborhood because we were circling around about ten times smoking out. So he pulled us over and he knew what he was looking for, he could smell it. He spent almost an hour searching my car and still couldn't find it.

Whatever the value of hiding spots for avoiding arrest during vehicle stops, the dealers obviously preferred not to get pulled over in the first place. They manipulated the likelihood of being stopped for traffic violations simply by trying to drive carefully. As Mark explained, "If I was driving when I was dealing, I'd follow the rules of the road." When dealers had drugs on them, they seemingly became some of the world's most diligent drivers. Christian said that whenever he had drugs in his vehicle, "I was a safe driver. I'd never speed or anything like that. Consciously be careful with the driving: make sure you don't run a red or anything, full stop at stop signs, use my blinkers." And Katie said her method of avoiding police stops was the following: "Don't speed when I have pills on me; use turn signals when I have a quantity on me." We see, then, that whereas driving under the influence can increase the likelihood of accidents, drug dealing may have actually done the opposite.

Another method for reducing the likelihood of being pulled over with drugs in the car was to limit the number of trips taken. As Ed explained, "The sketchiest part of the whole thing is driving around. Driving around is the only time I'm nervous, the only time I really could get fucked with it. I go to the supplier and then I stay at my place to sell it. When you do that, you don't have to drive around." Fred mentioned, "I try to keep all the drugs out of the car. That's one of my main things, keeping the drugs out of the car." It should go without saying that while this is a good technique for avoiding legal trouble in theory, it seldom was feasible in practice. To keep the drugs entirely out of their cars, the dealers would have to depend on suppliers to deliver them and buyers to pick them up. Not all suppliers were willing to make deliveries, nor did all dealers have a residence from which they could dispense drugs without attracting parental trouble or the wrath of neighbors.

Sellers were under the impression that the main difference between being charged with simple possession and with intent to distribute was the amount of drugs in their possession. Marijuana dealers, for example, thought that so long as they were not caught with an ounce or more, they could avoid a felony charge. Therefore, some of these dealers purposely limited the quantity on their persons in case they were apprehended by the police. Ed observed, "I know there's a law like about twenty-eight grams, enough to get to federal court, so I'd just get one ounce at a time. I will always pick up one at a time. As soon as you start grabbing two at a time, you're putting yourself at risk." Bruce told us, "I never carried a whole lot on me. I always left it at the house, the majority of it. I always kept enough to where if somebody wanted a bag, or maybe another bag, I could give it to them." As with customer filtering, when dealers limited the quantity purchased at any one time, it could restrict their ability to make trades and income. They forfeited the better prices that went along with larger purchases and risked running out of stock for trade, thereby losing potential customers.

Dealers also refrained from carrying a scale, small plastic bags, or other accessories because such items were thought to serve as evidence of dealing. For example, Robert said, "The only time that I was really at risk was when I had marijuana in my car and was driving. I didn't carry scales in the car, and try not to carry a shitload of bags and stuff. I would try not to transport more than an ounce, so if I did get caught, I wouldn't be charged with distributing."

As discussed in the previous two chapters, dealers did not simply *transport* drugs in vehicles but also carried out transactions in them. This exposed the dealers to police action. Here again, the key to minimizing the risk inherent in such situations was to create an impression of normalcy.[13] As normalcy is a function of conventionality, the dealers sought to conduct their trades in busy public places. To avoid detection, Jared would "try not to sit around in one place waiting for a deal, try not to just sit there and look suspicious. We had a certain parking lot that we'd meet at. It was pretty good, pretty big so you could blend in. It was a grocery store in a little shopping center." Another seller, Christian, explained:

> I just tried to pick my spots. I'd lived in the community long enough where I knew where the cops would be. I picked my spots where to meet people: grocery stores, pharmacies, restaurants, the movie theater, neighborhood pools, stuff like that. And I'd try to make the deal as quick as possible. It's the only way you can do a deal really with people looking at you but not necessarily know what you're doing 'cause you could have a reason to be there.

Phillip "preferred meeting at a really public place, like a place where there's a million people walking around, and you wouldn't think twice about a car just sitting in the parking lot. Places like grocery stores that are open twenty-four hours. I'd just stop by there and drop something off." And Frank claimed that he went so far as to "take my girlfriend with me to look like I was just taking her out." The fact that dealers sometimes preferred to transact business in busy places rather than more private ones might seem counterintuitive. But dealers realized that the very "publicness" of such settings served to normalize their presence, making them less conspicuous. Teenagers were recognized by the whole community as having few places to congregate; they could not go grab a beer, for instance. Thus, when adults saw them loitering in a parking lot, it was rarely construed as deviant or suspicious, at least not to the extent that anyone would do anything about it, especially because everyone was obliged to engage in civil inattention.[14] Moreover, the transient nature of parking lots meant that no matter how many people came and went, no one was there long enough to witness a drug sale or, if they did, to become invested enough in the problem to exercise control—assuming the traders did not take too long.

The dealers did not want to linger in such locations for fear of drawing attention to themselves. Yet it was not easy for dealers and buyers to coordinate their travel to arrive at a public place at precisely the same time. A variety of "things" could come up. Traders would underestimate how long it would take them to reach the agreed-upon meeting spot or would be delayed by their parents, traffic, or the need to fill up on gas. If everything went according to plan, one party might have to wait only a few minutes for the other to arrive, but sometimes this delay could stretch upwards of thirty minutes. With each passing minute, the lone trader assumed a greater risk of attracting attention; occasionally, they would become annoyed or develop a "bad feeling" and leave before making the sale.

Making a drug sale in a public parking lot offered some protection from the law, but obviously, it was not perfectly safe. Bruce, for instance, thought that to "meet in high-populated areas at certain times is some stupid shit"—although, we should note, that did not stop him from doing so. In practice, the alternative was for the dealer to sell out of his or her parents' home or that of a confederate or buyer. Such locales offered increased protection from law enforcement authorities by insulating the transaction from public view. Joe sought protection from the police by selling out of a friend's home whenever possible: "If I was there and his parents weren't, I wouldn't even have to go anywhere. They would just come to me."

An important question is why would anyone sell in a public place instead of their residence? One obvious reason is that dealing from home could raise the suspicion of neighbors—or simply annoy them—and thereby lead to a police report. Traffic in and out of a residence could draw the ire of neighbors, especially if it caused noise, parking problems, or other disruptions to peaceful living. Dealers were well aware of this possibility and sought to nip such problems in the bud. There were three ways of doing so. One was simply not to sell from a residence. More common was to limit the number of people allowed to come over or the times at which they were permitted to visit. These first two strategies could be costly by restricting the number of potential customers and thereby sales. The third strategy entailed no such cost, but it was time-consuming. Whereas drug dealing in public places required limiting the time that the seller and buyer spent together, some dealers operating out of residences demanded that visiting buyers "hang out" for a set period of time, lasting anywhere from twenty minutes to an hour. They reasoned that neighbors would be less suspicious if visitors stayed for extended periods of time because doing so signaled a normal social call.[15]

Trouble with Parents

The dealers knew full well that their activities could bring them into conflict with their parents. Although they believed that dealing was not "wrong" in and of itself, and should not be a crime in the first place, they had no illusions about where their parents stood on the issue. What truly mattered to their parents was not the morality of substance use and distribution so much as that engaging in crime could hurt their family's reputation and damage their child's prospects for achieving conventional success.

While we did not observe every dealer's parents in action, we did interact with many of them over the years. By middle-class standards, at least, these were "good" parents. They took care of their kids. They did far more than the minimum amount of caregiving that could be expected of them. Thanks to their parents' efforts, the dealers never went hungry; there was always food on the table, and much more stored away in the fridge and pantry. The kids were always clothed, and in fashionable attire to boot. They always had supplies for school and any sports or musical equipment they might need. They were treated to frequent cultural and recreational experiences, everything from being taken to the movies, to attending professional sporting events, to going on vacation.

These parents cried when their children suffered a setback and were filled with pride when they experienced even a modest triumph. Their emotional lives were a roller coaster, with great ups and downs. They undoubtedly would have been more comfortable and less stressed had it not been for having children. Indeed, we heard some of them say exactly that—with a sly smile—to their sons and daughters. But in the same breath, they would tell them that all the costs—financial, temporal, and emotional—of parenthood were outweighed by its benefits. Given the kind of parenting these parents engaged in, it seems unfair to blame them for their children's lawbreaking.[16]

The dealers' feelings toward their parents were mixed. They loved their moms and dads and were not shy about saying so. They knew that they had good parents, who provided them with a good life. They wanted to make their folks proud and to not disappoint them. In theory and practice, that amounted to doing well in school and avoiding trouble with the law. That is what parents wanted from their children, and their children knew it, because that was the surest route to conventional success. Parents taught their children that getting a good education would help them to secure a good job and that getting a good job would allow them to afford what they would want and need in the future, not to mention earning them respect in the community and a sense of self-accomplishment. Parents also taught their kids that getting into trouble with the law could put all that in jeopardy. In essence, what the dealers wanted for their long-term selves was what their parents wanted for them.

But those are long-term goals; achieving them takes many years. In the interim, the dealers experienced intense pressure to be cool. They wanted to be respected and socially desired by their peers. By choosing an outlawed path to coolness, the dealers put themselves at odds with what their parents wanted of them and with their perceived own long-term best interests. In time, this realization would lead many of the dealers to quit selling drugs. Until then, however, they would continue to worry about the consequences of getting caught by their parents without having a clear idea of what those consequences might be, unless and until they actually were caught.

What did parents do when they caught their children selling drugs? Their responses ranged from doing nothing to talking out the problem by expressing concern, withholding financial assistance, grounding them, or confiscating their contraband and any associated ill-gotten gains.[17] None called the police or resorted to any sort of corporal punishment.

To a large degree, parents handled evidence that their child was dealing drugs simply by looking the other way. This was accomplished by making use of two common tricks for minimizing conflict: denial of suspicions and acceptance of excuses. For example, drug dealers need a scale to transact business, so being caught in possession of one is bound to make parents suspicious. Consider what happened to Christian after his mother found evidence of a scale in his room:

> My mom calls me up and she's like, "I found a box to a scale. What is this?"
> I don't know what I'd done with the box to the scale. I had put it somewhere apparently and she found it. I was just like, "I have no idea what you're talking about"—just complete denial. I wasn't going to say anything. I was just like, "I have no idea what you're talking about. It must be a friend's." And

that was the end of it. She didn't press me on it 'cause she doesn't get anything, I think, out of pressing me on it. It's easier for her to just throw it away.

Another seller, Jeff, recounted an almost identical incident:

I don't think they ever suspected my dealing until one day they found a scale
downstairs. It was a big digital scale that I had that I used to weigh everything out. That set off a light in their head and they were like, "What's this?"
and showed it to me. I blamed a friend of course. I think they did believe
me; there is a good possibility that they did, but only because they wanted
to believe me.

Both of these events followed a similar pattern: a parent found a scale and
asked the child about it; the child blamed a friend; end of conflict. But why
did the conflict end there? Did the parents believe the excuse or did they
simply choose to turn a blind eye? One or both may have been at work
because they served a useful function: conflict minimization.[18] It would be
distressing for parents to discover that their offspring was a drug dealer,
which lowers the respectability of the child and the parents alike and en-
dangers the former's future. Plus, this kind of a problem creates a tense,
strained feeling in the household that is troubling to everyone therein. Fear
of these troubles, in turn, facilitates a situational gullibility in which it is
more comfortable for parents to ignore the evidence before them and accept the child's denial of responsibility.

There were cases, however, where parents uncovered clear-cut evidence
of their child's drug dealing. In theory, the parents could have meted out
some form of corporal punishment. In practice, however, this never happened owing to the parents' obvious disdain for open conflict, especially
violent retribution. For example, when Robert was asked if his parents punished him for getting "caught trying to get an ounce of weed dropped off in
the mailbox," he said, "I mean they couldn't really. It's like what are they
going to do—beat me?"

Robert's experience notwithstanding, parents did sometimes punish
their child's drug dealing by taking away various privileges and confiscating
their drug paraphernalia. Dealers' privileges included independence, an allowance, and luxury goods, especially a vehicle and cell phone. Without
these privileges, it was far harder for suburban adolescents to be cool. And,
not by coincidence, all of these privileges facilitated drug dealing. Perhaps
understanding this, Dave's parents took the following action when they
discovered a large quantity of drugs in his room:

They found out once. They just found it basically in my room, probably about $1,000 of weed, and they knew that that was too much to be smoking. A quarter pound. They just took it away. They took a lot of money out of the monthly money they were giving me—just tried to make sure that I wasn't having money anymore. I wasn't able to do a lot of things.

The other major tactic used by suburban parents to punish their children for drug dealing involved confiscating the contraband. Ron, for instance, described an incident in which his parents flushed his drugs down the toilet:

My parents caught me with some weed at one point because I was living at home still. They flushed it down the toilet, like a lot, maybe an ounce. I mean we don't have a bad relationship, but that's just the one unspoken. It's like an unspoken thing that sometimes they're thinking about but they're not going to say anything—that kind of thing.

It is not hard to imagine parents flushing their child's drugs down the toilet. What is somewhat unexpected, however, is the consistent finding that parents frequently chose to minimize open conflict with their children. When parents found out that their "baby" was a drug dealer, they often responded by taking away privileges or destroying items related to drug dealing, but they were almost certain to sweep the matter under the rug quickly thereafter.

Preventing Parental Trouble

While parental punishment typically was neither certain nor serious, dealers nonetheless employed various strategies in an attempt to avoid this sort of trouble.[19] The most common tactics involved hiding their drugs and minimizing interaction with mom and dad. Home was the place in which parents were most likely to discover that their child was involved in drug dealing. To counter this risk, the dealers often found or constructed secure hiding spaces within the residence to store their drugs and paraphernalia. Jared, for instance, said, "I had a lot of places, hiding spots. I had to be pretty sneaky around the house." And Ed told us, "I had hiding places in my room. My room is like James Bond's room. I've got like floorboards that come up and I've got all kinds of shit."

Other dealers relied on friends to store their drugs for them. The dealers used this strategy when they feared that their parents were on to them. By moving the stash out of their own home, the chances of parental discovery or interference were reduced. For example, after Ron's parents caught him selling marijuana, he resorted to "putting my weed at a friend's house. I was leaving it there for a couple months." This preventive technique also was used when sellers reasoned that they had more stock than they could safely smuggle into the house or hide in their bedrooms. William had so many Valium pills that he thought it was impossible to sneak them past his parents without arousing their suspicion:

> The most I would keep was five thousand in my room because five thousand Valiums would fill about a whole gallon bag. The other stuff I stored at one of my friend's house that I trust. It just came to the point where I had picked up about five thousand and I had already had some more at my house 'cause I had paid for the ones at my house. I had about twenty-five hundred left at my house. You know, I was like I really can't sneak these in. So he had a basement and said I could store them there. I was always over there, so it wasn't a big thing for me to be over there, so there was no problem with access or anything like that.

In addition to hiding their contraband, dealers also tried to keep a low profile around their parents. Asked how he handled his parents, Robert replied, "Didn't talk to them. I would just try to avoid them." And Mark echoed his sentiments:

> When I was at home, I'd try to stay away from them. I usually didn't come home until they would go to sleep, just tried to stay away from them as much as possible. I would just try to never have anything in my house where they could find out. I would never use my house phone for any kind of deals or anything. I did my best not to get caught. I pretty much would just try not to talk about it while they're around or anything.

The dealers had to curtail their business temporarily whenever their parents were around. Cell phones provided dealers with some privacy, but even they could be a source of trouble. Dealers could not, of course, openly discuss business in front of their parents, but not taking calls translated directly into lost sales. Recognizing this, Christian elected to answer his phone and step outside when his parents were present, though it made him nervous to do so:

I had to be nervous about what I was doing all the time, going in and out of a room when you're with your parents to answer the phone and talk to people. You just have to be conscious of them. It makes you a little bit more nervous around them, but I don't know if they would have felt the difference. I just kept it out of their business as much as I could.

Two other techniques used by the dealers to maintain a low profile around their parents were to take periodic breaks from selling or to have a daily closing time. When asked how long he had been selling drugs, Dave replied, "I guess about two or three years on and off." He went on to explain the logic underpinning his occasional breaks from dealing:

> There's reasons for those breaks. I was living with my parents, so I didn't want them finding out, and my dad is paying for my cell phone bill, didn't want him to catch on with that. It's just a lot of things that you don't even think about that could happen, so if you take breaks, then you can think about those things, see what's happening.

Using similar logic, Christian restricted his drug dealing to the late afternoon because "at night my parents are home, so I have to take it easy." While these techniques helped to reduce the risk of parental sanction, they came at the cost of lost sales and the coolness that flows therefrom.

Earlier we noted that the dealers clearly thought that it was very risky to drive while in possession of drugs. Why, then, did many of them choose to engage in parking lot dealing? The answer is to reduce the odds of being discovered by their parents or neighbors. If it were not for parents and neighbors, traders could dispense drugs out of their own residences with little fear of detection and let customers assume the risk of transporting them. Consider, for example, how the threat of parental discovery shaped where Jared chose to meet his customers: "I always used to have parents around, so we had to be sneaky about it. We'd decide somewhere to meet up, preferably somewhere indoors where we can be more safe, but if we couldn't find that, we'd do it in a parking lot somewhere and just try to do it as fast as we could."

Although most of the dealers did not take up drug selling to make large profits, some of them still amassed a considerable amount of cash and had to be careful not to spend it ostentatiously, lest their parents become suspicious. For example, William said, "I could have saved up and bought a car, but my parents would be like, 'How the hell did you save up ten grand?'"

And Trevor commented, "I'd say I made—at the height of the thing—maybe $200 to $300 a week. I couldn't spend it on anything real public because my parents would catch on. I'd say most of my money went to food, better herb, CDs, and shit like that, and pipes, lots of pipes."

Some of the dealers used legitimate activities to cover their involvement in drug selling and allay parental suspicion.[20] Josh, for instance, held a legitimate job so that he could use his drug profits to buy things without raising any red flags in his father's mind:

> I was making about $1,000 a week. A lot of the time while I was still slinging I would have a legit job. I was either working for my uncle or working for a buddy that owned a garage or lifeguarding. Always had a legit job while I was slinging, just to make my dad not so suspicious, like when I am buying things and coming home with new stuff.

Mike, on the other hand, used soccer practice to deflect his parents' suspicions: "If somebody needed something, I'll do it after soccer practice because my parents are like, 'Where you been?' and soccer is a constant excuse: 'Oh, I was at soccer practice, I just got back.' Even though I've gone and bought some drugs, distributed some drugs, thirty minutes later I get back and it's a little late, but soccer was an excuse." Evidently, involvement in conventional activities sometimes can be employed to facilitate lawbreaking.

CHAPTER 5

Victimization

Even before they started selling drugs, the dealers knew full well that in doing so they risked legal or parental sanctions. They understood those risks from the beginning and were prepared for them, at least in theory. But what they were not prepared for was the very real threat of serious victimization. As users, many of them may have been shorted by dealers in the past, but few had been the victim of a major fraud, theft, or robbery—until, that is, they took up drug dealing.[1] How and why do such victimizations occur? What sorts of victimizations did the dealers experience? And what did they do to try to prevent them?

Preventing Victimization

Peachville had almost no serious street crime, and most of its adult residents devoted little energy to worrying about victimization as they went about their day-to-day activities. Indeed, many of them had moved there in the first place because they wanted to raise their families in a safe environment.[2] This meant that for all practical purposes their offspring inhabited a social world in which they had no need to be concerned about becoming a crime victim.

Like their Peachville peers, the dealers had given virtually no thought to the threat of victimization prior to taking up drug selling. But becoming a drug dealer changed all that. Once these previously care-free adolescents got into the illicit drug trade, it did not take long for them to start worrying about predators who might be tempted to take advantage of them. And they had good reason to worry. For one thing, the very fact that they were engaged in the process of making and executing trade agreements made them vulnerable to the risk of being cheated by customers or suppliers. For another, because the dealers possessed more cash and drugs than most of their peers, they were attractive targets to predators. Yet another thing that put the dealers at greater risk of victimization was their reluctance to go to the police for help or redress. It goes without saying that a black-market contract cannot be enforced in court. But the dealers were not inclined to report offenses against them in any case for fear of exposing their own illicit conduct. And they understood that their hesitance to seek police assistance increased their chances of being targeted by thieves.[3]

Knowing all this, the dealers employed a variety of preventive strategies to reduce the risk of victimization.[4] These included target hardening, hiding possessions, customer and supplier filtering, keeping business straight and minimizing the seriousness of frauds, avoiding credit, and paying down debts as quickly as possible.

The dealers used target hardening primarily as a way of combating the risk of stealthy or unseen thefts. A ubiquitous method of preventing such thefts was simply to lock the door. This is a routine precaution widely used across the United States, and the dealers had been taught to do so as young children.[5] They acted on this lesson to protect themselves and their property without even thinking about it; consider what Christian said: "I always lock my doors, even in my driveway. I live in one of the safest neighborhoods you can live in. I'll go into my house for like two seconds and I'll lock my car door. It's just habit."

Another approach to target hardening employed by some of the dealers involved locking possessions inside a personal safe or strongbox. The dealers did not learn this strategy from their parents or neighbors but rather picked up the idea by watching movies and television. They would buy something to protect their drugs or money, believing that it offered them an added layer of protection. But as Stephen found out, not all strongboxes or safes really are strong or safe: "I bought a safe. I bought a safe for the pills. It was in the closet for a while. It was an $80 piece of shit, and one day I just hit it with a hammer to see what would happen, and it popped open! Then I just kept the pills in a false bottom in a desk drawer."

The other problem with a safe or strongbox is that it represents an obvious target for thieves. Recognizing this, the dealers often took steps to hide these containers. As Jim told us, "I've got one of those strongboxes you can buy. All my money I pretty much stash in there. I put it under my bed. I just pretty much restrict the mugger that goes into my room from having access to my things."

As with locking the door, hiding possessions was a routine precaution. Everyone knew how to do it. Hiding things was a popular preventive measure because it was effective and inexpensive. Fred hid his drugs so well that even he had trouble finding them: "I hide my stuff really good. I have about four or five really good places that I hide things. I won't remember which specific spot I hid it in, but I'll just check and it will usually be in one of those five spots." Other dealers made the practice less complicated. Brendan, for example, said, "It's always in the same place. It's in a cabinet nobody goes in." At the end of each day, Bruce would move his product out of his car and into a hiding spot in his house: "I never left my weed in my car. I always took it inside at night and put it somewhere. Nobody knew where I kept my weed either, so they couldn't take it from me." Similarly, Jared said, "I liked to keep it in a safe place at my house."

But storing drugs and large wads of cash in the home heightened the risk of trouble with parents. Understanding this, some of the sellers traded an increased risk of victimization for a decreased risk of trouble with their parents by keeping contraband in their vehicles. Christian explained, "I kept it in my car because it didn't make any sense for me to bring it in and out of my house 'cause that would be the primo time to get caught by my parents."

Keeping drugs in their vehicles helped the dealers to avoid parental sanction, but it heightened the risk of being busted by the police during a routine traffic stop. Clearly, then, the dealers faced a complex set of choices. While the risks associated with selling drugs could be reduced by employing various preventive techniques, choosing which technique to use often was tricky—a good method for avoiding one sort of threat could increase the likelihood of another.

Recall from the previous chapter that customer filtering is the process whereby dealers refrain from trading with certain individuals to reduce the various hazards associated with selling drugs. One reason that the dealers conducted business only with friends, friends-of-friends, and workplace colleagues was to guard against legal trouble. But another reason they did so was because such individuals were perceived as being far less likely to victimize them. In this sense, customer filtering served to kill two birds with one stone. As Jason explained:

> If anyone had called me, like when people called me if I didn't really know who they were, they would say they got my number from somebody who knew me, then I would just hang up. I was at work one night and I had a cell phone call and this guy was like, "Hey, I'm a friend of John and he gave your number and said it was cool." I asked for his name and had no idea who he was, and I got a real weird feeling from it so I just hung up the phone. I

mean at that point you just hang up. And another time a similar situation happened, but I didn't just hang up the phone. I was just like, "I don't know what you're talking about, dude; sorry I can't help you out, 'cause I have no idea what you're talking about." I just kept saying that and he was like, "Whatever man," and I was like, "No, dude, I don't know what you're fucking talking about," and just hung up the phone in the end. I was just worried about either it was somebody that I didn't know and that they were trying to pull a quick move on me and like snake some weed from me. Like I get out [of the car] to drop the bag off and like the dude when he sees it, he just grabs it and takes off. I go to drop him the bag and two dudes come up out of nowhere and like choke me or something. Seriously, I get beat up just thinking about it. Or maybe if I agreed to meet with that person and I didn't know who they were, they could be like an authority or something, you know, and at that point when they call you say, "I don't know what you're talking about," and that would cover the authority thing. "I don't know what you're talking about; I don't know who you are."

And Jeff echoed his observations:

> I bought and sold carefully, I guess you might say, try to use some kind of caution. I guess profile the people that I'm selling it to or buying it from. But usually I didn't even need to do that because I already knew them previously. They were friends or acquaintances. I can't think of anybody that I ever sold to that I wasn't at least acquainted with because, of course, that's always kinda risky. If you don't even know somebody's face, then how you gonna do something that shady with them if you're playing smart? If you keep it in a tight circle, there's less worry about getting ripped off or mugged, reported to the police.

The dealers identified two kinds of potential customers whom it was best to avoid: unknown persons and so-called "sketchy" or "shady" individuals. By definition, sketchy people were risky to deal with.[6] Asked to define the term, Christian said, "Somebody who doesn't play by the rules necessarily or does shady shit, just do stuff that's not right—rob people or whatever." Not surprisingly, people perceived to be sketchy were spurned by most dealers. Tom put it this way:

> You have to make sure that they're straight and they're not sketchy, they're not going to rob you or anything, make sure you know them from a friend or something, make sure it's not some person that you don't know that's

going to try to jack you or anything. I mostly only dealt to my peers, mostly only my friends or friends-of-friends. But if you find some sketchy folk, it's not cool, so that's the only thing that I was really worried about.

A proxy for sketchiness employed by the dealers was perceived addiction to certain "hard" drugs, such as methamphetamine or cocaine, and they differentiated between drug use and drug abuse. Many of them refused to deal with those they believed to be using too much of the wrong kinds of drugs, even though this meant forgoing potential profit in favor of enhanced ontological security. Nathaniel, for instance, said, "If they're sketchy, I don't deal with them. Like if, honestly, anybody that has a coke problem. Those people are sketchy as hell, dude."

Some of the dealers also used perceived social class as a proxy for sketchiness. Asked how he avoided potential predators, Dave told us: "Just don't hang out with those kinds of people. There's enough people that buy it that are in the upper classes that you see that are your friends, that hang out at parties, and they always want some; it's most of your business." When asked whether upper-class people ever tried to cheat him, he responded, "Not as much, you don't see that a lot because they have money, so why would they need to do that?"

A number of the dealers relied on race as a proxy for sketchiness. Everyone knows that America has a long history of racial prejudice and discrimination directed against Blacks. That discrimination extends from the social life of conventional institutions, such as work, to the criminal underworld. The stereotype that Blacks are dangerous was more or less ingrained in all of the dealers' minds.[7] They believed that racism was wrong, but they could not seem to help themselves.[8] It is unsurprising, therefore, that some of the dealers regarded Blacks as too risky to do business with. Those who took the chance—and were victimized in the process—adamantly refused to ever do so again. Fred, for instance, explained, "I don't like to buy drugs from Black people 'cause I've had deals that have gone wrong in the past. Purchases will be shorted or contaminated with like oregano mixed in." Clay's commentary is interesting in that it betrays awareness that his strategy for protecting himself from victimization is inherently discriminatory:

I've had a gun pulled on me once. It was this Black guy. I went to buy from him, and it was completely shit weed. He asked me if it was straight, and I said, "No. This isn't straight." And he pulled a gun on me, and he said, "Is it straight now?" And I said, "Yeah. It's straight," and I got the fuck out of there. It was scary. It sounds really bad, but I kind of stopped dealing with most

Black drug dealers. Every time I went to like a Black person, it was always really sketchy, and then I got a gun pulled on me once.

Jason's friend was defrauded out of $800 by a Black man posing as a supplier. Afterward, Jason strongly concluded that it was inadvisable to deal with Black males:

> You don't deal with Black guys. You do not fucking deal with niggers—sorry, excuse the fucking racist term—'cause they're looking to fuck over the little White kid. They see an opportunity when they look at somebody like me or they look at the situation. That's all they see. That's how they are. And that's why we don't fuck with Black guys. Because they're trying to look for opportunities and this looks like an opportunity. They're gonna try and get one over on you. Always. Always looking for a deal. Always looking for something. They're always looking to figure out a different way to make things work or whatever. They're always trying to screw with the plan. That's why we don't fucking deal with them. It's just too much of a risk.

Interestingly, the dealers did not have the same response to intraracial victimizations, which were far more common. When wronged by a White person, the dealers attributed the incident to that individual's character rather than interpreting it as symptomatic of a race-based proclivity to try to cheat them. Such thought processes and concomitant actions served to amplify the already-striking racial homogeneity of the dealers' black market.

While customer and supplier filtering helped the dealers to prevent problems, this benefit came at the cost of lost sales and smaller profits. If dealing did not entail risk, dealers could sell to and buy from everyone. They would function more like bars and gas stations that sell alcohol and tobacco to anyone who putatively meets the minimum age requirement. Legal markets, after all, need not fear police detection and can count on them for help if the need arises. Illegal markets, on the other hand, do not enjoy such advantages, so some participants attempt to protect themselves by discriminating against groups regarded as especially risky. But obviously not everyone can be avoided, because, by definition, dealing requires interaction. For the dealers, deciding who was safe to interact with and who was dangerous was fraught with uncertainty.[9] They did not always make the correct call and sometimes paid a steep price for their mistakes, as we will see soon enough.

The fourth set of preventive techniques employed by the dealers consisted of tactics designed to prevent each and every kind of victimization, from unseen theft to fraud to robbery, as well as nonconfiscatory violence, like assault, and those of a destructive nature, such as vandalizing a home or vehicle. The reason the following preventive measures apply broadly is that they are focused on reducing the possibility of retaliation, which itself can take a wide variety of forms.[10]

One way that the dealers sought to avoid retaliatory victimization—and the reputational damage that flows therefrom—was to forgo ripping off their customers in the first place, thereby giving them no reason to strike back. Jeff put it in these terms: "I didn't want to make anybody mad. I was just trying to relax. I'm a pretty easygoing guy." To demonstrate their honesty, dealers who sold a weighed product, like marijuana, often ostentatiously weighed the purchase in front of their customers. Adam, for example, explained, "Most of the time I'd weigh it in front of them. I just always made sure that they knew that they got it." Pete reported, "I just don't want to short anybody anyway. I'm not that type of person. I don't like being a dick. A lot of people, I'd weigh it out in front of them so that way they had no questions at all. I would do that to let them know I'm not fucking them." And Ron said virtually the same thing:

> I keep them all exactly on the dot. The amount is always what it's supposed to be. When you don't, that just causes problems. If you don't use scales, if you don't use scales, somebody will call me back and be like, "Oh, I weighed it out on hand scales and it doesn't weigh." So if you just always weigh it on digital scales, you can just be like, "No, that's not true. I weighed it out on a scale." I just don't like feeling shady at all; it causes you problems.

As discussed in chapter 3, some of the dealers did occasionally cheat their customers. But the amounts involved in such scams usually were so small as to be virtually undetectable: enough to offset the cost of hooking up a more favored customer but not enough to provoke undue suspicion.[11] Dave admitted that he sometimes slacked customers, but not by much:

> Most of the time, I really don't slack people. If I'm supposed to give them 3.5 [grams], I might give them 3, 3.2, depending on what the weed looked like. If you got some fluffy-ass weed, then you can just rip somebody off because you know they're not going to weigh it out because you know they don't have any scales. I have a pretty good clue that they're not going to weigh it out.

Tom reported that he only ripped off people whom he "despised." Even then, however, he kept the fraud to a minimum to avoid conflict. When asked how much disliked buyers typically were shorted, he answered, "Not too much, maybe a gram at the most out of a quarter sack or something like that. Nothing too, too much because if it was, they would know that it's slack." Christian made a similar observation, adding that a major benefit of limiting the size of fraudulent drug transactions was that it gave the dealer an element of plausible deniability:

> Whenever I slacked people, I never slacked them big. Like I'm talking a tenth, two-tenths. I never slacked anybody where they'd have any chance of knowing. The people I'd slack were basically just the people who I knew I could get away with it because they wouldn't have a scale. It's a rare thing to have a scale. Like even if somebody weighed it out on a digital scale, I'd be like, "It's 3.3, dude. I fucked up. Here, 0.2," which is like nothing. I never slacked anybody big.

This dealer went on to say that customers who did not have their own scale were dependent on "eyeing" their purchase to determine whether or not it was fair. But as he explained:

> It is practically impossible to tell by eyeing the difference between a sack that weighs 1.7 grams and 1.5 grams. This made me feel fairly confident that people would not know I was underweighing them. Besides, a tenth or two of a gram will not get a person high at all. Therefore, I felt as though I was really not cheating customers out of the reason they came to me—to get high.

Christian clearly had weighed the risks and rewards associated with slacking his customers, justifying his predatory behavior by denying that it caused any significant harm.[12]

Customers were not the only trade partners with whom it was important to keep business more or less straight. Dealers wanted to keep their suppliers happy too, or at least satisfied. The major way in which a dealer could get into trouble with a supplier was to be given drugs "on the front" with an obligation to pay off the debt at a later date but then take too long to do so. To avoid potential conflict, some of the dealers consciously sought to minimize the amount of time they were indebted to a supplier. Bruce summed up this approach, saying, "Anytime I'd get it on a front, I'd make sure the kid got his money back as fast as they could. That way they'd have no reason to be pissed about it." An even safer approach was to avoid such indebtedness altogether, which is how most of the dealers aspired to operate. As Jason explained:

I was getting fronted for about a month, and then I made it enough that I
didn't have to get it fronted anymore, and then I could just go ahead and
pay for what I needed. I like to front people. But if I was getting fronted and
fronting out at the same time, then it kind of causes a problem 'cause I'm
waiting on money from them and at the same time he's trying to get the
money from me. So I got to the point where I didn't have to get fronted.

Taken together, these examples of the ways in which young, middle-
class, suburban drug dealers conducted business with trade partners indicate that they had a general disdain for conflict. Defrauding customers or
suppliers could invite retaliatory victimization, be bad for business, and
warrant the dealer being labeled "a dick." Recognizing this, the dealers
kept business largely straight with trade partners and minimized the size of
frauds or the length of time for any credit granted or accepted.

Noticeably absent from the reports provided by these suburban dealers was any mention of the use or threat of violence to prevent victimization. Asked what she does to protect herself, Andrea responded, "I don't
believe in guns." In fact, none of the dealers ever carried a firearm to ward
off victimizers.[13] When asked whether he ever had considered using a gun
as a preventive measure, Bruce said, "It's more dangerous than it's worth.
It'd create more problems than it solved. I'd try to pull a gun on someone
when getting robbed, and they'd just shoot me instead." There was a general feeling among the dealers that resort to serious violence, even in self-
defense, was unimaginable. Indeed, the only weapon used by any dealers
was their fists, and even that was extremely rare; more will be said about
this in the next chapter. For now, suffice it to say that violence was not a
prominent feature of their victimization prevention repertoire.[14]

Being Victimized

Precautions notwithstanding, the dealers were not able to insulate themselves fully from victimization.[15] Fraud was by far the most common form
of victimization experienced by them. They were conned by their customers and suppliers and, in some cases, by people merely posing as potential
trade partners. One, albeit atypical, way would-be customers ripped off the
dealers was by running or driving off with drugs without paying for them.
William described just such an incident:

Do you remember the pool hall? We were up there and a kid from school, one
of my close friends, wanted a twenty pack [of pills], so I said, "Okay, no prob-

lem." They came up there and I kind of had a feeling; it's kind of weird but you kind of get a feeling. You just don't know, but you're like, "Yo, wait, this could be a bad situation." And so I called my buddy and I was like, "Hey, bring some people out here; this might go bad." So I walk up to the car and I say, "Where's the money?" And the guy says, "Here." He says, "Where are the rolls [ecstasy]?" I said, "Here." Then he grabbed my hand and they drive off. When he grabbed the stuff, I jumped in the car 'cause I'm thinking this is $320. So I jumped in the car, and he just nailed the shit out of me, right swing to the face. So my feet are dragging on the ground; I'm trying to get the rolls or the money. The money's been thrown in the backseat of the car. I'm just grabbing and trying to hold on and I just let go. I bust up my jeans, bloodied my knees and everything. I mean my whole leg was just torn to shreds by hanging on.

More common was for a customer to be given credit but then to renege on the promise to repay, which is what happened to Joseph: "I let people keep tabs on the mushrooms. I let people keep tabs, which was not the greatest financial decision, but it totally contributed to how I wanted to be about it. One guy owed me like about $80 or something. Once he mentioned, 'Oh man, I owe you that money,' and he took my number, but I never saw him again."

Scams by would-be suppliers were a little more variegated but, compared with frauds by customers, often were more serious in the sense that they typically involved greater amounts of money. One type of supply-side scam involved the provision of cash for drugs that were never delivered. Mark, for example, told us how he had been ripped off by a putative supplier:

Me and my buddy were going to get some herb. We had like four or five hundred dollars. I didn't really know the guy we were getting it from; it was the only guy we could find at the time. We picked him up at a restaurant near the mall and took him all the way back to his house near the old dollar theater. The dude was like, "Hey, give me your money. I'll go inside and get it and I'll bring it right back out." Then he ran around the house straight through the backyard and went and got in somebody else's car and left.

Not all of the scams pulled by would-be suppliers involved large monetary losses. Jared described a situation in which he received most but not all of his drug money back from a middleman who was unable to make the promised purchase: "I gave somebody some money for some quantity. He didn't get it and returned all of it except for $70."

Suppliers also attempted to con dealers by giving them less than they had paid for. Jim described one such incident: "I couldn't get in touch with my guys, my dealers. I ended up calling some random person. His girlfriend showed up and sold me about half as much as I thought I was buying—totally fucked me over. She left and I got shit." A similar experience was reported by Joe: "He shorted me like a quarter or so on an ounce of dank. It was kind of significant, really."

The third, and least common, kind of fraud perpetrated by suppliers against dealers involved the sale of low-quality or fake drugs. Joseph, for instance, described how he had been swindled by a supplier: "I bought two ounces. It was supposed to be dank, and we got shafted—it was mids. It was $300. It was kind of a lot of money. We were supposed to be getting dank and ended up getting more like mids, or it could have been quite simply shwag." Jeff thought he had found acid for a great price, but the deal turned out to be too good to be true:

> One time we got fifty hits of acid from this kid. We were just doing it basically so we could just take it ourselves. We were gonna sell it to a bunch of kids and take some ourselves, and it was gonna be an easy deal or whatever. We got it at a really cheap price, which was kind of suspicious. It turned out to be fake. I had to learn a little bit from that not to buy anything for that amount of money from somebody who you have no idea who they are and especially if it's kinda ridiculously cheap.

Christian arranged to buy what he thought was ecstasy but made a costly mistake, despite suspecting that he might be getting cheated:

> I had 180 bucks or whatever to buy ten pills. I remember it was me and my friend and we drove to the house and there was two guys and a girl. I had the money, and I was like, "Let me see what's going on here." I looked at it and I really didn't like what I looked at, and I felt like this wasn't right. So I looked at the girl and asked her, "Have you taken this?" and she was like, "Yeah." I was like, "Is it good?" and she was like, "Yeah, it's good." I was like, "Alright." It's hard to find, it's not easy to find at all, so I didn't feel good about it but I bought it anyways—and against my will basically, like I knew what I was doing was dumb. I wanted to find out if it was real because I was so suspicious of it. I took one of them myself and it wasn't real and I was pissed. It was almost a tranquil pissed, like I was like, "Man, I just got fucked over."

Unseen thefts were the second most common type of victimization experienced by the dealers. Frank, for example, had drugs stolen out of his vehicle: "Someone broke into my car and jacked like two ounces one day. I parked it, went with my girlfriend somewhere, came back, and the window was broken. They took fucking $600 worth of bud." Similarly, Robert had $360 in drug money taken from his car while he worked at a local fast-food restaurant. By coincidence or not, a couple of weeks later Robert's home also was burgled, and more than $1,000 in marijuana was stolen.

Not all unseen thefts were as serious. Stephen, for instance, said that friends sometimes took advantage of him by using some of his drugs in his absence: "A friend once in a while took a bowl, but nobody took money." Jim recounted an incident that illustrates just how easy it is to steal unguarded resources:

> There were these two random girls. They were both really spacey and stupid, but I had been hanging out with them; I had been selling to them. I also knew they did coke; the one girl was just really wacked out a lot. They knew where I put my money. It was a lot. They saw me weigh the stuff out; they saw me take the money; they saw me put it someplace—the whole shebang. These two sluts. They're in my room, and I went down to go get someone else and bring them up into my room. And I come up into my room, just the two of them, they're chilling out; they buy what they need to buy, then they leave. At the end of the night I am counting my money; I was pretty anal back then. I'm counting my money, and I'm $20 short. I counted it again; I'm $20 short. I count it again; I'm $20 short. I've been doing this for a year and a half—I never fucked up my account. So I'm sitting there going, "Huh, how easy it would have been. They could have stolen it all, but how much simpler is it to just pull it open and grab a twenty? He's not going to notice, you know, and that will be an extra half a gram of blow one night." And I didn't notice; I didn't notice until hours later when they were all gone. I could be wrong, but I don't think I am.

Unseen thefts also occurred in venues other than the dealers' own vehicles and residences, especially at parties, which, by their very nature, encouraged participants to let their guard down. William described a serious unseen theft committed against him at a party while he was too intoxicated to notice:

> I was at a party. I think we were just having a party just because, pretty much. There were about one hundred people at this party. I spent about $300 on liquor. We made hunch punch, a huge pot of hunch punch. So we were all drinking that and people were taking bars [Xanax]. Bars and liquor—that's

gonna be a disaster. It was a crazy party. I was fucked up out of my mind. And the last thing I remember was going back to a closet and fucking this girl, and she wanted like five rolls on the front, and I knew I would never see that money, but this was as we are fucking around, so I was like, "Here you go." So I had about fifty and that's about the last thing I remember. I woke up the next morning with no money, no rolls—and I probably had about $2,500 cash—that was gone. No rolls, nothing, and the problem was that everyone had been drinking the hunch punch, and about 90 percent of the people there had been taking bars, so no one remembered anything.

We noted in chapter 3 that Pete sometimes sold out of his friend's basement, where he and others would regularly chill and be stupid. When Pete was at work, his buddy occasionally would sell for him and, in return, be allowed to smoke "as much as he wanted." While both parties were happy with this arrangement, on one occasion Pete felt that his pal had taken advantage of his generosity: "One day all of my friends were over there, and they smoked a lot of it while I was at work, more than a quarter between the five of them, which was uncalled for. He could smoke all he wanted to, not everyone. It's kinda gay on their part to do that, to smoke it without me."

Recall that Ron turned to storing his stash at a friend's house after getting busted by his parents. Unfortunately for him, this preventive measure backfired when his drugs were stolen, not by the resident, but during a burglary. In recounting the events surrounding the theft, Ron points out that it is impractical to report a drug-related break-in, because doing so can damage the homeowner's reputation and standing in the community:

One day my friend came home and his house had been broken into. The weed had been taken; a bunch of his dad's shit got taken 'cause he lived with his dad. So, we were like, "Shit, dude. Who the hell did this?" And they didn't break in. The way they did it was they knew where the key was hidden because he had come over to his house like twenty or thirty times; he was supposedly a friend. He had stolen like three ounces of weed, stolen a lot of shit, and he broke into my friend's dad's room—like that was a pretty big deal. You can't really turn anyone into the cops for a drug-related robbery. Like his dad is a doctor, and his dad can't have that, you know what I'm saying? It would completely fuck his practice up; it would really hurt him. So we were looking for the kid, but he just dodged us for a long time until we just stopped fuming over it. About four months later we drove by his house, and we saw a kid in a wheelchair being pushed down the road and it was him.

He had gotten in a head-on collision and broke all his teeth out, shattered his jaw, broke both of his legs, one of his arms, three of his ribs—like he almost died. It was just really weird. Then we just had no problem and we were like, "I guess if there's karma, then that's what it is," and that was the end of it.

The third kind of victimization that threatened the dealers involved violence. Drug market–related violence has received more attention from the media and researchers than any other form of victimization that occurs in this context. This is probably because its consequences can be grave. But for the dealers we studied, violent victimization was extremely rare.

When we asked the dealers whether they had experienced violence of any kind, many of them simply laughed and said no. That these dealers found this question literally to be laughable suggests that violence was abnormal in their drug market and in their community as a whole. Referring to the drug scene he operated in, Joseph remarked, "I never heard of anyone getting beaten up." Even the dealers who had been robbed understood that their experience was far from commonplace. As Phillip said, "It doesn't really come about in a city like this and the people we're dealing with." And Pete recounted, "I hadn't been around an extreme lot of violence in my life. I wasn't scared that my customers were going to hurt me physically or hurt my business in any way."

When dealers *were* violently victimized, it was always in the form of a robbery. The resulting injuries ranged from none to minor. No one was shot. No one was stabbed. No one required hospitalization. The worst injuries were reported to us by Pete:

I was looking for a QP [quarter pound], and most of my regular guys [suppliers] didn't have it. I got a call from a kid that I thought was my friend, and he told me he could get it for me: "I hear you're looking for some weed and I can get you a QP." I said, "Yeah." He was like, "Well, come pick me up and we'll go get it." So I went and picked him up, met these people. We met at a neighborhood pool. They said, "You got the money?" I said, "Yeah, I got the money." They were like, "Okay, let me see it and I'll go get it." I was like, "I don't think so. I'll come with you, or you can go and get it and come back." So I got out of the car [and then] got hit in the side of the face. I acted as though I was knocked out and lay on the ground facedown. I had the money in my jacket pocket. I felt somebody drag me and roll me over to try and get the money, and when they did that, I grabbed them, pulled them down, got up, and got in my jeep and drove off. I didn't have any broken bones or anything. I think

I dislocated one joint, but that's about it, and I was beat up, dude. I was black-and-blue all over. I really can't even tell you what I was thinking when it happened. I didn't even realize I was getting jumped until I got hit in the face about three times. First time I got hit, it made me like dazed, you know, then I was like, "Shit, shit, they're trying to steal my money." I got out and started driving off. I was like, "What the fuck, what the hell, what the hell's going on?" And I was at a party at one of my friend's houses just before—not a party but we just had a little get-together—so I went back over there, went to his house, got in the shower 'cause I was bleeding everywhere.

One of us actually saw Pete the day after this incident. He had a nasty black eye but otherwise appeared to be fine.

Another dealer, Fred, received slight facial injuries after being punched in the face by a robber:

I sold a quarter to one of my friend's buddies. They were both in my car, and I sold him a quarter of marijuana, and he called me later that night for an ounce of marijuana. He wanted more because he said it was good, and then I went to go meet him and my friend. My friend called and said that he had to meet up with his probation officer and that I was going to be meeting up with that third party that I had sold the quarter to earlier. Then he ended up just punching me in the face and grabbing the weed and running. I was kind of hysterical for a little bit, didn't really know what had just happened, because it was one of my pretty good friends who had arranged everything.

Although the worst injuries sustained by the dealers consisted of facial bruises, these were not necessarily a result of the "most violent" victimizations. Three dealers were robbed at gunpoint, but none sustained any injury. One of them was Clay, whose case was discussed in reference to discrimination against Blacks. Another dealer, Nathaniel, was robbed at gunpoint twice within twenty-four hours:

Some kid, I called him, I had gotten stuff with him before. I knew him. A couple of my friends knew him. I mean he bought bud off me before, and I called him looking for some bud, and he was like, "Yeah man, I got you. I'll call around real quick." He calls me back. "I could only find you this much. I can't get you as much as blah blah blah." And so I went out and met with him. I was with one of my buddies. We met up with some guy at a Walmart parking lot. Got in the car with the guy and guy pulled a gun out and said, "Give me the cash." So we gave him the cash. And then less than twenty-four hours after that with my purp [a type of marijuana] dude going to pick up nine ounces of purp. We were going to meet with one of his friends. Walking through the front level of an apartment complex, and a guy came out of the corner with a shotgun. He stepped out too early and ended up giving us enough room to take off running, so we got away with that one.

And Phillip described a similar robbery:

I'd been smoking all day. I was chilling at Waffle House with a couple friends and I got a phone call from someone. I was high as shit. I didn't even pay attention to what their name was. I dealt with like twenty, thirty people a day, so shit, it was just routine. I get a call for like two ounces and I didn't have it on me, so I had to go drive by my guy's house and pick it up and go deliver it. So I go by my guy's house and I'm short on money, actually, so I owed him like 100 bucks. I take it to this place where I'm gonna meet this guy, pull into the back of this neighborhood, and there's three young Black guys chillin' at the end of this street, like a dead-end street, and I'm like, "This doesn't look good." This was someone I didn't even know. But I go ahead with it anyways, I don't know why, but I do. I pull up straight ahead and let one of them in the car. He sits in the seat, leaves the door open. I put the scale in the middle and show him, put two bags on top of it, the two ounces on top of it, and show him the weight. Right when he looks at the weight and sees that it's straight, he grabs them both off the scale, puts a gun to my head, and is like, "If you move, I'm gonna fucking shoot you!" I'm just like, "This kind of came out of left field; this kinda came out of nowhere." I'm looking at him like "What the fuck is going on? Like what the fuck?" And by then the other two guys have started running off. He starts running off and disappeared into the darkness, and I'm just like, "Fuck! I just lost $500, $600."

By now it should be clear that dealing was not always cool, even in the relatively safe environs of a solidly upper-middle-class suburban community like Peachville. The dealers were victimized at rates that far exceeded those of their peers. But even so, many of them never experienced any form of violence, and for those who did, such occurrences were rare and mild. In part this was because the dealers took security precautions and dealt almost exclusively with known customers who, like themselves, had no stomach for aggression.

CHAPTER 6

Hitting Back?

The dealers who fell prey to serious victimization quickly realized that they could not realistically go to their parents or the police for help. So how did they respond?[1] The short answer is that they typically resorted to the same conflict management strategies that their suburbanite parents used to handle disputes, which is to say they stomached the offense or avoided future contact with the offender. Sometimes, if it was in their own strategic interest, they sought to negotiate a settlement with the person who had victimized them.[2] The only significant difference between the dealers and their law-abiding parents when it came to managing conflict was that the latter relied far more heavily on legal assistance, whereas the former more often turned to sneaky or violent retaliation.[3]

Tolerating

Toleration involves absorbing and ignoring an offense.[4] Prior research shows that toleration is the strategy most commonly employed by American suburbanites to manage conflict.[5] It is perhaps unsurprising, then, that the dealers frequently responded to victimization simply by doing nothing. William, for instance, had more than one hundred Valiums stolen out of his pocket as he slept, but he made no effort to find the perpetrator because, as he explained, "It didn't matter to me at the time. Better to write stuff like that off." Another dealer, Brendan, had $50 in cash stolen from him and did nothing in return: "I'm not really the pursuit type, man." Yet another seller, Jared, was cheated out of $70 by a customer; instead of seeking revenge, he "just gave up on it." Jason explained, "I like to front people. If someone doesn't happen to have the money, then oh well; there's nothing I can do about it." When we asked Joseph why he did not do anything after being sold substandard marijuana, he said, "We were not looking into getting into any sort of altercation with anybody. I just wasn't looking for that situation at all. I didn't want to freak someone out on a bad day. I didn't want to get into that. If it wasn't going to be cool, then it wasn't worth it to me. We didn't really know this person and we were kind of scared." Nathaniel refrained from retaliation when guns were pulled on him; he justified his lack of response by saying that "there's nothing you can really do, especially messing around with people who have guns— unless you're willing to play with guns too."

Another case of toleration involved Robert, who had a few hundred dollars stolen from his vehicle while he was at work:

> My car got robbed while I was at work for $360, and I was gonna go re-up after work. It was Victor. He went to school with me. I didn't know him that well at all, but he knew Brian's older brothers, and shit like that, so he knew who I was. They thought I had weight, and I had money instead. They jim-mied it, you know, use the jimmy on the window, and then when I got out, there was no money. I started calling everybody, and Tommy was always good friends with my brother and he's friends with Victor and he told me that he did it.

When we asked Robert what he did upon discovering the identity of his victimizer, he responded:

> Fucking nothing. I mean what am I gonna go do—shoot him? It's not worth getting in trouble over. The only thing I could have done is went and whupped his ass, and at that point it wasn't worth getting in trouble, because I was trying to sell and make a little money, but I'm not trying to escalate in criminal activities. I'd try to be a nice person and not be too much of a dick, so that's another thing. And I never wanted to rob anybody. I never ever robbed anybody. I don't want to buy a gun or shoot anybody or fuck some-one up permanently.

It is obvious from Robert's description of this event that he lacked a cultural framework conducive to violent dispute resolution. His words betray a mind-set bounded by a particular kind of culture, one that sees violence as antithetical to "common sense."[6] For him, vigilantism was ir-rational in at least two respects. The first is that violence would deepen his criminal involvements. In Robert's mind it was one thing to deal drugs, quite another to be violent. He concluded that the legal risk of exacting vengeance was too great; it could result in arrest, probation, or prison, not to mention the negative effect a criminal record might have on landing a good job. Dealing, of course, entailed similar risks. But what separated drug selling from vigilantism and constituted the second reason that Robert rejected retaliation is that drug selling could make someone cooler, but hurting someone—even if they "deserved it," so to speak—was a "dick" thing to do. Far from representing a source of status, violent retribution risked making Robert less well liked among his peers and members of the wider community.

As already noted, the dealers did not want to hurt people. They had been raised in a peaceful community and, at least prior to taking up drug selling, their safety and security had not required them to project a "badass" image.[7] Indeed, their parents literally had taught them not to strike back if attacked. In Peachville, to be seen as violent was lame. No one wanted to hang out with hotheads. Violence only invited problems; it had practically no protective benefit. There was not much to protect against in the first place.[8] If anything, retaliating served to increase the risk of being injured. That is how the community regarded the prospect of vigilantism, and these dealers were no different.

In Peachville, young and old alike subscribed to what might be called the "code of the suburb," which maintains that when it comes to conflict management, less is more.[9] In such a cultural context, toleration is an especially popular response to victimization because it consigns the event to the past and keeps it from escalating, thereby allowing victims to get on with their lives. Continuing conflict is costly. It can be time-consuming and emotionally exhausting. Worse yet, it can make all involved in the conflict seem lame and therefore socially undesirable. Toleration largely avoids these costs. Needless to say, the dealers did not respond to victimizations by calculating the costs and benefits explicitly; their reactions were as much subconsciously generated as they were consciously deliberated.[10]

Avoiding

Avoidance is known to be a ubiquitous conflict management tactic in middle-class suburbs.[11] It is perhaps to be expected that the dealers often responded to victimization "simply by withdrawing from relevant dealings with the offender."[12] Jim, for instance, described an incident in which he suspected that a female friend had stolen $20 from him during a drug buy. Instead of seeking vengeance, however, he decided to cut his losses and simply avoid her in the future:

This is fucked up. A good friend of mine, she comes over. She is buying an eighth; she gives me the money, I take it. I take it into my room, and she is sitting in my common room. I take it into my room, get her her sack, and come out and give it to her. Then one of my other friends, who is also someone I sell to and I had become very buddy-buddy with, he rolls up and he is buying a twenty bag and I specifically remember this. He put the twenty on my coffee table; I watched him drop it on the coffee table. He didn't give it to me; he just put it there. I watched this; I don't remember picking it up. I go into my room to get the thing and he follows me. He talks a lot and he was talking to me. He comes into my room, he's talking to me, I give him the sack. I come back out. We're sitting there and we're chilling for about a minute or two and then I'm like, "Let me grab that twenty." It's not on the coffee table. I go, "Where is it? Where's the twenty? Where's the twenty? Let's look around for it." We're looking around for it and it's not anywhere to be found. This girl is sitting there, saying "Oh!" I said, "Did you see it?" She said, "Oh, I thought you took it in there." We're looking around for it; she's going through her purse looking through. You know finally it's like, "It's gone, whatever, fuck it, no big deal, fuck it." And then they were like, "Hey dude, sorry." So I'm like, "Okay, see you guys later," and they both left. And before they left I pretty much suspected this girl slightly because the $20 was sitting on the coffee table. Me and this dude went into my room. She's out there alone, and suddenly everything this guy said made sense. Everything she said didn't. She's like, "I saw you take it in there. Are you sure it's not in there with your other stuff?" 'cause I usually stick it in a little Tupperware thing and she knows that. My brain is telling me I don't remember taking it and sticking it in there. No. This guy is saying, "I threw it down there on the coffee table." I remember that, I remember watching him do that, but all the shit she is saying don't make any sense. So she leaves and ten minutes later I'm continuing to look 'cause you know it could be under a pillow, I've got no idea. I look everywhere. At this point I'm like this girl's fucking swiped $20 from me. I'm processing it 'cause it's the whole idea of how could someone do that? Right in front of me. She's someone who I thought was like my friend. But then I'm thinking the only logical explanation here is that she just swiped that twenty off the fucking desk. And I'm thinking that doesn't make any sense. It doesn't make any sense whatsoever or I just don't know this girl at all. And that's a side of her that I'd never seen, and that's something that she would be willing to do that I just had no idea about. And also apart from the fact that, yo, it's me. Unlike some people, I didn't meet her through dealing drugs. I met her through something else, through a different social situation, but in this one she swiped it. Ten minutes later I called her on the phone. I was pretty sure that she took it. And I was just like, "Hey, how you doing? Just wanted to know if you saw it, if you checked your bag again?" She was like, "Oh no, I checked it, I'm pretty sure. I hope you find it. I just feel terrible." I'm like, "No, it's okay. I'm sure it will turn up. Take it easy." And I haven't spoken to her since because I'm pretty convinced that she took it and that she lied to me to my face in front of me right there. She just swiped it the three seconds I was in the other room, and then she proceeded to lie, lie, lie, lie, lie about the entire thing. You know she wasn't just some shady customer. I thought she was like someone I knew. But no. I think she fucking knows. I've bumped into her once or twice and she's real kind of awkward. I mean 'cause who does that? And she knows that I know, I think. So I don't speak to her anymore. Like once or twice I've seen her, and I don't know, but I feel there's a real hesitation like she doesn't even know what to say to me. I think she fucking knows, 'cause she did it and I think she knows that I know. She can probably sense, like, "Hey, how you doing?" She probably senses that I am seeing right through her. It's like now I know that you are that type of person, that's disgusting. She doesn't call me anymore. She never called me that often, but she certainly doesn't call me anymore. And that doesn't surprise me.

Note that Jim had several opportunities to avenge his loss, but he made no effort to do so. He merely asked her whether she knew anything about the lost cash in a nonconfrontational manner. This casual mode of questioning was potentially beneficial for both the dealer and the suspected thief; the alleged perpetrator could have saved face by explaining the theft as an accident, and therefore, the victim had a chance of getting his money back. But there was another advantage to Jim's nonconfrontational, inquisitorial style: it minimized the dispute's effect. By not accusing the suspect of wrongdoing, the problem was partially contained. But their relationship was contaminated. Their interaction thereafter became "awkward"; a cloud hung over it. He stopped calling her and she stopped calling him. They walked a fine line between toleration and avoidance. They knew they had an unresolved conflict, but they avoided discussing or fighting over it; they just severed their preexisting ties.

Another case of avoidance was described to us by Frank, who responded to a perceived robbery attempt by cutting off the would-be perpetrators:

> I almost got jumped at [a neighborhood near the high school]. My girlfriend was with me that night. She was freaking out. There was one guy—I owed him money, something like $40 or something like that. He just lent it to

me for nothing particular. This was my supplier [before I was dealing]. He wanted a quarter for that [which is worth $100], and I told him I'd give him the money [instead], and it turned into a huge problem. I thought that I did pay him back and that was the biggest issue. I told the guy, "I thought I'd paid you back. And now that I'm selling, you just want free bud?" He had an attitude. I was at his house one day and he turned all badass and shit, so I got an attitude and said, "Fuck you, I'm not giving you shit now." He ended up trying to jump me and shit one night. I was at some party and he said he wanted to meet me; the whole thing was sketchy from the beginning. He said that he wanted a sixteenth. He was like, "I'm in my parents' car. I can't come. I'll meet you at the party." So I'm like, "Okay, I'll come and meet you." He wanted me to meet him at a neighborhood pool at the very back. So I get there and nobody's there yet, and all of a sudden someone else comes driving up in this guy's car. Nobody else is in it but him. So I said, "Okay, what the fuck is going on here?" The whole time he's like talking nonstop, and I'm like, "Hey, I've got to get back to this party; get to it." I got out to go over there, and he was just talking pretty normally on his cell phone, then went and started peeing in the bushes by the tennis courts, and I was just kind of looking around and I looked over to my right and I saw three guys behind a bush. I thought, "What the fuck?" They were about to come out and I was like, "Fuck you! Fuck you!" and then jumped in my truck and sped off. I cut them off completely. I had nothing against them before that; I'd give them bud all the time, but after that I thought, "Fuck you."

Christian described how his moral compass served to promote toleration and avoidance over retaliation in the face of predation. He was the victim of a fraud, subsequently becoming suspicious—perhaps even paranoid—that others were trying to victimize him. Instead of taking matters into his own hands, Christian's negative attitude toward violence led him to tolerate the instigating fraud and ultimately to avoid the suspected predators:

So [this guy's] like, "I want a quarter," and I was like, "Alright, let's do it." And he was like, "No, follow me to my house 'cause I don't want to do it here." And I was like, "No, I'm pretty sure we can do it right here." And I look at this, and I say to him, "Why do you have a bat and a crowbar in your car?" And he doesn't really give me an answer, so I kinda knew what was up. So I was like, "Whatever, I'm gone, give me a call later or something." And so he calls me back like hours later looking for a half ounce, and I should have known when he upped the weight that this is definitely not right, but we decided to meet at a pharmacy. This is one of the most embarrassing stories I have, but he opens the door, and I was like, "You got the money?" And he throws down a roll of bills with a five on the outside, and I'm like, "Alright, here's the weed." He runs off, and, sure enough, I open it up and there's $18. My loss on it was $142 or something. So I was like, he can have it 'cause it's not worth getting shot, 'cause this is somebody I didn't know and he had just gotten out of jail and he had a crowbar and a bat, so at that point I pretty much committed to that I'm either wrong about this person or I'm right and they can have it anyways, and it was dumb but I did it anyways. At this point it's like, "It's not worth getting shot; flat out, I don't give a fuck about $150. I'll pay somebody $150 not to shoot me."

Just a few days after this episode, Christian became suspicious that he was being "set up" for another scam—or perhaps even a robbery—by a different predator:

This kid I knew called me up and was like, "Hey man, can I get an ounce?" And I would sell an ounce every now and then, but I really wasn't too up for it because I was only making like 50 bucks profit off it compared to 100 bucks profit off selling small bags. And so he basically called me up looking for an ounce, and I was like, "Dude, I dunno, I don't have a lot, and if I get rid of this ounce, I have to re-up, so it doesn't make sense, so no, I don't want to do it." And he told me who gave him my number, so I called that guy up and was like, "Dude, what's the deal with Rick calling up for an ounce?" and he was like, "Dude, don't deal with Rick. I gave him your number but don't deal with him; he's been a sketch lately." So the kid calls me later and he's like, "Dude, you got to let me get this ounce. I'll buy it for 400"—which would give the same profit as selling small bags—and at this point I'm like, "Bullshit." And you could tell by the tone of his voice that it wasn't right. Like you can tell when somebody's lying to you if you really listen to them; especially if you do like ten deals a day, you can hear the hesitation in their voice. And if somebody starts messing with prices in terms of they're just getting fucked, then you shouldn't deal with them, 'cause that's the point where you know they've said, "Okay, I don't care. I'm going to make it profitable for this person—because I'm not going to pay it anyways—where it's gonna be profitable enough for this person to do it, I'll tell them I'll pay them $1,000 for an ounce, 'cause they're not going to get the money anyways. All I need to do is to get them where I need them to be in order for to jack them." And that's what this kid was trying to do and I knew it, and obviously, I can't be sure, but I would put anything on it. And that incident happened a few days after the first jacking, so I felt like something had gotten around to him and like now I was somebody that people could take advantage of. So pretty much at that point I stopped dealing with anybody in that crew. I don't remember dealing with anybody who I thought would know them or be a part of them.

Christian realized that a past victimization could mark him as easy prey for others, and in this case he played it safe. Theoretically, he could have acted on his intuition by preparing himself for a fight designed to show that he was not to be messed with. But instead he chose to avoid the would-be predator. The toleration and avoidance exercised by Christian reflect a rationality bounded by the cultural commitments that shaped his identity. As demonstrated in the quotation below, Christian had strong reservations about the use of violent retaliation, which, by its very nature, involves hurting someone:

I've never been in a fight. Like I've always thought, like I remember being eight years old and thinking, "If I get in a fight, I'm kinda screwed 'cause I don't want to hurt somebody." Like I can't imagine punching somebody in the face and hurting them, and I've always been like that. So it's like the idea of physical violence as retribution has never been something I wanted.

In short, the suburban dealers were uncomfortable with the idea of violence and largely incompetent in its execution. They were both uninterested and unschooled in the ways of the badass.[13] Their parents had not instilled in them a need to project a violent persona or to stand their ground in the face of challenges to deter predators. Nor had they learned how to fight on the school playground. Fighting was not tolerated in Peachville's schools, and those who did faced immediate suspension or even expulsion. Simply put, violence carried little or no cultural currency in Peachville, and engaging in it risked being labeled as lame and excluded from the group. This is a major reason that the dealers steered clear of vigilantism. It is embarrassing to be victimized, but it is worse to be identified as a vigilante by police, parents, or the wider community. It is better just to avoid the individual in the future.

Another reason that the dealers favored avoidance over violence is that by retaliating they would open up the prospect of counterretaliation, whereas avoidance minimizes that possibility. It is less risky to cut off an offender than it is to strike back. After all, "[t]he surest way . . . to prevent threats to face is to avoid contacts in which these threats are likely to occur."[14]

But why avoid the offender instead of simply tolerating the offense? Avoidance is at least as much about preventing future problems as it is about punishing past ones, whereas toleration does little to minimize the chances of further victimization. Responding to offenses by cutting off contact with wrongdoers may not have much deterrent value, but it does have strong preventive effects by reducing or eliminating the dealers' exposure to individuals proven to have predatory tendencies. Avoidance, of course, comes at the cost of lost sales by cutting off potential clients, suppliers, and go-betweens. Whether any given offense ends in avoidance or toleration, then, seems to depend in large part on a subjective weighing of the perceived certainty and severity of future threats relative to the perceived benefits of continued interaction with the offender.

Negotiating

Negotiation was yet another strategy used by the dealers to manage conflict.[15] They often tried to resolve disputes over underweighed sales or unpaid debts by talking out the problem. Whenever Fred, for instance, was unhappy with a purchase, he would "call the person back immediately to see what they had to say on the subject and work something out. Sometimes you'll be able to call them and work something out." When Brendan was underweighed by his female supplier, he "just went back over there and told her and she didn't even have to see. She was just like, 'How much was it?'" He told her "'2.5' and she was like, 'Okay,' and she went and got 2.5 grams and brought it over, gave it to me, and never questioned it at all." Christian recounted resolving an incident by talking it out with his supplier: "There was one circumstance where he underweighed me like two grams, like instead of weighing fifty-six it weighed like fifty-four." Rather than tolerate the incident or avoid the supplier—upon whom he depended for product—Christian instead decided simply to "ask him about it. And he was like 'fine' and gave me two grams." As these incidents demonstrate, a major benefit of negotiation is that, when successful, it can serve to make things right, thereby saving face for both parties and allowing them to remain cool with one another. Business then can continue apace. Consider what happened with William, who described a conflict with his middle-class, suburban supplier:

> One of my suppliers was from a very nice family in the area. His dad was fairly wealthy; his mom was a housewife. That's where I got all the Valiums, Xanax. And then the other guy, he was probably from a lower-middle-class

family. Lived over there in Flynton. Decent home. He had a car; his dad had three cars; his mom had a car. His brother, who was fifteen, had a car, so he was kind of well-off. The guy I got all the rolls [ecstasy] and the Lortabs from who was the lower-middle class. He was actually six months younger than me, so he was born I think in eighty-four. One time when I first started dealing, I bought a twenty pack [of ecstasy] and I had sold it for a decent amount of money. Me and my friends went out, and I figured I still had ten left to sell and that would make my money back and I could still pay him back, so we went out and blew the money, you know, and I still had these ten. Well, me and my friends went back to his house. We went back there and we took off the next day. My guy fronted it to me 'cause I wanted to get on my feet, and I was like—but I had to call him and say, "I haven't got the money. You'll have to front me some more to get it." And I thought he was going to beat the hell out of me. This is the guy I got the rolls from. He was like, "Oh, you need some more. Let's sit down and talk about this." And I'm like, "Holy shit!" I thought he was going to beat the fuck out of me. It would have been an even fight, if I fight him and I want to get stuff from him again, so I'm gonna have to let him win! I mean I need him! So I went back to him and sat down and he was like, "All right,"—'cause he knew I ate them too—"I don't want you to sell anything less than $20; here's a ten pack." I had bought the twenty pack for $280. So he was like, "Here is a ten pack and I don't want you to sell [for] any less than $20 [apiece], and I want at least $200. I want you to come back with more than $200. I'll give you a price break since you're getting back up. So I'll give them to you for $12 apiece." So I had $120 worth of product and I had to come back with 200 so I'd knocked out 80 of my debt. And I came back two hours later with like 240, so I'd knocked out $120 of my debt, 160 to go. I did the same thing again and made it up to 160 bucks and that's when he bumped up my price back to $15. He had done the $12 apiece to help me out. But when he was on the phone and was like, "Let's sit down and talk about this," I was like, "Shit, I'm gonna get my ass beat and I've got to let him too." But it was nice of him to do that, and both of them were real nice guys. They were kind of like me; we're all three nice people.

This incident is noteworthy because William recognized the potential for violence but was more concerned about preserving his business ties than in proving his toughness. While he believed that in a fight he and the supplier were evenly matched, he nevertheless was intent on letting him win. Clearly, William did not want to get his "ass beat," but he viewed this as a potential cost of doing business. He figured that to fight back too aggressively would reduce his chances of maintaining a connection to a critical source of supply. As William put it, "I'm gonna have to let him win! I mean I need him!" It is not hard to imagine that the supplier felt the same way about William and therefore sought to negotiate a resolution rather than fight it out.

The problem with negotiation is that it requires compromise and is subject to failure. When that happened, the dealers typically turned to avoidance or toleration. Tom, for example, described an incident in which he and a customer could not agree about the fairness of a recent drug exchange:

> I can only remember one time when that happened—when somebody actually got pissed off at me—but it wasn't anything heavy. I completely remember that day. I hooked them up straight, and they were just trying to play me off like I didn't give them enough because I didn't weigh it out in front of them, and when they weighed it out on their scales or whatever, they thought differently. They were just trying to get me to give them more weed. I kinda got into it with them, and we just—we never got in a fight or anything—I told them, "Whatever, dude, go to somebody else." We just stopped being friends, stopped talking to each other.

Another dealer, Josh, fronted two ounces of marijuana to a customer without being repaid. His first response was to seek a joint resolution. When that proved unsatisfactory, he resorted to avoidance:

> I gave two ounces to a friend because he said that he knew somebody that wanted to buy two ounces, and he ended up selling one of the ounces and smoking the other one. He ended up telling me like a few months later. I ended up seeing him a few weeks after I loaned it to him. I sat down and talked with him and I said, "Hey man, you owe me money" and stuff like that. He gave me the money back for one of them but then just kind of bummed out on the other one, and I had to pay for it out of pocket. I kept on bothering him about it, but I wasn't gonna be like a bitch about it. I wasn't gonna try to start a fight over it or anything, just because I figured it would be better off just not to sell to him ever again. I just brushed him off, "Hey, whatever man," and never sold to him again.

Both Tom and Josh claimed to be uninterested in resolving their problems through combat. Although the nature of their victimizations was substantially different—with one experiencing an attempted fraud and the other suffering an actual loss—they both felt that negotiation was the appropriate response, followed by avoidance when it failed. What is evident in their cases is that the way in which victimizations were handled depended more on the victims' culture than on the seriousness of the instigating affront. Whether the loss was zero or far greater and resulted in no injury or bruises, the dealers rarely were inclined toward violence. By and large, their willingness to confront victimizers extended no further than negotiation. Fighting was lame. It could result in their being labeled an "asshole" by their peers and get them excluded from social gatherings. Plus, if the fight was reported to their parents or the police, serious consequences could follow. So when talk failed to resolve a dispute, the dealers felt they had little choice but to absorb the loss and move on.

Failed negotiations, however, did not always lead to avoidance. Sometimes the dealers opted for another nonconfrontational strategy—toleration—instead. Toleration became more likely than avoidance as disputants became more dependent on one another. Adam, for example, believed that his supplier "always" ripped him off, yet continued to do business with him because the price per gram still was better than he could get elsewhere:

> One my best friends from middle school, high school, still now—he was always three grams short. Always like one, two, or three grams. Like a QP [quarter pound], it'd be three grams short. Or if I got an ounce from him, it'd be short; it was always one to three short; it was never right on or over. He'd be like, "You can weigh it on my scales," and I think his scales were just messed up; it'd always be under. I'd tell him and he would just say, "Bullshit." Most of the time he'd be like, "Sorry, I weighed it." But sometimes he'd give me some but make me feel bad for it, like even though it didn't weigh on my shit. He'd either give it to me or not give it to me—however he felt. I'd usually just go with whatever he said, 'cause he was giving it to me for real cheap anyways.

Some of the dealers had more than one supplier to buy their drugs from, but this was not true for all of them. With few sources of supply at their disposal, dealers often reasoned that they had little choice but to absorb losses imposed on them by suppliers. They could complain about it to the suppliers, who would, on occasion, make things right by providing compensation. If that did not work, the dealers theoretically could try to take their business elsewhere, provided that they could locate an alternative source of supply. Doing so, however, exposed them to unknown costs and risks. Faced with such uncertainties, many of the dealers simply decided to stick with the devil they knew.

It is important to point out that the dealers turned to negotiation only in certain circumstances: namely, where they had a preexisting relationship with the other party and the dispute concerned an alleged failure to fulfill the agreed trade terms. Put differently, the dealers seldom tried to negotiate with new trade partners or those who tried to steal from or rob them outright. The closer the dealers were to those who victimized them, the more likely they were to feel that the problem could be talked out on the basis of mutual respect. Frauds between friends or long-term trade partners were often cast as unintentional or, at least, not interpreted as a personal affront. But when the dealers were less close to their victimizer, the transgression was more easily viewed as intentional and personal, which undermined their incentive to negotiate.

Sneaky Payback

Few of the dealers sought to strike back against individuals who victimized them, but those who did opted most often to avoid direct confrontation by relying on some form of sneaky retaliation. Sneaky retaliation involves rebalancing the scales of informal justice by getting even through fraud, vandalism, or unseen theft. Instead of making it obvious that retaliation is taking place, sneaky strategies are employed to impose secret punishment, thereby ensuring that the avenger remains anonymous.

Fraud is one kind of sneaky retaliation used by the dealers. This involved righting a perceived wrong via an unfair sale accomplished with deception. Recall that the dealers were especially likely to defraud customers whom they disliked, and of course, customers who tried to cheat them were especially likely to be disliked. In the dealers' tight-knit drug network, what went around often came around. For example, once Clay became a dealer, he took the opportunity to pay back any dealers who had cheated him: "When they ever shorted me in the past, I would short them." Mark described a different sort of customer conflict that ended in a retaliatory rip-off:

> I can remember this one guy that called me up and I knew his bag was straight and he called me up saying it wasn't and then he forgot about it or whatever, and then the next time I hooked him up [fairly] again, and I had just weighed it out, I knew it was straight, and he called me up complaining about it being slack again, tried to [get me to] give him more or whatever. So the next bag he came and got, I ripped him off hardcore.

Something similar happened to Bruce. On two separate occasions, custom-ers tried to get him to use inaccurate scales tilted in their favor, leading him to cheat them in return:

> I never specifically really tried to rip anybody off. There were times when I did short people—if they went out of their way to be a dick to me. Like if they came to me, and if I told them that I didn't have scales and that I couldn't sell to them right now, they'd come to me with their scales that would be off; I'd fuck them over. These kids would come to me wanting a bag of weed, and you can't sell it them because you don't have scales at the time—your friend or whatever has it—and I'd be like, "I can't do it right now." And this kid would go—it just happened like twice—these two different kids, they'd go find these crappy scales and bring them to me, and I mean I'd throw a nickel on it—a nickel is supposed to weigh 5 grams when you weigh it out on a digital scale, and you can use that to measure the accuracy of a scale—and it'd weigh like 3.6 or something. It would just be completely off, totally off. It was just twice, but both times the nickel weighed like 6.4 and 3.6 on one of them. And I was just like, "Alright, I'll eye it for you."

It is clear that Bruce was not the kind of dealer who typically ripped off his customers. Doing so was not in keeping with his perception of himself as a fundamentally fair, likable person. But he was willing to defraud individu-als who "went out of their way to be a dick." To act like a dick, after all, made someone lame, or at least lamer, the consequence of which is to re-ceive less favorable treatment from peers. In the instance described above, Bruce was not inclined to make the sale in the first place. He did not have his scale and was trying to be fair. He explained this to the customers, yet they pushed him to do the deal using their inaccurate scales instead. Upset by the forceful nature of the exchange—and by the potential loss that could have resulted—Bruce decided to short them as a form of punishment.

Stealthy or unseen theft is another form of sneaky retaliation, whereby victims punish those who have victimized them by secretly stealing some of their possessions. Dave, for instance, used stealthy theft to get even with a person who failed to pay him back for $300 worth of marijuana:

> There was one time when somebody didn't pay me back, it was just about $300, and I had trusted the kid for a long time. He wasn't paying up front. I was just giving him the bud and he would sell it and give me the money later, and then it took about three weeks once, he still hadn't given it to me,

and I was trying to call him and get it from him. And another week or two
passed and I started talking to a lot of people and I was putting some time
into it trying to figure out what was going on, and they all said he wasn't
going to pay me, and the way he was talking about it was just really disre-
spectful. I just went over to his place with a couple other kids that I know to
do shit like this, but I don't do shit like this unless someone has my money.
We just went up to his house and knocked on it for a little bit, but the music
was so loud they couldn't hear us—I guess his mom was out of town—and
I saw that his car was right there, and I opened up his car door and stole his
TV that he had actually stolen from somebody else. I needed something that
was worth that money.

Dave was not initially interested in retaliation. He called the defrauder several times, hoping to negotiate some kind of resolution to the conflict, but
the offender was not willing to talk things out. Fearing that he was being
made to look lame, and anxious to recoup his financial loss, Dave turned
to sneaky theft as a last resort.

A third way to exact vengeance "on the down low" involves surrepti-
tiously damaging or destroying the offending party's property. After William was defrauded, for example, he and his friends resorted to property
destruction in an attempt to get even:

We tried to find the guy, and so after we couldn't find where they went, we
retaliated against the associate. He was at his momma's house at the time.
We tore up to the house, bust all the front windows, slashed all the tires
on the mom's car—you know we were angry. We threw rocks and baseballs
and all through the front of the house, broke all the glass at the front of the
house. We did it and ran of course.

This case highlights the potential diffusion effects of retaliation. When
the actual victimizer could not be located, William and his friends instead
took out their anger on his "associate," who had set up the deal.[16]

Sneaky retaliation was beneficial for the dealers to the extent that it re-
lieved the stress caused by the precipitating injustice and helped to compensate them for their losses. Nonetheless, this form of conflict management was rare because, generally speaking, the dealers shared a cultural
commitment to minimizing conflict. In their eyes, escalating a conflict
risked making you appear to be an asshole in the eyes of your peers and
could draw the attention of parents or police to your drug-dealing activities. An important question to ask, then, is why some of them chose to

strike back instead of relying on negotiation, avoidance, or toleration? That question can only be answered in probabilistic as opposed to deterministic terms. In other words, although certain conditions appeared to increase or decrease the chances that any given dealer would resort to retaliation, they did not guarantee such an outcome.

The retaliatory cases that did occur—sneaky and violent alike—do share several common characteristics that may help to explain their occurrence. For one thing, in virtually all of them, more peaceful means of dispute resolution had failed or were logically impossible. Recall that Dave had tried to negotiate with the debtor, and that those talks got him nowhere.

Retaliation also appeared to be more likely when a dealer had been victimized previously. Once again, Dave's experience is exemplary. He was victimized by someone else prior to being swindled out of $300. He tolerated the first incident but retaliated in the second. Asked to explain his differential response, he said of the first defrauder: "He's just a psycho case who does way too much crack and stuff like that, so it just wasn't worth it. I don't even deal with stuff like that. I've never done it. I don't want to deal with people who do that." But Dave apparently felt differently about the second offender, perceiving him to be less of a risk. He went on to say that he had had enough of being taken advantage of, so he stole the TV "because you can't let people keep doing that to you, taking money from you and getting away with it."

In order to retaliate, of course, the dealers had to have a realistic opportunity to do so.[17] Had the individuals who defrauded Bruce or Clay not sought to trade with them thereafter, for instance, they could not have been cheated in return. It is not difficult to imagine that many defrauders simply avoided conducting business with their victims rather than take the chance of being treated in kind.

A final question is why, when faced with a choice between sneaky and violent retaliation, the dealers usually opted for the less confrontational approach. In large part, this is because the code of the suburb that these dealers lived by militated strongly against the use of violence with all of its attendant personal, moral, legal, and physical liabilities. From their perspective, violent vigilantism was far riskier than its sneaky counterpart. It was more likely to get them into trouble with their parents or the law and, in turn, to jeopardize their long-term goals, as well as to make them appear lame in the eyes of their peers. Plus, and as already noted, they were inept in the ways of the badass. They were uncomfortable with the idea of fighting and even more so with the possibility of being beaten up. Although sneaky retaliation was discoverable by the victimizer-turned-victim after the fact, this form of payback was designed to go unnoticed during its execution, thereby reducing the chances of a physical confrontation.[18]

Hitting Back

By this point it should be clear that the dealers seldom resorted to even the mildest forms of violent retaliation. Their reluctance to respond to victimization with violence can be tied to at least three interacting factors. First, the use of violence to settle disputes received little cultural support in their community or among their peers; people who did resort to violence were likely to be shunned. Second, the dealers were incompetent in the use of violence, at least in part because they had little familiarity with it.[19] And third, they feared not only the short-term harm that might result from the use of violence, such as physical injury or loss of likability, but also the long-term damage it could do to their employment prospects. Overall, the dealers regarded themselves as peaceful and peace-loving individuals. We asked Joe, for example, whether he fought back after discovering that something had been stolen from his residence, and he responded, "It's not really my thing to go pursue something like that." Similarly, Ed told us, "I'm not aggressive. I haven't hurt anyone. Never fucked up anybody's life. Never done crazy shit. I deal with nice people; nobody's a hothead."

While violent retaliation was extremely rare among the dealers, it was not wholly unknown. Conceptually, this form of conflict management includes everything from threats to murder. Threats, the least serious form of retaliation, were meant to impel the victimizer to pay for or return what rightfully belonged to the victim. The dealers sometimes resorted to verbal threats when they perceived that there was little chance of talking out the problem. "Pay up, or else" was the message, but as illustrated below, such threats seldom generated compliance; deep down both parties "knew" that virtually everybody in Peachville was opposed to violence and incompetent in its application. Consider how Adam handled the following situation:

> My friend, he got fronted and didn't pay me. He lived [in a town an hour away] so we'd meet somewhere on [the highway connecting the towns], usually in between. He paid me right and everything and so asked for a little bit more: he wanted an ounce of weed and two ounces of mushrooms. I drove it halfway there like I always did, gave it to him, and two weeks later I started getting suspicious because he wasn't calling me. He's like, "Yeah, I lost my job" and all this shit and ended up never paying me. That shit pissed me off. It was right at like 400 or 500 bucks. I remember he Western Unioned me

a $100 one time when I was real pissed, after I rode him like every day for about a month straight. I'd call him every day and he'd answer and be like, "I'm working on it man." I think I told him I was going to kill him one time. And he was like, "You're going to kill me over $400?" and I was like, "Yeah, I guess not." I didn't want to hurt people. And that was kind of the end of that, stopped calling him, just stopped telling him to come hang out. It kind of ruined our whole friendship, actually.

Adam's account demonstrates how conflict management strategies can shift over time. His initial reaction was to talk out the dispute with the defrauder. When that failed, he issued an unconvincing and wholly unrealistic threat: pay or die. The person he threatened called his bluff, asking rhetorically, "You're going to kill me over $400?" Both parties understood that this was not going to happen—as Adam said, "Yeah, I guess not." Finally, he resigned himself to the fact that the debt would remain unpaid and handled the problem simply by terminating the friendship.

Among all the dealers, there must have been several hundred victimizations that theoretically *could have been* handled with violence. In practice, however, just three victimizations actually *were* handled in such a way.[20] Not only was violent retaliation rare, but when it did occur, it was strikingly mild. Indeed, the instances of violent retaliation reported by the dealers amounted to nothing more than old-fashioned schoolyard fights. No weapons were used. No one was hospitalized. The worst injury suffered was a nasty bruise. Thus, the few exceptions to the pattern essentially prove the rule: violence was a minor part of the dealers' suburban drug underworld.

The first example of violent retaliation was reported by William. One of his acquaintances covertly stole between three hundred and four hundred Valium pills from him and then "disappeared." Later on, this same thief broke into a house belonging to one of William's friends, stealing several items. With the transgressions multiplying, William and his friend "showed up at [the offender's] house, beat the hell out of him, and took every dollar he had, you know, just two guys on one." They "weren't gonna bloody him up or anything, just kind of beat the hell out of him, held him, took all the DVDs. Obviously, he had sold some [of the Valium], probably got about $600 back."

Another dealer, Ron, retaliated with violence after a customer drove off without paying him, using a mutual friend to set up the fugitive for revenge:

I had mushrooms and I was selling those. I was riding with this kid and it was his friend, so it was someone I didn't know very well. This kid, like we were meeting at this church, and he pulled in next to me and he came to the window and I gave him the mushrooms and then he put his hand in the car and started counting out the money and then he just like pulled it out real quick and drove away. And he was real scared, like we called him immediately, and we were like, "What are you doing?" So we called that kid who had stolen it right back and he was like, "Oh, I'm going to get the money." And we were like, "Shut the hell up, you're not getting the money." So then for a couple weeks I couldn't get in touch with this kid. I was going to kick his ass, get my money back, just generally do something, 'cause I was just pissed off. I knew where he lived, but he was one of those kinds of kids—'cause he sold drugs and shit too—so he was never at his house. So over time, the kid that I knew that was my friend that had known him tried to call him back like a week or two later, and he was just pretending like it was all cool, like maybe he was fucked up and didn't remember doing that, like a younger kid who's just really stupid or something, and he started talking to my friend again. So my friend was going to get weed from him and shit, and I was like, "Dude, you're not my friend if you're going to fucking deal with this dude who stole shit from me because of you." So then I was like thinking that this kid that I thought was my friend maybe is not my friend. And then I'm like, "Dude, when you go and meet him for weed, you have to bring me with you so I can kick his ass; like, you can't not bring me with you and still deal with this kid; you're a fucking idiot." What I did is let [the mutual friend] drive my car, and I got in the trunk and hid in the trunk, right? And he picked up this kid from a party. They rode around, I [had given the mutual friend] some weed, they smoked weed in the car in the neighborhood riding around, and then they like drove around. And the plan wasn't really going right, you know what I'm saying? He was supposed to let me out in the neighborhood so I could kick the kid's ass, but he left the neighborhood and went into a gas station to get gas, and then he cracked the [trunk] and was like, "Okay, man, we're going to pull out of the gas station, we're going to go somewhere, and I'm going to stop, and that's when I'm coming out here." And I was like, "Okay," but he's like, "I'm going to leave the trunk open for you, a crack." Like when we pulled out of the gas station, the trunk like comes all the way open. The trunk flies up, so I hear the two kids in the car like, "What the fuck was that? What the hell was that?" So they pull into this hotel, and he comes out and lets me out. I roll out of the car, and I could see him in the rearview, and my friend gets back in the car and is sitting in the driver seat, and I just open the door and try to pull the kid out, but he has his seatbelt on, so I can't pull him out. So I just started beating the shit out of him, like I just started punching him in the face, and then he got all down in the seat to where I couldn't really get at him. So I just kept kicking him; like I kicked him twenty or thirty times. Then finally he was like, "No, stop," and I pulled him out of the car and fucking took his shoes and threw them in the road. I took his money. He probably didn't give it all to me—he only had like 10 or 12 bucks—and then he had this bag full of sugar cubes that I thought was LSD and I took those too. And those ended up not being real, or so I thought, like this is the funny thing, before we drove there I was like, I was telling my friend, "You know this kid, if you don't hit this kid, if you don't, like, do something to this kid, he is going to call you up every day and come to your house, and if you don't beat his ass right now, he's going to come back at you, and I'm not going to be there to defend you, so you better do something." And he was like, "Ah, naw, man." And he didn't do anything. So we drive away. I'm like, "Here you go, here's your present," and I gave him the acid, and I was like, "If they're real, if they're good, give me like two of them." And there was like fifteen or twenty and I took the 10 bucks. That's all I really wanted to do, just leave [the kid who cheated me] somewhere random in the middle of the night. It was like two thirty in the morning and he was stranded somewhere. That's all I really wanted to do.

The third instance of violent retaliation involved Robert, the same dealer who had tolerated an earlier victimization because he was trying not "to escalate in criminal activities" and "at that point it wasn't worth getting in trouble" over. Shortly thereafter, however, he was victimized again, this time deciding to strike back:

I come home from school and I go to where I had my herb and it was gone. Roughly like twelve, thirteen hundred dollars. I had just gotten a QP and broken it up into quarters the night before. And I was freaking out, and then I look around the house, and then I go down into the basement, and the garage door—one of the windows was busted out. And then I started making phone calls, and you get leads but you're dealing with a bunch of fucked-up people. Everybody's full of shit 'cause everybody's on drugs for the most part. No one is really honest, but I never really found out who did it. But I ended up getting in a fight with [my friend] because he had to have been the one who told them where the weight was because only my friends knew where I had my herb in the house, and all they stole was the herb. All of a sudden his brothers had weed that was very similar to mine, and they were selling it, and they weren't really petty pot salesmen, so that threw up a red flag. It was very similar if not identical to what I had, and not a lot of people our age got from the guy I got weed from. That's why it was very peculiar that all of a sudden the day I'm robbed they have weed to sell. I was pissed the whole day. It was the next day, and then I had the same gym class as [the friend], but it wasn't like the same class but you go to the same changing area, and I threw him up against the caged locker and one of the coaches called us off and I was like, "I'm going to fucking whup your ass after school." And then immediately after school, the person who he rid with parked exactly where I parked so [he] knew I'd see him, and I just got out there before he could get out there.

Robert did not describe the confrontation itself. Coincidentally, however, it took place directly in front of the first author's eyes; he witnessed it unfold in real time. The disputants were evenly matched in size, each being a little less than six feet tall and weighing approximately one hundred and fifty pounds. A crowd of spectators gathered.[21] Who would strike the first blow? Would the other guy fight back? Who would win? No one seemed to be taking sides, as they were all friends, but emotions were running high.[22] The two combatants circled each other with eyes locked and fists raised, staring each other down. Robert pushed the wrongdoer, who pushed him back. Seconds passed with nothing happening until one of the bystanders suddenly sucker-punched Robert in the back of the head, inflicting no damage. And with that, the confrontation seemed to run out of steam.[23] The fight ended and people got in their cars and drove off.

In the hours immediately afterward, Robert continued to pursue the idea of getting even, but despite his purported readiness for combat, it was clear that he had no real heart for it: "I was fucking ready to go, I was pissed. I made certain phone calls to certain people, but nothing ever happened."[24] When asked why not, he said, "I don't think anyone wanted to get fucked up that day." Within a short time, Robert and his friend had reconciled. They remain friends to this day.

Robert's failure to make good on his promise to "fucking whup" his friend's "ass" reflects the cultural commitments that shaped day-to-day social interaction in Peachville. Indeed, whenever the code of the suburb was pitted against a fleeting urge to get even, the code ultimately seemed to prevail, even in cases in which some form of "violent" payback actually took place. None of the cases of violent retaliation reported by the dealers betrayed any evidence of a determined attempt to inflict serious harm on the wrongdoer.

Figure 5. The parking lots of fast-food restaurants were one of the dealers' favorite places to buy and sell drugs; the very nature of these business establishments encouraged people to come and go quickly, thereby normalizing brief meetings and exchanges. And when one trade partner arrived before the other, he or she could simply go into the establishment and grab a drink or bite to eat without drawing suspicion. The theft from Robert's vehicle occurred in this parking lot.

Figure 6. Pete was robbed in this swimming-pool parking lot. The dealers frequently made exchanges in the parking lots of neighborhood swimming pools because, from May to September at least, they are a legitimate place for youngsters to congregate. An advantage of such places over the parking lots of businesses is that, except on the weekends, few adults are present.

Figure 7. This is the back of the pool hall frequented by William and his friends and also where he had $320 worth of drugs snatched from his hand and was dragged alongside the victimizer's vehicle. The advantage of making sales at this location is that it is shielded from the adjacent road and also from patrons of the pool hall itself.

Figure 8. This neighborhood recreational area, which consists of a swimming pool and tennis courts, is where Frank met with the "sketchy" customer who appeared to be setting him up to be beaten or robbed.

Figure 9. This parking lot is located behind a church and is shielded from the main road. It was a popular place for making exchanges and also is the spot where Ron was defrauded in the course of selling mushrooms. Previously, a public volleyball court was located behind the basketball goal. It was frequented by many of the students at Peachville High, and therefore, it was common to see youngsters there. Drug traders made deals here, with the volleyball court legitimizing their presence.

Figure 10. Robert's fight with his friend occurred in front of the large bush near the center of this picture, on the street where they both routinely parked their cars on their way to Peachville High.

CHAPTER 7

The Triumph of Conventionality

On their face, becoming the victim of a serious offense, being arrested for a felony, or getting into serious trouble with one's parents may appear to be wholly negative events. But for the dealers, such events, though rare, often marked a positive turning point in their lives. The dealers initially entered the drug trade with only a vague theoretical appreciation of the risks involved. Once they actually encountered one of those risks, however, many of them were moved to terminate their drug selling to protect their short- and long-term identities and life prospects.[1]

The Good of Victimization

The most common problem that led the dealers to reconsider the wisdom of selling drugs was serious victimization. Recall, for example, that Frank had "fucking $600 worth of bud" stolen from his vehicle and was almost robbed at a neighborhood pool. He identified these two events as instrumental in convincing him to quit dealing. When asked why he got out of the illicit drug trade, he responded, "I guess the car getting broken into and getting jumped. I figured something was going to happen if I just kept doing it. I knew I had to change, stop dealing drugs."

Robert dealt drugs without incident for "six or seven" months, but then was victimized twice in thirty days, losing roughly $1,500 total, a considerable sum of money for a sixteen-year-old. He tolerated the first incident, a stealthy theft, asking rhetorically, "what am I gonna do—shoot him?" But the second time around he fought back, albeit ineptly. These bad experiences had the effect of turning Robert away from dealing. As he explained, "It was probably great that it happened to me, reflecting back, because then I stopped. It wasn't worth it." He quit dealing, concluding that continuing would require a willingness to resort to violence that ran counter to his cultural commitments:

> If I wanted to I could have progressed easily. I knew enough people. But the thing is, when you start selling more weight, you're taking on more consequences of getting robbed. You gotta worry about being robbed, and then that's gonna escalate to more crime, because if you actually want to be pushing that weight and actually make a business off of it and make a profit, then you have to be willing to protect your crops, your weight, and that means if they try to assault you, then you have to fuck them up. There's got to be repercussions if someone steals. If there's no repercussions for what you are doing, then people will continue to do it. You'll get robbed again. I mean word gets around. What am I going to do—start fist-fighting people or knifing people or shooting people? It wasn't worth that. I didn't want to go to jail. That's why I never progressed. I wasn't willing to take the next step in progressing. I was just trying to have a good time, smoke for free, and make a little money.

Robert was not prepared to use violence to protect his business from predators and calculated that this made him an increasingly attractive target to them. To continue in the drug game was going to put too much that he valued in jeopardy: his health; his finances; his identity as a cool, peaceful person; and his ability to achieve conventional adult success.

Not only did experiencing victimization lead the dealers to reconsider their chances of being injured, but it also prompted them to reevaluate the odds of getting into trouble with their parents or the law, and thereby putting their future educational and employment prospects at risk. Earlier, Christian described being defrauded and then set up for a scam. In response, he initially just "stopped dealing with anybody in that crew." Those incidents happened to him about two weeks before going on a family vacation, during which he began to question whether the benefits of drug selling were outweighed by its potential costs:

> We go to [this place] for vacation because that's where we're from. I remember being in the airport about to come back. I had been gone for like ten days and didn't bring my cell phone with me or anything. I remember sitting in the airplane and I remember thinking to myself, "When I go back, do I want to keep doing this?" 'Cause I knew I was eighteen and that if I got caught I was fucked. I would have gone to jail for a good while, I think, long enough, and my parents would have been so disappointed in me, they

would have been decimated by that. I can't even imagine what they'd think, but I just know they would have been so disappointed. I mean, I know they could have took it, but they wouldn't have taken it well at all. I basically decided that when I got back that I needed a change. I was going to stop dealing, and the other thing is I knew I was coming to [college]—like, I remember thinking to myself, "I'm going to [college] and I'm not going to make enough money to make it worth basically fucking up your life and not being able to go to [college]." 'Cause it was basically like I was on the right track and I was done with high school and it was finally time for me to go off and make something of myself, and I just knew that if I was going to continue to deal, I was going to put that at a heavy risk and it just wasn't worth it. I mean having the money was nice, but the rest of my life wasn't worth the money. The chance of getting caught wasn't worth it compared to any of the positives. I'd had a good time, the best months of my life; everything was good. I had a best friend that I worked out with every day, I had a girlfriend, I had a successful business so to speak, I was smoking all the time, I had everything I wanted, and I was like, "Alright, I'm done." Dealers are smart when they know to get out, and I'd had enough positives where I was okay with getting out and I'm not going to regret it at all. I remember coming back and giving my mom $1,000 in twenties. I didn't tell her where it was from; I told her it was from the hundred bucks I would get from weekly allowance—"I'd save a little bit every time and that's why I had that amount of money"— 'cause there's no other way to explain that amount of money, especially in all twenties. I told her to put it in the bank and that was supposed to get me through fall semester partying, and then I had $500 that I kept for myself— like that she wouldn't know about it. I had basically smoked a thousand dollars' worth of free pot, so I had had a good enough time where I didn't mind giving it up.

Although victimization did not cause Christian to terminate his drug selling immediately, it did set the desistance process in motion. He started to reevaluate the risks and rewards of drug dealing in relation to alternative lines of culturally prescribed action available to him. The vacation that he took with his parents subsequent to being victimized offered Christian an opportunity to reflect on his current and potential future life trajectories. He realized that he was eighteen years old and no longer a minor, that he was going to college soon, that the profit from dealing was not sufficient to offset the risk, and that it was time for him to go and "make something" of himself—to achieve conventional success. In the end, Christian decided that he should quit dealing, thereby giving him greater control over his own future.

Given that serious violent victimization was virtually nonexistent in Peachville, it perhaps was inevitable that parents there would be highly suspicious when dealers came home with visible injuries. What were these adolescents doing that caused them to be targeted? That is how Pete's family reacted after he told them that he had almost been carjacked when, in fact, he had been beaten up by two assailants who wanted to steal his drugs:

That's the thing in my life that I regret most in my life ever, having my whole entire family having to see me all beat up because I was selling weed. They knew. I told them someone tried to steal my car and blah-blah-blah. I told them a bullshit story, but everyone knew. My whole family, my parents, everybody. My parents didn't buy it. Everyone else was like, "Oh really, that's awful!" But I know everyone in my family, and they knew I was bullshitting to them. Eventually, I told my parents what really happened. About a week after that happened. Christmas Eve. My mom asked me if I was selling drugs because she knew nobody was going to steal my fucking car. She said, "I know you're selling weed." I was like, "Why?" She said, "Because of this," and she showed me $1,000—just a stash of cash [I had] in my room. I was like, "Damn." I got mad at first and said, "No, I've just been saving up money," and just kept trying to lie. I didn't want my parents to think that I was selling drugs. I didn't want them to be disappointed in me. It's just the concept of "He's a drug dealer," you know. All these women say, "Oh, he's a drug dealer, he's a drug dealer, scum of the earth," like that's the fucking title given to drug dealers, and I didn't want to be that and I didn't want anybody to know that's what I was. I didn't think that I was [a bad person]. I still don't think I was for selling weed. I wasn't a bad person. Yeah, I sold drugs that were illegal—I mean I don't think they should be illegal, but that's not what it's about. I dunno, I just don't think I fit the description of what everyone thinks a drug dealer is—what everybody makes out a drug dealer to be. Like a violent person who steals, fucking has guns, is sketched out, all tripped out on drugs and all, has no self-control. I quit like two weeks after I had that confrontation with my mom. I got jumped and then I kept trying to buy the weed and then I found the weed and then my mom was like, "Yeah, you're selling, blah-blah-blah," and I sold the rest of the weed I had, like a QP [quarter pound]. I bought a QP and sold it in ounces, and then I had that confrontation with my mom, on Christmas Eve. I was down and felt like shit. My parents knew that I was selling weed, and my parents thought that I was a bad person because of it. My dad said I was an idiot. He just talked down to me like I wasn't a person, you know, like I was a fucking dog or something. For about a week, two weeks, I felt like shit. My mom was like, "I can't believe this has happened, but it's alright, I still love you." She said I was lucky they didn't kill me. Mom was just scared. She told me that.

In Pete's mind, the victimization was his fault because it would not have happened if he had not been a dealer: "That's the thing in my life that I regret most in my life ever, having my whole entire family having to see me all beat up because I was selling weed." His immediate and extended clan knew he was "bullshitting to them" when he lied about being carjacked. While suburban parents prefer to avoid conflict, some problems nevertheless are too obvious to ignore. Not buying Pete's carjacking story, his parents investigated, and after finding $1,000 in cash stashed in his bedroom, they confronted him. They scrutinized and shamed their child.[2] Pete's father told him he was an "idiot" and treated him as if he "wasn't a person" and like "a fucking dog or something." Pete's mother, on the other hand, applied social control through expressions of caring and concern. She "was just scared." In response, Pete felt "down" and "like shit." He was embarrassed and ashamed.[3] He had lost the respect of his family, and his reputation as a good kid was damaged. By giving up dealing, Pete sought to eliminate the potential for further problems and to reinstate his identity as a good kid in the eyes of his parents.

Another dealer, Phillip, had a gun put to his head and two ounces of marijuana forcibly stolen from him. This victimization, coupled with a desire not to let down his parents, led him to give up drug dealing:

I was on cloud nine [while dealing], seriously. The king pretty much, like the main, main marijuana dealer for the high school for that year. It was a monopoly pretty much. Everybody would come through me, everybody. I felt good about it, but I felt even better about it after I got out, like officially, because you know everyone says, "Get in and get out before it's too late." You either have trouble with the police, or you know, you end up getting hurt, so I felt like I was lucky. I quit after I got jacked for $600 and it started to seem more risky than it's actually worth. You get a gun pulled to your head, you start to think about things like, "Is this really worth it?" It's a serious situation to be in just for some extra change. And my parents, my parents knew; well, my mom knew. She kept it from my dad 'cause she just didn't want him to know, she didn't want him to deal with that. Yeah, she knew for a good amount of time. She never really found anything; she never had hard evidence; she probably maybe found like a glass piece [pipe] or so here and there, but that doesn't necessarily mean that I'm dealing. But people would come over to my house; like at the beginning of it I was stupid, just have people over to come get it and leave. People would stop by for like two minutes, and I mean she can pretty much put two and two together. I come up like all red-eyed, and you know she knows what's going on, she's not stupid. That was, aside from getting jumped, that was the other main reason for me quitting. I just knew that she was really disappointed in me. She knew that I could make more of my time than that: I could be doing more useful things; I could have a more legitimate job, be working more towards a career instead of backtracking, in a sense.

Phillip's victimization caused him to question whether selling drugs was "really worth it." In thinking about the risk posed to his health by continued dealing, he also started to consider what selling was doing to his relationship with his mother. Like many Peachville parents, she never confronted her son about the matter. She even kept her husband in the dark to reduce the possibility of open conflict between him and her son. Nevertheless, Phillip perceived that she was "really disappointed" in him, and this hurt his self-image. He feared that he was "backtracking" in life at the exact time that he was supposed to be growing up and becoming a successful adult. Phillip had a stake in conformity, but with every drug sale he put his future prospects at risk. The combination of being victimized, feeling bad about what he was doing to his mother, and a realization that he could make more of his life convinced Phillip to get out of the dealing.

Too Loving?

It does not seem that parental action, on its own, was sufficient to convince the dealers to stop dealing drugs permanently. All of the dealers who quit selling after experiencing trouble with their parents eventually went back to it, unless they also were seriously victimized or subjected to law. That said, parental conflict did lead some dealers to stop selling drugs temporarily. Trevor, for instance, told us that he gave up dealing for some time after his parents punished him for selling drugs and drug paraphernalia:

I cut out altogether because I got in some trouble, not a lot of trouble, just parent trouble, and I had to chill out—got my cell phone nabbed and all that kinda shit. My parents actually busted me selling glass pipes out of my trunk. I had a buddy who had some friends who blew glass. I was really into smoking and really into pipes and stuff at the time, and I was selling, so I had some cash lying around. He introduced me to these guys, and I got some pipes from them, just bought some pipes, and they were these really awesome blowers. After a while they were like, "Hey, you can help us out by taking this case of glass," and they'd basically give me a case of glass and say we need a thousand [dollars] back for it, which would be much less than the pipes were worth, and they'd give me a little card with their recommended prices for each pipe and then I could either sell them at those prices or do whatever the hell I wanted with them really, and they just wanted whatever they wanted back for them. They would basically make it to where I would basically make maybe like a 100 bucks or something, enough where it was worth my trouble. I did that for a while. The thing was I ended up with most of them, which is how it goes with the herb and everything else. But I got into some trouble with my parents, which at the time seemed like a big deal. It was over that glass thing. Being as swift as I was at the time, I was just running fucking shop out of my trunk while my parents were home. Kids would be coming over and like stand there at my trunk and pointing inside at all these pipes. My parents come out and I slam the trunk, and my parents are like, "What's in the trunk?" I'm like, "Nothing." So I got nailed on the pipes and then they just looked through my car and they didn't even find any herb; they just found like my little backpack with baggies and a scale or something in there. It was pretty obvious as to what was going on. They definitely knew that I was selling pot. I got in all kinds of trouble. They just got really pissed, and they took my car, my phone, and a bunch of other shit. They just kinda basically really put their foot to it in a way that they hadn't before. They did what parents do, tried to get their point across. I think I got the point. It just made me completely unhappy. That was when I quit dealing for a while, just chilled out for a while. I quit messing with that shit for a while, quit messing with dealing, that is. I chilled out until college, which was about, at that point, about a year and a half later.

Trevor's parents meted out an array of sanctions in an attempt to deter him: they "nabbed" his cell phone, took his car, "and a bunch of other shit" too. And it worked. Trevor got out of drug dealing and, at the time, had no intention of ever getting back into it. He returned to the drug business only after going away to college, beyond the bounds of day-to-day parental supervision.

It perhaps is surprising that parental punishment alone was insufficient to prevent the dealers from eventually resuming their drug selling. This was not because all the dealers evaded detection; several of them were caught red-handed by their parents. Why did parental discovery not cause them to turn away from dealing permanently? After all, parents carried a pretty big stick in the sense that they could withhold financial and emotional resources that the dealers valued. Indeed, parents sometimes *did* apply these sanctions, but only to a limited degree; they abhorred the stress that confrontation put on family life and sought to minimize it as much as possible. But because parental sanctions tended to be mild, the threat of receiving them was insufficient to deter future dealing. This is not to say that the dealers did not fear trouble with their parents. They clearly did. Yet its effect was largely interactive, producing desistance only in tandem with serious victimization or punishment by the law.

Punishment Works

The dealers rarely were sanctioned by the police for their drug selling. It did happen twice, however, with the same effect each time. In each case, the dealer felt disgraced and was ashamed to face his parents, who were obviously disappointed by what had happened. These moms and dads had invested much in their kids, and their children, in turn, had high expectations for their own futures. Yet the dealers and their parents alike realized that a criminal record could seriously undermine prospects for success by making it difficult to be admitted to a good college or to land a well-paying job. After apprehension and shaming by their parents, then, the dealers quickly concluded that their drug selling had to come to an immediate end so as not further to jeopardize their futures. Even so, the dealers paid a hefty financial penalty in the form of attorney fees to minimize the negative consequences of their encounter with the criminal justice system.

One of the two dealers arrested was Josh, who was charged with felony possession of marijuana. This led his father to search his bedroom, discovering evidence of dealing in the process:

> I quit 'cause I got arrested for possession of marijuana. I was on my way down to Florida for spring break and got arrested. We were speeding, I guess; well, that's what they said. That's why they pulled us over. The reason they searched the vehicle, what the cop told my friend who was driving, was that his license smelt like marijuana and that gave him probable cause to search our car. So they get us all out, and there's three of us in the car. They cuffed me 'cause I'm up front and he's up front and there was pot that they found that was up front. I had an ounce, so it was felony possession. My friend got

busted for DUI drugs, which is driving under the influence of marijuana or whatever. Then I had another friend that was with us who was in the back and got off clean. But usually if there are drugs in the car, everybody gets arrested. I said that the pot was mine, and I ended up spending four days in jail. After I got arrested, I pretty much got out of it. Once I got arrested, I was done. I got arrested for possession of marijuana, and I went to court for it and everything like that. I had to get an attorney, and actually it ended up the attorney got me out of it because they said it was an illegal search. For one, they didn't have a legit reason to search the vehicle, because saying someone's license smells like pot doesn't hold up in court, and that's what the judge felt. My dad was just like, "I'm not mad at you, I'm just disappointed," and that's just as bad as saying I'm really pissed. "But you're just going to have to pay for it yourself and deal with it on your own." I mean that was punishment enough, because I had to work to get all the money I could just to pay for an attorney. I had to pay for my attorney's fees. I had cash that I had saved from slinging, but my dad found it and I don't know what happened to it. I asked him for it and he said he didn't know. It was about $2,000, $3,000. I got out of jail and my sister picked me up and I got home. I took a shower and the first thing I did was go check my stash. I go where I normally keep it and everything is turned about. All my stuff, how I had it organized, was all thrown about, and I came to find out that my dad went through my room and took everything. So he took my money and I asked him about it and he just didn't tell me an answer, didn't give me any reason as to what I think he should have used it for or whatever. He never said anything. So I was pretty pissed about that, but I was happier that he found it instead of the cops, 'cause then I had intention to distribute. So once I got arrested, I was done selling pot, and that was it. It kind of hit me that making all the money and everything like that is definitely a plus side, but then there is the downside that it is illegal and you're gonna get caught sooner or later. Or you're gonna end up getting jumped and lose all your money and all your product.

As with serious victimization, punishment by the law can trigger a chain of events that lead adolescents away from dealing. Josh believed that his legal troubles were the main reason that he decided to give up dealing. But there is more than this to Josh's desistance. The legal trouble caused familial conflict that surely also contributed to his decision to quit selling drugs. The sanction meted out by his father was severe. Not only did his dad shame him, but on top of that, he also confiscated thousands of dollars in drug money. Yet again, we see that suburban parents were prone to minimize open conflict to the extent possible; when Pete asked him about the money, itself a bold move, his dad "never said anything."

Josh's experience with the criminal justice system also served to make him more concerned about being robbed. For this dealer, and others like him, there was something about experiencing one kind of trouble that increased the perceived threat of others. Perhaps this is because all risks are abstract until any one of them actually is experienced, after which the danger presented by each becomes more salient. Josh's legal trouble not only reminded him of the threat of formal sanction but also made him more aware that continued selling could hurt his home life and make him a target for predators.

William, the other dealer to be arrested, also was busted as the result of a traffic stop:

> So we go to a fast-food place, and we're going to head back home, me and two of the guys I got busted with. I'm in the back of the car; the owner of the car was sitting in the passenger seat; the driver, of course, is driving. He was speeding, doing about twenty over. So we see a blue light and he took off. Pulls down first street on the right—a dead end. We pulled on to this street, we're sitting there, and we sit there for a few minutes and it's like, "Hey, we're cool." Cop comes over the hill. We're like, "Fuck! Fuck!" At this point I was kind of in and out of it [from drinking and taking pills the previous night]. I don't really remember much. The first thing I really remember that sticks in my mind is a cop walking over there, seeing how fucked up I was, and opening the door to say, "Get the fuck out of the car!" And I was like, "What?" and there was a brown bag with all the shit in it sticking up through the seat. He grabs the brown bag and looks in it, drops it, and says, "Get out the car now!" They put us all on the hood of the car, take us to jail, and I had to call my grandmother 'cause my mom wasn't in. Told her about the five counts of drug trafficking, and it was ecstasy, Xanax, Valium, Percocet. Once you get charged with one count of possession with intent, once you get felony, if they find anything else you get possession with intent. So if you had a hundred Valiums, you get possession with intent there, possession with intent for that little weed, anything they find in there. Same thing once you're done for trafficking: once you have trafficking for one thing, everything becomes trafficking. Now those four were large quantities, especially with the amount of cash we had, so those were legit. My friend had an Ativan in the car that was his girlfriend's, so they said, "Oh, that's trafficking too"; so we got one charge of trafficking for that because of everything else that was in the car.

William's situation was exacerbated when his legal difficulties forced him to seek financial help from his family:

> I woke up, 'cause I was still fucked up when I went to jail. I woke up after the next night, and it was like, "Gosh, that dream was horrible! Holy shit, I'm in jail! Oh, this is not good, not good!" We got busted on Saturday and we got out on Tuesday. We didn't go in front of the judge, but our case had to go in front of the judge, and he set it as five counts of drug trafficking, about a little over $25,000 fine. We made bail, and so afterwards I had to tell my family everything, everybody in my family. It was like an intervention; it was real fun. They had had suspicions. They'd found like fifty pills and they had taken them, and I just never noticed they were gone. They never found my big stashes. They found my little one, and they never thought it was on the scale that it was. They knew I was using, but I sat down with my whole family, little brother, little sister, their faces were just—God, I just felt so bad. I called my lawyer, and it was fifteen grand. My parents, my mom, and my grandmother were just like, "Holy shit, fifteen grand!" And so some of the money I had earned paid for that. They will never to this day admit that it did, it was all from my grandmother and my mom, but I said, "What else am I going to do with this money?" I had this money to sort of try to save my ass, about three grand. My grandmother and my mother put some money in, and I put some money in. And to this day, they will of course claim that it was all theirs, 'cause they won't admit that they used drug money to get a good lawyer.

What had been a profitable business for William up to that point suddenly turned financially ruinous. And this created problems for his family too. William's parents "had suspicions" but had not done much about them up to that point. They confiscated his drugs but never confronted him about it. What might have happened had they spoken up is unknowable, but as fate would have it, their son ended up getting arrested. Once this happened, the family took an unanticipated financial hit. William's family was not poor, but they were not rich either. Luckily, William had saved some of his drug profits, which helped to cover the cost of his legal defense.[4] Of course, his mother and grandmother were ashamed to accept this money, but they took the cash and, in true suburban fashion, never admitted its source.

> I had a pretty good lawyer. My lawyer had known that judge. The prosecutor came back with five counts of possession with intent, which is what they

were going to charge us with, and then we knocked down to about three. Every time we'd go to court, it would be, there would be so many cases that day—crack possession, cocaine possession, meth possession, child support, these were the only four things there—and there was our little case that was just kind of a little weird one, these little suburban White kids and then all these rednecks for child support and meth and then you got the Black people downtown in the road doing crack and doing coke. So we kind of stuck out a little bit there, and it just progressed and progressed and progressed. The DA just formally discharged us all eventually, and we all got out of it good.

Having narrowly avoided conviction on serious drug charges, William concluded that the time had come for him to stop dealing, before something worse happened to him. Viewed in this light, William's arrest and trial served the positive function of deterring him from continued involvement in the drug underworld, with all of its attendant risks:

I learned a lesson. I could probably have ended up dead from drug use or dead from a bad deal gone bad, stuff like that. It could have all ended a lot worse than it did. I had great times and I wish instead of me getting busted I had just completely quit, but I didn't. The guilt from the family kind of over-weighs the good. The guilt thing about my family, I didn't feel that until after I got busted. I mean I just can't imagine how they felt. That would be like if you were drunk-driving and you killed someone. That was the type of guilt I felt. My family's very open and knows everything that is going on, and they were kind of hurt that I had this usage problem and had not said anything. Of course, I'm not going to say anything about selling drugs. They were kind of hurt because they knew something was weird because I was never home and all that, but they thought it was weird that I didn't come to them with that. I have a good family that's very accepting. I made a dumb mistake and they understood how it started out; hey, you get taking pills for free until the next thing, you know—drug trafficking. It was just boom, boom, boom, and the next thing you know you're doing big drug deals in bad areas with people that you don't know that well. They understood how it happened. But they set me up very well; we have a family business, and I started working for them, and I've worked for them ever since.

As already noted, the young suburban dealers started selling drugs first and foremost to subsidize their own drug use and to generate a little extra cash that they could use to enhance their perceived coolness and, relatedly, to secure a more central place among their peers. In doing so, the sellers had some notion of the risks involved, but those dangers were so far removed from their day-to-day experience that they had little or no deterrent force in the face of the obvious benefits. Once the dealers actually experienced one of those risks, however, the balance shifted such that they attached far greater weight to the potentially negative consequences of continued selling. In effect, they asked themselves, "Is it really worth the risk?" The answer typically was that it was not, and the dealers responded accordingly by deciding not to sell drugs anymore.

Before It Is Too Late

Some dealers terminated their selling careers *before* serious problems emerged, concluding that if they continued dealing, something bad was bound to happen sooner or later. Jared, for example, said that he gave up drug selling because "It wasn't worth it. Just the getting caught, legal reasons. It's just not worth it in the long run because if you're caught with just like an ounce, you go to prison." Asked why he quit dealing, Clay explained, "It was just to the point where I was just tired of it. I kind of got a little like paranoid about it. I feel everyone that sells, if you continue, it's just inevitable that you're going to get caught." Another dealer, Joe, recollected:

> One day I just woke up and was like, "Man, this is stupid. If I get caught with any of this shit, I'm fucked." So that's why I quit selling drugs, and I really did quit selling drugs. Definitely worried about the law, not really too worried about my parents. I mean, it would suck if they caught me, but I mean, it's way less worse than if the cops caught you. That's definitely the thing I was most worried about: the law. Anyone who called me, I'd tell them to quit calling me: "I'm not selling shit."

And Justin's exit from dealing too was motivated by a desire to protect his future life chances for conventional success:

> I never had any reason to suspect I was in any legal trouble, but I started thinking that a selling-pot charge would not be a good thing to have on my record. If you're going into a professional career, that's not something I wanted on my record. I felt that the amount of money I was saving was not worth anything that could possibly happen as far as legal repercussions.

It is clear from the account above that Justin had a stake in conformity and that this is what convinced him to turn away from drug dealing. He perceived his future to be bright and believed that one day he would have a professional career, which he did not want to jeopardize by acquiring a criminal record.

At the time of the study, the dealers featured in this book had graduated from high school and most were attending college. The vast majority of them had not attained full adult status, which is to say that they were yet to secure a respectable career position. Two, however, already had taken their first steps into the adult world of employment. Recall that William had skipped college and gone straight to work in his family's business, having given up dealing after being arrested and charged with drug trafficking. Joseph, when we interviewed him, had just finished college and was about to be married; he planned to live on his wife's earnings while he pursued an acting career. Financially secure and about to take on the responsibilities of adulthood, he had no intention of going back to drug dealing, which he saw as being too risky and not in his best long-term interest:

> Well, I'm getting married a week on Saturday, and she is going to be working as a registered nurse. I have absolutely no need for money. I'm trying to act and go to as many auditions as I can. I might be working in an outreach teaching acting high school program. I might be doing that depending on how large the program is and if they can use me, but I'll try to find some kind of job that I can do on a flexible schedule. I was thinking of substitute teaching, but you need a degree to substitute teach unfortunately, and there are a lot of people with degrees in drama who are looking for temporary work as teachers. It's very competitive to get a substitute drama teaching job and you have to put two hundred hours in, so maybe sometime in the future I'll go into that, but not right now. Right now, I want to try auditioning to see what I can do. With my fiancée's income, she is going to be making between 58 and 60 thousand dollars the first year, so that monthly income is plenty for us to get by, more than enough for us get by. So I don't really have to make a lot of money, so it would be almost more useful for me to put as much time as I could into auditioning to get my career going, so that I can hopefully make money the way I want to sooner than later without getting bogged down waiting tables or something like that. But I'm not going to not work forever. If after two months or so I can't get a job, I'd have to get something; I couldn't handle that. I'm definitely not selling. That's not worth it at all—too risky.

Joseph's case is instructive in that it provides some insight into the transient appeal of drug dealing for suburban adolescents. Having left youthful pursuits behind, about to be married, financially secure, and chasing his dream of an acting career, he already had attained a measure of conventional status and planned to do better still. He was well on his way to securing an enjoyable middle-class life and felt far less pressure to be seen as cool by his peers. Indeed, his reference group was changing such that drug dealing was no longer "worth it."[5]

The dealers who continued to sell drugs during college had every expectation of getting out of the game once they entered adult life and started earning serious legitimate money, if not sooner.[6] When asked if he planned to quit dealing, Ed told us: "Oh yes, absolutely. Maybe next year. Definitely as soon as I get out of school. I'll be making money legitimately. Then I won't be risking anything." But he went on to say that he was beginning to realize the importance of getting out of drug dealing before something bad happened:

> Everyone, at the end of it, had that one close call and they were like, "Shit," and they don't do it anymore. I think it's that same kind of thing where I feel like I'm getting to a point where I'm like I'll do it for a while, but you don't do it for so long or you're going to get into trouble. You have to stop or you're going to get into trouble, so I'm kind of getting to the point now where I'm like getting to that point.

The bottom line is that these suburban middle-class dealers viewed their involvement in drug sales as nothing more than a phase, something to fulfill their short-term desires, which revolved around a pressing need to be cool, until they assumed professional careers and achieved financial independence from their parents. Once they started to perceive dealing as a potential threat to their future prospects for conventional success, therefore, they had little inclination to continue. For them, drug dealing was never intended to be a career—better to get out before it was too late.

The Bigger Picture

The adolescent dealers featured in this book do not fit the academic or media image of the drug seller.[1] The dealers we studied are suburban, White, affluent, conventionally oriented, and peaceful. Practically all of their Peachville peers are the same. Their parents are well educated and enjoy lucrative careers. The young and old in Peachville are similar because adults there serve as role models. They teach their children to value conventional success: to "work" hard to earn educational credentials and to land a well-paying job, to avoid trouble, and, failing that, to minimize its negative effects.

This contrasts starkly with the portrait of drug dealers painted by social scientists, journalists, and television and movie producers alike. The stereotypical dealer is urban, Black, poor, street culture oriented, and combative.[2] Many of the same-age peers in their neighborhoods share these characteristics. These adolescents also learn what to value by observing and listening to the adults around them, who are often uneducated and unemployed or in low-wage labor—or criminal work. What they learn is that their status, financial well-being, respect, and safety require a willingness to be combative and to break the rules of law.[3] While they may be told that conventional success is important—that an education and profession are goals to strive for—the cultural tool kit needed to attain these goals often is not successfully transmitted to them.[4]

In past projects we have interviewed these stereotypical drug dealers, as well as robbers, burglars, carjackers, and other violent offenders from their community.[5] In the pages that follow, we draw on our research and that of others to explore not just the differences but also the similarities between dealers who—for the sake of succinctness—we refer to as "suburban" and "urban." We use the terms "suburban" and "urban" as shorthand; it should go without saying that not all suburban residents are White or affluent nor are all urban ones Black or poor.[6] Compared with Whites, however, Blacks disproportionately reside in neighborhoods of concentrated disadvantage, where rates of poverty, unemployment, low educational attainment, family disruption, victimization, and legal trouble are all high.[7] For this reason, and also because urbanites (as we define them) have been the focus of most prior examinations of drug dealing, our urban-suburban dichotomy serves as a useful point of comparison to explore how social structure, culture, class/status, identity, and rationality move people to action.

The "Obvious" Differences

The suburban dealers we studied would stick out like a sore thumb in "the streets," as too would the urban ones in Peachville. There are distinctive cultural dissimilarities between the two groups tied to where they grew up and live. For one, the suburban dealers speak "conventionally," meaning in Standard American English, except for a few interspersed words deriving from their youth and drug subcultures.[8] The urban dealers rely heavily on a dialect known as "street language" or Ebonics, which draws on conventional English but makes greater use of original words, meanings, and pronunciations.[9]

The suburban and urban dealers we studied look different too. The color of their skin is the most obvious and enduring difference, although this is not culture *per se*. Culture does include material possessions such as clothes and accessories. The urban dealers sport flashy jewelry rarely seen on a suburban seller.[10] And we have never seen a street seller dressed in a tie-dyed T-shirt and Birkenstock clogs. Even when members of these groups wear the same items, they wear them in distinctive ways. Polo shirts, for instance, are owned by suburban and urban dealers alike, but those of the former group generally fit more tightly; and both groups wear baseball caps, but the suburban dealers round out the bill while the urban ones keep it flat. There certainly is overlap in how suburban and urban dealers speak and look, but they are distinguishable—on the average—in their modes of cultural expression.

Not only do the suburban and urban dealers look different; so too do their communities. In the eyes of the suburban dealers at least, Peachville looks "nice": clean and well preserved, with spacious buildings organized by social function. Detached houses of 1,900–4,500 square feet are grouped into subdivisions and placed along through streets. Each home has its own yard, and every household member has his or her "own room."[11] Stores, gyms, movie theaters, gas stations, and restaurants are mostly confined to shopping centers, and other sorts of firms are zoned into "business parks." The outside of every building, whatever its function, is not allowed—by law or custom—to fall into disarray; when repairs are needed, they are made voluntarily or to avoid fines.[12] Green space is tidy, with regular mowing in the warm months, leaf blowing and raking in the colder ones. In a word, Peachville is orderly.

By suburban standards, the physical appearance of urban disadvantaged communities is "rough": dirty and run-down, with everything cramped together.[13] Urban residents' homes typically are small, often consisting of no more than a thousand square feet; it is not uncommon for household members to share bedrooms and sleep on the floor or living-room couch. There is more mixed land use, with homes next to and on top of businesses. Most troublesome, from a suburban perspective, is how derelict and messy everything appears. The roofs of homes and businesses alike are in desperate need of repair, broken windows are left unattended to or covered with plywood, wall siding needs to be painted, and yards are overgrown. Throughout the streets, graffiti is rampant, cars are abandoned, and buildings are vacant. Not only is trash strewn about, but so too are used syringes, crack vials, and condoms.

Another "obvious" difference between the suburban and urban dealers we studied is their status or class. Of course, part of this dissimilarity has to do with how we have defined the two groups: by definition, suburbanites and urbanites live in, respectively, middle- or upper-class and poverty-stricken communities. Although whether someone is middle or lower class cannot be determined definitively by looking at or listening to him or her, it is routine—if regrettable—to make inferences about people's social class based on their cultural expressions, race, and where they live. People's educational background, profession, and income—as well as their criminality—are presumed to correlate with their manner of speaking, appearance, and home address.[14] For this reason, many onlookers would be able to stereotype the suburban and urban dealers we have studied as "middle class or better" or "lower class" by simply asking them a face-to-face question: Where do you live? Upon receiving an answer, the onlookers would hear and see everything they needed to know: White or Black; conventional or "street" apparel; Standard American English or Ebonics; and suburban or urban residence.

The Pursuit of Coolness

Yet for all the apparent differences between suburban and urban dealers, these two groups are in many respects similar. One major similarity between suburban and urban dealers involves the largely subconscious motives that lead them to selling. Both groups venture into dealing as a way to satisfy their pressing need for coolness. And the reason they want to be cool is to feel and be respected and sought after by others.[15]

Attraction is one part of the coolness equation. Onlookers are attracted to "stylish" items, but looking good can be expensive. Urban youths deal drugs to afford and display fashionable products: clothes, shoes, jewelry, and even motor vehicles.[16] For instance, an urban dealer explained his motives for taking up selling thusly: "I seen everyone else with all this jewelry, money, clothes, new cars. I wanted that. My partner who was slingin' had all the stuff I wanted."[17] These material items confer status, a symbolic beauty so to speak, that makes their possessor attractive, especially to members of the opposite sex.[18] As another urban dealer explained, "See, when you selling big, you the Godfather. . . . I was riding around in a red Bronco, . . . gold jewelry on, . . . [G]irls saying, 'Oh, he's so fine.' Now see, they didn't notice me when I didn't have no drugs, but now I'm the finest thing that walks."[19] Explicit in this seller's statement is that the value of hip material goods resides in their ability to garner positive evaluations of one's looks and exert a pull on others.

The suburban dealers spend some of their drug profits on automotive accessories, clothes, hats, jewelry, and shoes too. But these purchases usually do not account for a large portion of their monthly expenditures. Buying too much, recall, can invite parental interrogation. Besides, parents and part-time work provide for the "basic luxuries" anyway. Drug money is not needed to buy such things. Urban youths, conversely, are not so advantaged and may see dealing as one of the few practical ways to afford fashionable luxuries, as their parents and the lawful work available to them are less lucrative sources of money.[20]

What suburban parents do not intend to pay for, or to allow their kids to work for, are drugs. The consumption of psychoactive substances is a ubiquitous form of recreation among the suburban dealers because this staging activity gives them the chance to show off a cadre of admirable personality traits like being generous and fun. In this way, drug use—when done in a group—facilitates the acquisition of likability. The "problem" young suburban drug users confront, however, is that their habit is expensive. While allowance and part-time work cover some of that expense, mainly because their parents pay for many of their other needs and wants, it is nonetheless difficult for teenagers to maintain a fifty- or hundred-dollar-a-week drug habit alongside the other costs of adolescent life, even with a part-time job. Dealing is a way to offset that cost. By earning "free drugs" the suburban dealers can afford to participate in peer interactions, act cool, and appear desirable (by being included in peer activities) while gaining respect and desirability (by demonstrating likability). Better yet, in their minds, is that they earn so much in free drugs that they can increase their pre-dealing level of consumption, which means even more opportunities to win over and be with others.

Urban and suburban adolescents, for all their seeming differences, are the same in that their dealing represents a route to coolness and, thus, to being more respected and socially desired.[21] Disadvantaged dealers buy trendy material goods with their drug profits not because of those items' intrinsic value but rather because they confer status in the dealers' community.[22] Suburban dealers are less commonly motivated to obtain such possessions via dealing because their parents and, for some, part-time work already provide them. Instead, the suburban dealers covet illicit drugs. This is not simply because of the drugs' psychopharmacological effects; it has more to do with the social effects that accompany getting high. Whereas all of the suburban dealers cited free drugs as a good reason to sell, urban dealers were less likely to feel this way.[23] Moreover, while suburban dealers sold only substances that they also used, urban dealers were more apt to express disgust for their product and to be repulsed by it.[24] As one urban dealer explained, "I ain't messin' wit' that. Get sprung or somethin' [start an all-consuming addiction]. Don't ever wanna start off like that for real."[25] Another urban seller said of his product, "I don't fuck with it. . . . Just sell it and go."[26]

There is a further "dissimilar-similarity" in these groups' actions that springs from a commonly held concern for coolness. Both sets of sellers sometimes give their drugs or money to others. The motive for this altruism, if only subconsciously, is to increase their likability. In effect, the dealers are using resources to buy companionship.[27]

Prior research suggests that urban dealers, who, like their suburban counterparts, are overwhelmingly male, largely are focused on attracting the attention of females.[28] As an urban dealer said, "You can't get no girl with no money."[29] As already noted, one benefit of money is the ability to buy attractiveness. A second is to afford generosity. As described by one seasoned observer of the urban social scene: "The kids are making the money off the drugs—they're the only ones who have money. Everybody wants to be associated with somebody who has money, and they're the only ones who have the money to really show the girls a good time."[30] While growing up, urban children may learn that neighborhood drug dealers—but few others—have money and, by no coincidence, have the girls too. Wanting the same for themselves, some of these youngsters grow up to sell drugs.[31]

The suburban dealers also spend some of their money on females. But compared with their urban counterparts, they seem far more likely to spend their profits on male friends. They buy these "dudes" drinks and food and give them free drugs or the hookup on purchases. Everyone expects the dealers to do this, including the dealers themselves. This altruism is by no means necessary for the survival of the group; these friends, like almost every other teenager in Peachville, can get by on "their own" due to parental generosity. But there is a norm in Peachville that giving is good and whoever is financially better off is obliged to be generous. Throughout their lives, these dealers have seen their parents fight, figuratively speaking, with other adults over restaurant bills and pick up the tab for visitors. Watching this, these young suburban dealers have learned that generosity is a good trait, that whoever has more should provide for those with less, or that if it is a tie, then they should negotiate over who gets to pay the bill.[32] The suburban dealers understand that generosity has costs, but that those expenses are outweighed by the benefits of increased likability, respect, and desirability. This sort of financial generosity and culturally based system of rewarding altruism appears less pronounced in disadvantaged urban neighborhoods; people there have a hard enough time paying their own bills, let alone those of others.

While some scholars have suggested that drug use and dealing are antisocial behaviors,[33] in many respects this label distorts our understanding of these practices. While drugs can cause social problems, for many people the allure of drug use and dealing resides in their social benefits. These activities provide people with a reason to socialize and an opportunity to demonstrate their coolness, thereby earning respect and desirability. Dealing, moreover, offers people the means to engage in such activities, look good, and be generous. If the genesis of crime is our main concern, then the "problem" with many dealers is that they care too much about social life, not too little.[34]

Coolness versus Conventionality

But why do suburban and urban dealers care about being cool and socially desired? The second major similarity between suburban and urban drug dealers is that their relatively low social position in the broader society at least in part explains their inordinate concern with status among their peers.[35]

In Peachville the minimum requirement for conventional success is to have a middle-class income.[36] There is an important difference between being brought up in a middle-class household, as the suburban sellers were, and being conventionally successful, which they were not. It takes time to graduate from high school and college and then to establish yourself in a successful career. Very few teenagers are able to do so. The American educational and economic systems are not structured to promote early success, and most people do not fully attain it until at least their midtwenties, if they attain it at all.[37] Until then, most suburban adolescents—when measured independently of their parents' status—are objectively lower class and unsuccessful: with no job at all or only a low-wage one.[38]

So what are young suburbanites to do in the meantime—that is, until they can claim to be a success in their own right? It is unrealistic to think that all suburban teenagers will simply bear being lower class until adulthood. A plausibly successful future cannot fully discount the importance of a person's evaluation of whether they are "somebody" today: somehow valuable and worthy of respect. An adolescent's stake in conformity—meaning having something to lose in the future by being bad now[39]—does not fully negate their stake in coolness: what is lost in the present by being disliked or unattractive.[40]

If conventional success is at best years away, then how can someone achieve status in the here and now? There are always subcultures that place more or less emphasis on one or another marker of success or that emphasize another set of markers altogether.[41] An alternative to the conventional system of success is one that emphasizes coolness. In this subculture, persons who are both likable and attractive are cool (high status or upper class); persons who are dislikable and unattractive are lame (low status or lower class); and persons who are somewhat likable or attractive or both are in between (middle status or middle class).

Being cool is beneficial; it leads an individual to be treated well and sought after by peers. By being cool, a person gains a sense of value, just as he or she would from earning a middle-class income or better. But unlike that marker of conventional success, coolness is imminently attainable. To be cool, all someone has to do is develop a subcultural understanding of what looks good and then look that way, and to discern what traits are likable and act that way in the company of others.

As explained above, urban adolescents are motivated to sell drugs to buy fashionable items and attract female company. In theory, they could get a legitimate job instead. In practice, however, such individuals have a tough time landing a job at all, never mind one that offers a solidly middle-class income.[42]

One reason for the lack of good-paying jobs for urbanites is that structural changes have adversely affected inner-city residents far more than they have suburbanites, who actually have benefited from some of these changes. Those changes include the building of highways and freeways, which has led to jobs being dispersed out of cities and into suburbs and which has also disrupted the "pedestrian patterns and economic" logic of inner-city neighborhoods.[43] Additionally, urbanites' real wages have been hurt by the failure of the minimum wage to keep pace with inflation and by regressive tax policies that have cut into what little income is provided by low-wage work.[44] And urbanites' prospects for conventional success have been undercut further by declining demand among US employers for low-skilled labor, by the relocation of industries to the suburbs (and eventually overseas), and by urban sprawl generally, which further reduces job opportunities near where urbanites live while increasing them closer to the suburbs.[45]

Another factor that serves to limit employment opportunities for urbanites is racism, both overt and subconscious. Research has shown time and time again that Blacks have less favorable employment outcomes than Whites.[46] Blacks are less likely to be hired than are Whites of similar qualifications; part of the reason for this is that Blacks are less likely to receive an interview.[47] When Blacks are hired, it is more likely to be for a lower-wage job relative to those of Whites.[48] And when working the same job, Blacks tend to earn lower wages than Whites.[49] What has to be remembered about discrimination is that it cuts both ways; when Blacks are getting a raw deal, this is often to the benefit of Whites.

The third reason that many urbanites have a difficult time finding a good job is that they lack the necessary qualifications. The accumulation of education positively impacts a person's ability to land a job, especially a higher-wage one. Part of the reason that urbanites, especially males, have poor rates of employment and make low wages is that they lack important educational skills, diplomas, and job training.[50] Some studies even suggest that the Black-White gap in employment and wages is largely or entirely an artifact of such factors.[51] While that may be true, what is indisputably true is that Black youth disproportionately reside in disadvantaged neighborhoods that make it difficult to acquire the sort of skills that could make them competitive on the job market. Children who reside in neighborhoods marked by lower median family income, for example, have been shown to have lower scores on scholastic achievement tests that measure symbolic learning, reading, and mathematical reasoning.[52] Likewise, being raised in a severely disadvantaged urban community is known to substantially impede the accumulation of verbal skills.[53] Related to this later finding is that such communities have particularly high rates of violence[54] and that children's exposure to extreme violence lowers their scores on vocabulary and reading assessments.[55] And growing up in a disadvantaged neighborhood can lower an individual's odds of graduating from high school by 10–20 percent.[56] The flip side of all of these examples is that Whites are relatively competitive on the job market because they tend to grow up in more advantaged communities and therefore to have better educational outcomes.

As a result of structural barriers, racism, and a lack of qualifications, urban adolescents understandably may conclude that their employment and wage prospects are poor. A culture of widespread pessimism emerges, in which achieving conventional success is perceived to be a losing battle.[57] Many urban dealers believe that they have little or no hope of ever landing a well-paying legitimate job. Consider one urban dealer's experience on the job market: "Went lookin' [for work] but nobody call me for jobs. Have to . . . deal [drugs to make money]."[58] Another urban seller made a similar statement: "Tried to get hired, but [they] never did holler at me. That's what makin' me sell. . . . I can't get no job."[59] The jobs that are available to urbanites often pay at or near the minimum wage, and so dealing comes to be seen as worth the risks. One urban dealer explained, "I make just as much as this motherfucker in Hardees [the fast-food restaurant]. I make more than that. I make three Hardees' checks in one day!"[60] Although working a low-wage job is conventionally more respectable than drug dealing, it is a lower-class job all the same. Recognizing their poor odds of achieving conventional success, some urban adolescents refocus their attention on dealing to make money, look good, get the girls, and be respected.

Like the urban dealers, the suburban dealers are motivated to start selling drugs in pursuit of coolness, respect, and social desirability. And, again like their urban counterparts, their pursuit of coolness is a way of compensating for their lack of conventional success. The suburban dealers we studied knew what constituted conventional success and they aspired to it. They also knew that they were years away from achieving that goal and thus pursued a more immediately attainable form of status: coolness. They wanted to be more than good kids striving for conventional success; they also wanted to be popular teenagers. Dealing drugs was a way to do exactly that, and more. Dealing paid for drug consumption; earned extra cash to spend on group activities and attractive material goods; and made dealers more integral and high-ranking members of their subcultural peer network because they had what others wanted, drugs.

A third major similarity between the urban and suburban dealers is that their illicit entrepreneurship puts them at increased risk of parental and legal trouble as well as various sorts of victimization. This similarity, however, is also where differences between urban and suburban dealers become more pronounced. In part this is because such problems arise with differential frequency and seriousness for the two groups and in part because the knock-on effects, or "collateral consequences," of those problems are vastly different for them.

Dealing in Spite of versus for the Family

It should be clear by now that the suburban dealers we studied wanted to avoid parental trouble. The costs associated with being caught dealing by their parents were emotional and social. The psychological pains included feelings of shame, regret, and embarrassment for having disappointed their parents.[61] The social costs included having their drugs or drug money confiscated, being "grounded," and the loss of parent-provided luxuries such as cell phones, allowances, and access to a vehicle.

Because these teenagers shared a close bond with their parents and were provided with ample amounts of financial support by them, the parents had the ability to impose meaningful punishments. The parents could have "cut off" their offspring in various ways, most damning of which would have been to kick them out of the house and withhold any financial help. In all likelihood, this would have devastated these adolescents emotionally and financially, jeopardizing their prospects of achieving conventional success.

But such a severe punishment would have had serious emotional consequences for the parents too. They had spent years grooming their offspring for conventional success. For them, accepting that their child is a drug dealer was tantamount to admitting that they had failed as parents. They had good reason to look the other way when faced with circumstantial evidence of their offspring's drug dealing and to temper the punishment when such evidence became too obvious to ignore.[62]

The suburban dealers felt guilty about the prospect or actuality of parental trouble. Yet this problem—on its own—did not carry enough weight to motivate them to cease their drug selling. For parental trouble to move a suburban seller to quit, it had to occur in conjunction with legal problems or victimization. This may be because these dealers implicitly understood that their parents did not have the stomach for inflicting any sort of punishment that might jeopardize their futures.

The situation is similar in many ways for young urban dealers, despite significant differences in their family lives. It is no secret that the family lives of urban residents often are attenuated.[63] There are more single-headed households among them than in the American population generally; only a few of the suburban dealers' parents were unmarried, for instance. Not only are urban homes more likely to be run by a single parent, but the other parent—usually the father—is more likely to be entirely absent from his children's lives.[64] And compared with suburbanites, both parents of urban youngsters are more likely to be absent, with the caretaking performed instead by a grandparent.[65] While a few of the suburban dealers did not live with both biological parents, they did have regular contact with each of them via phone and visits.

On average, urban parents have less emotional and economic capital to hold over their children's heads to prevent them from dealing drugs or to encourage them to quit doing so. For one thing, the bond between urban adolescents and their parents often is weaker because they are less involved in each other's lives. For another, the fact that many urban residents are poor means that they cannot give as much financial support to their children; these parents cannot afford to buy their offspring a vehicle or a cell phone or to provide them with a significant allowance. This lack of emotional and economic resources means that urban parents have fewer mechanisms for punishing their children to deter them from crime. Instead, many of these parents resort to the use of corporal punishment, thereby perpetuating a culture of violence that teaches their children that might makes right.[66]

Like their suburban counterparts, however, urban parents are known often to look the other way, to "see but not see," their children's drug dealing.[67] But whereas suburban parents temper sanctioning their children largely to avoid familial conflict and jeopardizing their child's prospects for conventional success, urban parents may withhold punishment—despite their disdain for drug dealing—for purely financial reasons. As urban ethnographer Elijah Anderson notes:

> Many [urban] parents . . . realize that their own son is probably involved in the trade. They disapprove of it, but they also benefit from it. A mother who

receives money, sometimes even large sums of money, from her son may not ask too many questions about its source. She just accepts the fact that the money is there somehow. Since it is sorely needed, there is a strong incentive not to interrupt the flow. Some people are so torn over what they are tolerating that they pray and ask forgiveness from the Lord for their de facto approval. Yet they cannot bring themselves to intervene.[68]

Thus, the parents of urban and suburban dealers behave similarly despite their differences. Those differences provide different motives for action that, perhaps paradoxically, lead to the same result. Suburban parents would not dream of withholding punishment for fear of losing the income associated with their child's drug dealing; it was never calculated into their budget in the first place and they did not need it to provide for their families. The economic position of the parents of urban dealers typically is far less fortunate. Caretakers in disadvantaged communities are often unable to find well-paying jobs. Many work at or near the minimum wage and therefore can barely afford to pay for their rent and groceries. Others have no job at all and depend on government housing and welfare. There is little or no money left over for the purchase of luxury items, despite the subcultural importance of such possessions for being cool, respected, and socially desired. In response, some urban youngsters come to see drug dealing as a way to afford not only their own wants but also the needs of their family. For example, an urban dealer explained, "I sellin' for a good reason. Give my mama money or buy me some clothes, so she won't gotta buy me stuff all the time and I don't have to ask. I be gettin' older, and I gotta help with the house. My daddy died, and sellin' dope helps with the stress of bills."[69] And another urbanite said, "I too old to ask my mama for somethin'. I need to be givin' Mama somethin' she need. Dad died two years ago."[70]

Legal Discrimination

The formal justice system poses a threat to suburban and urban dealers alike. Yet compared with their suburban counterparts, urban residents have a far rockier relationship with legal officials, especially the police.[71] A constant refrain among urbanites is that they are disrespected by the cops.[72] The police are viewed as too zealous, as enforcing and punishing minor offenses.[73] As one urban resident put it, "I can't stand [the] police. . . . They crooked, . . . pull you over for shit like not having a light over your license plate or something," and then they "end up running you name and searching your car."[74] And another alleged that the police would "stop [me] for anything . . . ; [walk] across a street and the light is red . . . , [stop me] for that."[75] A separate but related indictment is that the police *illegitimately* detain, investigate, use physical force against, arrest, and otherwise punish urbanites (e.g., through confiscation of possessions) on a frequent basis.[76] As one urbanite contended, "[E]very time I have an encounter with [the police], . . . it's some shit that I ain't had nothing to do with."[77] Yet another recounted what was for him an especially vexing incident:

> We was standing on the corner, police pulled up, . . . told us all to get against the wall. . . . We asked them, you know, what did we do, what we gotta get against the wall for? [They replied,] "That ain't none of your mother-fucking business! . . . Just turn your ass around and get against the wall!" [T]hey searched us and shit, grabbed us, threw us against the wall . . . and all this stuff. Told us to sit down on the curb and . . . handcuffed us and made us sit down on the curb and told us that we weren't supposed to be on the corner . . . and we wasn't doing nothing but standing. . . . They handcuffed us, made us sit out there in the rain for about twenty five minutes while they ran a police check on us, and then after that, when it came back clear, they come back and threaten us if they catch us on the corner again, "We gonna lock you up," and this and that.[78]

Police may even go so far as to plant evidence on suspects.[79] For instance, one urban teenager claimed that an officer "always checks us for drugs. Sometimes if you don't have no drugs on you he will put some on you."[80]

Urban adolescents exacerbate their already-tenuous relationship with the police if they deal drugs. Of course, selling drugs is a felony offense and inherently risky, but the policing of urban drug markets is notoriously aggressive. The police crack down via buy-busts and reverse stings, flooding hot spots with officers, conducting "street sweeps" as well as "stop-and-frisks," and raiding private property.[81] A major reason why these tactics are effective is that drug markets by definition are social. Buyers, dealers, and suppliers all need each other. One implication of this is that traders congregate; to the extent that these meetings become spatially fixed, the police will know where to target their efforts. A second implication of the drug trade's social nature is that apprehended offenders can be used against each other. Often there are less than five degrees of separation between a lowly user and a big-time supplier. It is well known that the police, especially those working the streets, take advantage of this by offering bargains to apprehended drug offenders in which they receive leniency in exchange for their cooperation in busting others.[82] These informants provide the police

with valuable gossip—such as that needed to execute a search warrant—
and sometimes participate more directly in undercover operations by wear-
ing a wire, setting up a buy, or testifying in court.[83] More than anywhere
else in America, urban drug markets are policed with a vengeance.[84] Thus,
to be an urban dealer requires you to be on your toes and, for many, to be
arrested and serve prison time.[85]

Suburbanites, by contrast, have far less contact with the police and
therefore have little to complain about. So long as they obey the law, there
is little chance of being confronted by the police, especially in comparison
to those living in disadvantaged urban neighborhoods. When the police
do initiate contact with suburban residents, the nature of the interaction is
totally different from what urbanities experience. A suburbanite may grum-
ble about being ticketed for running a red light, not making a complete
stop, or exceeding the speed limit. But otherwise, suburbanites, at least
those in Peachville, seldom perceive themselves as having been stopped by
the police for no reason or as having been treated disrespectfully by them.

Obviously, dealing is a crime in the suburbs too, and as such, doing
so entails some degree of legal risk. Yet twenty-eight of the dealers in our
study *never* experienced any drug dealing–related legal trouble. Two of the
dealers were arrested for reasons stemming from their dealing, but these
exceptions prove the rule insofar as they happened, not in Peachville, but
rather in rural Georgia. While all of the suburban sellers were worried, if
only a little, about getting caught by the police, they reasoned that this was
unlikely to actually happen to them—and they were right.[86] Partly this was
because they took precautions to lower the odds of apprehension.[87] But the
fact is that the police in Peachville displayed little interest in proactive drug
control. We never heard of anyone's home being raided by the cops; there
was no obvious hot-spot policing and there were certainly no street sweeps.

This means that urban adolescents involved in drug selling are assuming far greater legal risk than their suburban counterparts. The Peachville
dealers had little experience with the law, and those who did seldom felt
the full force of its sanctions.[88] Urban dealers appear far more likely than
suburban ones to know what it is actually like to be investigated, arrested,
jailed, tried in court, and imprisoned or otherwise punished. Quantitative
studies provide hard evidence in support of this assertion, though they are
admittedly imperfect because they compare Whites and Blacks rather than
suburbanites and urbanites as we define them. With that caveat in mind,
the statistics bear out two basic points. The first is that Whites are equally
or more likely than Blacks to sell drugs.[89] Based on that finding, we should
expect Whites to be no less likely than Blacks to be arrested and impris-

oned for this crime. But that is not the reality: the second consistent statistical finding is that Blacks are far more likely than Whites to be arrested and imprisoned for dealing.[90] When added to the qualitative evidence, it seems fair to infer from these statistics that being an urban dealer is more "dangerous" than being a suburban one.

Legal Problems and Conventional Success

Legal trouble is detrimental to an individual's prospects for conventional success. In the United States, between one-quarter and one-half of employers perform official background checks to screen job applicants; others simply ask job seekers to disclose their criminal record.[91] In practice, applicants with a known criminal record are less likely to be hired than are their competitors without one.[92] This is true for several reasons.[93] Employers may surmise that a criminal record is suggestive of character flaws that would make for a poor worker, or they may reason that the past is a reliable predictor of future behavior and therefore seek to avoid those who could pose a risk to employees, customers, suppliers, and business partners. Additionally, workplace-related offending can cause financial and reputational harm to the organization, which provides yet another reason not to hire ex-convicts.

While arrest and conviction can result in a criminal record and negative employment prospects, imprisonment appears to be especially detrimental to the odds of achieving conventional success.[94] Time behind bars is time out of the workforce. When in the workforce, a person acquires human and social capital that serve to further his or her odds of subsequent employment.[95] It is possible to accumulate some of that capital while in prison, but not to the same extent as when working on the outside. Thus, ex-prisoners find it hard to get a job not only because they have a criminal record but also because they are less well trained, experienced, and connected to persons who may know of job opportunities or can serve as references.[96]

There is another way in which being incarcerated makes it difficult to achieve conventional success. Time in prison does more than undermine an individual's chances of landing a job; it also lowers the wages earned for the work that is done. The underlying causal factors are the same as those outlined above: imprisonment can impede the development of human and social capital, and a criminal record can stigmatize an ex-offender as a poor worker or risk.[97] For these reasons, going to prison makes it harder for individuals to land anything but low-wage work and, once on the job, more difficult for them to be promoted.[98]

To our knowledge, no prior research analyzes how legal trouble differentially impacts the employment prospects of urbanites and suburbanites as we define them. However, one study finds that employers in the central city and the suburbs have roughly equivalent rates of administering background checks on job applicants and display similar rates of hiring ex-offenders.[99] This suggests that legal trouble is equally detrimental to urbanites' and suburbanites' labor prospects.

However, it is reasonable to speculate on the basis of studies comparing Whites and Blacks that in reality urban drug dealers are more likely than suburban ones to be unemployed or to lose out on income as a result of legal trouble. As reviewed above, Blacks are disproportionately arrested, convicted, and imprisoned for drug dealing relative to Whites. For this reason alone, urban drug dealers might be expected to be more likely than their suburban counterparts to suffer the collateral consequences of legal trouble with respect to employment and wages.[100] Moreover, compared with White ex-convicts, Blacks with a criminal record are less likely to be hired or to earn as high a wage.[101] One study even finds that Whites with a criminal history are more likely to be hired for positions than are Blacks with a clean record.[102] Extrapolating from these studies, it is highly plausible that drug dealing is more costly for urban adolescents than for suburban ones: the former group is not only more likely to suffer legal consequences but also is more likely to have its prospects for conventional success—as marked by a well-paying job—jeopardized in the process.

Being Hit versus Getting Shot

Another problem experienced more commonly by urban dealers than by those in the suburbs is victimization, especially the violent kind. For almost a century, crime has been a bigger concern in the cities than in the suburbs in the United States.[103] As an example, consider the serious crime rates for Peachville and its parent city, Atlanta, during the years when most of the suburban dealers whom we interviewed were in high school, 1998 through 2002. During those years, there were no homicides in Peachville but 722 in Atlanta, or about 34 murders per 100,000 persons annually. The annual rates of violent and property crime, respectively, were 26 and 3 times higher in Atlanta than in Peachville. More precisely, the robbery rate was 20 times higher in Atlanta; aggravated assault, 34 times higher; burglary, 5 times higher; larceny/theft, 2 times higher; and motor vehicle theft, 11 times higher. Such differences are by no means unique to Peachville and Atlanta. Throughout the country, central cities experience more

serious crime than the surrounding metropolitan areas.[104] And within cities, the areas with the highest crime rates are those characterized by social
disadvantage.[105]

Compared with their suburban counterparts, all urbanites have a relatively high risk of victimization, but drug dealing amplifies that risk. As
one urban dealer put it, "To me, when you get money like that, when
you in a game like that, you are bound to run into some problems. . . .
[R]obbery and sneakiness, it all goes with the package."[106] Urban-based defrauders, burglars, and robbers target drug sellers in and near their neighborhoods because they have valuable possessions.[107] As one urban robber
explained, drug dealers are ideal targets "'cause they have all the money on
them. . . . They carry all the money, jewelry, and all that on them, and all
they drugs."[108] A mugger added that a dealer is a sure bet: "You know he
gonna have some money. . . . Either he got some money or he got something in his pocket that's gonna make some money."[109] An additional reason why predators focus on urban dealers is that they are unlikely to report
offenses committed against them to the police. "That's all I done robbed
is drug dealers," said one street offender. "[T]hey not gonna call the police. What they gonna tell the police? He robbed me for my dope?"[110] And
even if a dealer reports the victimization, which does happen,[111] the police
are unlikely to do much about the incident.[112] One robber figured, "[The
police] gonna [say] that, 'Okay, this is a drug robbery. We really don't care
about this [incident]. You shouldn't have been out selling this bullshit.'"[113]

The suburban dealers also experienced victimization rates far exceeding
those of their non-dealing peers. In their pre-dealing days, they may have
been cheated out of a few dollars when buying drugs for personal use, or
they may have had something like a smoking pipe stolen at a party. These
were inconsequential losses. Dealing-related victimizations were different.
They often were far more serious as measured by the amount lost. And they
frequently were more disturbing too in the sense that the dealers' homes
and cars were broken into; money and drugs were stolen from right under
their noses; and people aggressively came after them, on a few occasions
with a gun.

While urban and suburban dealers are similar insofar as their illicit
business increases their risk of victimization, the implications of being victimized tend to be much graver for those who ply their trade in the inner
city. In urban neighborhoods, dealing drugs poses a realistic risk of being
shot or killed. Indeed, the homicide rate among urban drug dealers is re-
markable. Two studies are especially telling: one found that for members of
a drug-selling gang in Chicago, the death rate was 7 percent annually;[114] the

other calculated that about one in a hundred dealers in Washington, DC, was killed per year.[115] These homicide rates are many times greater than the average for the American population as a whole and, more narrowly, for urban residents, who historically are overrepresented among murder victims.[116]

Conversely, the victimizations experienced by the suburban dealers were almost never even remotely life threatening. Punches were thrown and guns were drawn a few times, but no one was ever actually shot at; no one was hospitalized; no one was killed; nor was anyone seriously injured. This is not to deny that some of these incidents were serious by suburban standards. But the fact of the matter is that what constitutes serious violence for the suburban dealers we studied is nothing like the deadly reality faced by urban dealers or urbanites generally. The worst—and also the rarest—dealing-related victimizations reported to us by the suburban dealers are an everyday risk for many urban residents.[117]

Combativeness and Peacefulness

As noted above, predators choose to target drug dealers because—compared with most other potential victims—they have more worth stealing and are unlikely to report their victimizations, and the police are unlikely to take such incidents seriously even if they do come to their attention.[118] For these same reasons, dealers are more prone than law-abiding citizens to retaliate against their victimizers. If an individual cannot turn to the government for help, then vigilantism emerges as the primary way to enforce justice.

Urban drug dealers are infamous for violent retaliation.[119] They have numerous motives for striking back violently. One is simply to relieve their negative emotions and restore cognitive balance. Bad feelings, especially a sense of being disrespected, can push people to seek vengeance. An urban seller who was robbed explained his retaliatory strike as "just doing it 'cause I was angry."[120] There is more to it than just that, however. Victims try to make themselves feel better by making the victimizer feel pain. An urban dealer gloated while noting that "I love to see the motherfuckers down like they did me."[121] Another explained his motive for retaliation as wanting to let the victimizer "know what I'm feeling."[122]

A more tangible benefit of retaliatory violence is that it can help victims to recoup lost resources. One urban dealer who was robbed of more than $1,000 in drugs and cash, for example, described his thinking afterward: "It's like I work too hard to let somebody to just take something from me like that. . . . It's like I worked for nothing. . . . What was going through my mind is I need my shit back, either he gonna give it back or either he gonna die."[123] An urban seller recently robbed of his heroin and jewelry was yet to retaliate, but he had every intention of doing so, explaining, "That's a loss. If I see them, shit, if I see them I'm gonna have to do something to them. I got to get mine back. That's just common sense, you know, I mean that is nature, I got to get that, . . . I got to get 'em."[124]

But urban dealers are not the only ones who violently retaliate against victimizers because they are angry or want to recoup their losses. While rare, the suburban sellers who retaliated, violently or sneakily, did so for exactly those reasons. But that's the only significant similarity between the urban and the suburban dealers who resorted to vigilantism. Urban dealers have three motives to retaliate that distinguish them from the suburban dealers we studied. Unlike their suburban counterparts, urban dealers learn and live by a "code of the street."[125] This is a set of informal rules that arise out of the social disadvantage of inner-city communities. This culture endorses the threat and use of violence, especially retaliatory violence, as a good way to garner safety and status.

For urban dealers, violent retaliation represents a method of deterrence. By striking back, these dealers hope to scare off would-be victimizers. In other words, the violence is intended not only to teach the victimizer a lesson but also to send a message to anyone else who might be tempted to attack the dealer in the future to think twice before doing so. As one urban dealer explained, "You mess with my product you going down. . . . That message gets around. . . . It gets around."[126] The flip side of this philosophy is that by not retaliating, dealers increase their odds of being preyed upon. When an urban dealer was asked why he killed the man who robbed him, he said, "See, you have to realize if I didn't get back at him, you and him could say [I'm] a punk. Everybody can go take [my] shit. . . . You need to let it be known you not gonna take no shit [because otherwise] you would be out of business . . . or dead . . . 'cause you would have people . . . coming up trying to rob you [thinking] he gonna do nothing."[127]

Urban dealers come to see violent retaliation as a viable method of deterrence because they view the police as generally ineffective and unconcerned with enforcing the law.[128] For example, one urbanite said this about the police: "It's gonna take them five or ten minutes to get there. . . . [W]hoever did it [robbed me] . . . gonna be gone and went on."[129] And another observed, "If you tell the police" about a crime, "they tell you they gonna investigate but man [they don't]. . . . Shit, somebody stole my car and the police honestly told me [they] weren't lookin' for it."[130] A prevalent— if cynical—view among many urban residents is that law enforcement officials simply do not want to fight crime in their neighborhoods. As one such resident remarked, "[O]n the [police] car it says what? To protect and serve. . . . [M]ost of the time there's no service. . . . [T]hey really don't give a fuck."[131] Another urbanite was equally discouraged about police officers' desire to serve justice: "Those motherfuckers ain't gonna do nothing. . . . They'll take our statements and send us on our way home."[132] Seeing the police in this light, many urban residents come to rely on themselves for protection, be it in the course of selling drugs or simply walking down the street.

Another motive for violent retaliation among urban drug dealers involves the pursuit of street status. In urban communities, violent retaliation often represents a way to gain rank among peers.[133] Whereas coolness amounts to how likable and attractive someone is, combativeness amounts to an individual's willingness and ability to use violence.[134] On the basis of these characteristics, individuals are said to be "hard" or "soft," meaning, respectively, capable of violence or not. As with likability and attractiveness, these traits can be inherited, learned, or purchased. Individuals, for example, may be genetically predisposed to violence; may learn from their parents that being violent is important; and may buy a gun or another weapon.[135] For persons subscribing to the code of the street, the payoffs of combativeness are psychological and social. In urban disadvantaged communities, to be a badass makes some individuals feel good because it confers status and respect while protecting them from predation; to be soft does the opposite.[136]

Combativeness determines a person's degree of coolness, although whether its effect is positive or negative depends on the subcultural commitments of the evaluator.[137] On the streets of urban communities, individuals gain coolness as they become more combative.[138] People who are hard are recruited into peer groups because they have status and the ability to deter predators. Those perceived to be soft are excluded from the cooler, combative groups and must stand alone or with other noncombative persons.[139] On the urban street corner, then, being combative is a way to earn cool points and social desirability and, in theory at least, protect yourself—which takes on special importance in communities characterized by notably high victimization rates.[140]

Urban parents teach their kids to stand up for themselves with violence.[141] This is not to say that all of these parents relish doing so; the more "decent" among them would prefer otherwise. But a reality of living in a violent community—where victimizations of all sorts are commonplace—is that a willingness to fight back is a necessary survival skill. In the streets, people who are not willing to portray themselves as violent invite attacks against themselves. Thus, urban youth are taught that violence is a necessary evil.

Combativeness is more than protective; it also can be employed to steal from others. Being able to take what you want by force raises your status on the street corner. What is taken through force—be it a pair of shoes, a jacket, or a gold chain—serves as a "trophy" that testifies to the robbers' combativeness.[142] By displaying stolen possessions, street offenders dually signal their attractiveness and their combativeness, thereby gaining status, respect, and social desirability among their peers.[143]

Decent parents in urban areas are not teaching their offspring to prey on others; they communicate the opposite. But not all urban parents are so conventionally oriented. Youngsters who are raised by street-oriented adults learn, if only implicitly, to be combative for the purpose of self-defense and as a way to get what they want.[144] This lesson is reinforced on the street corner. Children lost or left to the street by their parents may be exposed to and come to acquire a set of cultural commitments that lionize violence as a way to be cool and socially desired, thereby becoming a danger to themselves and others.

Those on the street corner interpret not being victimized by others as a sign of respect. As one urban drug dealer explained, "I'm the kind of guy that's not to be betrayed, . . . because if you do something to me then 99.9 per cent chance I'm going to retaliate on it and with a vengeance. I gained a lot of respect . . . because I took care of my business."[145] Being victimized, conversely, sends a message that the person attacked is perceived as being "soft" and, in the streets, this equates to being lame. Anyone who hears of the victimization may lose respect for the victim, concluding that he is not a combative, cool person. The best way for victims to counter this perception is to retaliate with violence. If successful, vigilantism sends a signal to everyone—the vigilante, the victimizer, and third parties—that the victim is not someone to be crossed.

Unlike their urban counterparts, the suburban dealers did not talk about the importance of retaliating in order to deter predators from targeting them again. Yet they recognized that by not doing so, they invited predators to take advantage of them. Robert, for instance, said exactly that: "There's got to be repercussions if someone steals. If there's no repercussions for what you are doing, then people will continue to do it. You'll get robbed again. I mean word gets around." After Christian was defrauded out of almost $200 worth of marijuana and then did nothing in response, he came to believe "something had gotten around . . . and like now I was somebody that people could take advantage of." Despite knowing the risks, however, neither of these dealers nor any of their peers sought to deter predators by enacting serious violence. The few suburban dealers who did resort to violence against predators did not explain their response as a deterrent, save perhaps for the time Dave stole a TV in retaliation for a buy gone bad. There is an incongruity here: the suburban dealers clearly recognized the deterrent value of violent retaliation and the cost of not striking back, but this recognition seldom resulted in the use of violence.

This incongruity might be explained by several factors. First, there is not very much violent victimization in Peachville, which means that there is little need for adolescents to cultivate a reputation for combativeness to deter predators. Second, suburbanites are far less antagonistic toward and far more trusting of the police than many urban residents; the citizenry of Peachville do not feel that they are overly or discriminatorily policed, and they assume that if they are seriously victimized, the police will take the crime seriously and do everything they can to obtain justice on their behalf. Third, few of the suburban dealers had the stomach for engaging in serious violence. Their parents had not schooled them in the ways of the badass, nor did they encourage such behavior. These suburban dealers lacked the mind-set to be combative. They did not know how to fight, and more tellingly, they did not want to inflict serious injury on anyone.

And because being combative is not protective in Peachville, it is not perceived as being cool either. People do not need to surround themselves with fighters to be safe and do not seek out their company. Indeed, combative individuals may actively be shunned by their suburban drug-dealing peers, who fear that they will turn on them or invite legal trouble.[146] That said, in practice, Peachville adolescents did not spend much time considering whether to associate with combative individuals; there were not many around in the first place. Those few combative suburban youths who were around, moreover, were soft in comparison to their street-hardened counterparts in disadvantaged areas.[147] They made empty threats and at most shoved or punched to back up their tough talk.[148] Weapons were not part of the retaliatory equation, nor were ambulances, hospitals, or morgues. Even the tough talk surrounding these incidents lacked conviction, as when William claimed that he and his accomplice "weren't gonna bloody [the kid who stole his drugs] up or anything, just kind of beat the hell out of him." Compare his response with that of an urban dealer who retaliated after being victimized in much the same way as William: "I'm like, 'What's up player?' . . . He tried to break out and just run 'cause he knew he was guilty. . . . I swung the bat. . . . Hit him in the back. He fell. Boom! Then I broke two of his legs."[149] It seems that "beating the hell out of" someone means something different to middle-class suburban drug dealers than it does to lower-class urban ones.

On the rare occasions when the suburban dealers retaliated at all it was far more likely to be sneaky rather than violent in character. Like retaliatory violence, sneaky acts of fraud, unseen theft, and destruction allow a victim to dissipate his or her negative emotions and recoup lost resources. Urban dealers do not seem proportionally disposed to sneaky retaliation. From their perspective, the defining attribute of sneakiness—namely, its covertness—is problematic.[150] If the retaliatory act is so sneaky as to prevent anyone, including the victimizer, from knowing who did it, then it carries limited deterrence potential and does little to enhance the victim's reputation for combativeness. But suburban dealers do not care as much about deterring victimization or being perceived as combative, so such considerations are of less concern to them. In truth, they favor sneaky retaliation for the very reason that it allows them to enact justice secretly.

The suburban dealers' preferred forms of conflict management were negotiation, avoidance, and toleration.[151] Negotiation's major benefit is that it can result in compensation and restore harmony to the disputants' relationship; the drawback is that it requires compromise, whereas other potential responses can be implemented unilaterally. The foremost virtue of avoidance is that it reduces the odds of further problems by cutting off potential victimizers, but it comes at the cost of fewer trade partners and lost profits. And toleration is a good response in that it minimizes conflict and, in doing so, keeps the immediate problem from spiraling out of control, although it may attract victimization in the future. In Peachville, the benefit of these approaches—relative to retaliation—is that they are less likely to stigmatize the victim as being a so-called dick, and because they are not outlawed, they are less likely to result in legal or parental trouble.

In the urban streets, however, the situation is different. While retaliatory acts are illegal there too, being peaceful does not have as positive an effect on one's coolness in that social context. Urban dealers do in fact tolerate, avoid, and negotiate with people who cross them, but they explain these peaceful approaches as a way to make more money by not wasting time on retaliation; as a way not to lose trade partners by scaring them away; and as a way to avoid prison, serious personal injury, or death.[152] Put differently, they do not avoid violence to keep from hurting others.[153]

The Future?

For the suburban dealers, falling prey to serious victimization or getting into legal trouble often served to turn them away from drug selling, especially when it alerted their parents to their illicit activities. Experiencing such problems led many of them to reevaluate whether the benefits of free drugs, extra cash, and a more central and high-ranking place in their peer network were worth the costs of being targeted by predators and getting into legal and parental trouble.[154] They were faced with a choice: "Should I prioritize my short-term or long-term self?" Put differently, "Is it more important to be cool now or to be conventionally successful later?"[155]

The suburban dealers imagined their future selves as successful, by which they meant earning and living a middle-class lifestyle. Yet experiencing dealing-related problems or being close to those who did made them realize that the pursuit of coolness was just a transitory stage in their lives, and that the need for coolness would dissipate with the accumulation of conventional success. They reasoned that however rewarding it was to be cool, it was not worth risking their chances of achieving long-term success. And that realization put them on the path of desistance.[156]

Urban dealers fear victimization and legal trouble too. Experiencing either of these consequences personally or vicariously can motivate them to stop selling drugs.[157] For example, one urban dealer explained his desistance as flowing from the following: "Some people got pissed off. . . . A lot of people started steppin' up to me, like, 'You can't sell on my turf, you're not in this neighborhood.' And when I got the message, I stopped. It was like a gang thing. . . . I saw death. I knew I had to get out of that life."[158] And another urban seller explained his decision to get out of drug dealing this way: "[I]t seemed like things started happening, police was, I wasn't going to jail, but they was on me. And people all of a sudden want to stick me up and beat me up for the stuff. So I just stopped, you know. . . . It got violent. That's what happened."[159]

The difference between suburban and urban dealers, however, resides in their tolerance for such risks.[160] Urban dealers persist in the face of threats that would discourage even the toughest of their suburban counterparts. Urban dealers know full well that their activities put them at increased risk of being attacked, getting in trouble with the law, and never achieving conventional success.[161] They do not need to read social science research reports to know that they live in violent communities that are subjected to heavy law enforcement and that produce relatively few well-paid professionals. From an early age, they see neighbors, friends, and family members being sent to the hospital or morgue as a result of gunshot wounds; being sent to prison as a result of a criminal conviction; and not being able to land a job at all or at best getting a low-wage one.[162] In short, urban dealers see with their own eyes that the odds of victimization and legal trouble are high, but they also see that the chances of achieving conventional success are low, whether or not they sell drugs. In the process, they become realistically pessimistic about their futures[163] and focus on the present.[164]

The streets are so dangerous, in fact, that individuals who grow up in disadvantaged city neighborhoods often conclude that they have little chance of living into adulthood. Asked about his odds of living to age twenty-five, for example, one urban adolescent in Atlanta responded, "[F]lip a coin. I say an equal chance, a good chance, I could be dead."[165] Urban youth assess their chances of survival in light of the violence that permeates their day-to-day world; as one such person said, "I grew up with shootin' and fightin' all over. . . . Where I'm from you never know if you gonna live one minute to the next. It's like a war out there. People die every day. You can go to sleep and hear gunshots all night man, all night. Bullets be lying on the street in the morning."[166] Offenders and nonoffenders alike are at grave risk. "You hear . . . about the little 3 year old kid got shot? He ain't in the game . . . but he got shot anyhow."[167] Simply put, the residents of poor urban neighborhoods know that "their time" may come any day. As one remarked, "Every day there's a chance I will get robbed, stabbed, or killed. . . . You put your life on the line every day, every motherfuckin' day. I just take it a day at a time."[168]

Realistically speaking, then, why should people delay gratification and focus on obtaining conventional success if they do not believe that they will survive long enough to enjoy it? One urban adolescent put it this way: "Might be dead by 25 so who cares?"[169] Another bluntly stated, "[F]uck tomorrow. It's all about today. Might not be a tomorrow. Might get shot. . . . So get it now. Now, now, now. Next week might as well be next century. Fuck next week. Fuck tomorrow."[170] With a precarious expectation of living a long life, urban drug dealers understandably are inclined to focus on the here and now: the short-term self. High status and respect on the streets of urban America do not require a college education, a legitimate job, or a clean criminal record. All that is needed is the ability to demonstrate likability and attractiveness in subculturally prescribed ways. As we discussed above, one way of doing so in both the streets *and* the suburbs is to buy drugs and resell them for profit.

Urban and suburban dealers know that by selling drugs they are inviting problems into their lives. Neither group wants to be victimized or arrested by the police. Nor do they want to disappoint their parents or other adult caretakers. But the prospect of encountering these problems is far less of a deterrent to urban dealers because they are far less confident about living a long life and, relatedly, far less motivated to do what it takes to achieve conventional success owing to the structural barriers they face in trying to do so. Thus, experiencing legal trouble or victimization is less likely to serve as a positive turning point toward conventional success for urban dealers than it is for their suburban counterparts.

As noted earlier, urban dealers are more inclined than suburban ones to retaliate violently because they perceive a strong need to deter further victimizations and reinstate or amplify their combativeness-based status. Another factor is their prevailing focus on the present self.[171] The suburban dealers claimed that they did not violently retaliate because they feared legal trouble and its collateral consequences for conventional success. Urban dealers do not relish the prospect of these problems either, but their realistically gloomy perspective on the future means that they attach less deterrent weight to them. The flip side of this is that preserving their present status is all the more important, which makes violent retaliation a rational response.

It is clear that selling illegal drugs increases the dealer's victimization risk. One way to counter that risk is to retaliate violently, but doing so increases the odds of legal trouble. Once the suburban dealers came face-to-face with this, their response often was to give up dealing. Urban dealers, however, are more likely to conclude that they have no realistic choice but to continue selling because they lack competiveness in the labor market and yet—unlike their suburban counterparts—need the money to pay not only for luxury goods but also for basic needs. When victimized, then, urban dealers are more likely than suburban ones to assault, rob, or kill whoever crossed them.

By contrast, suburban drug sellers are more likely to respond to dealing-related problems simply by retiring from the game and reverting to their former status as lowly users. It is easy to see that people's various identities do not always mesh.[172] Someone can be "good" and "bad" in the same day, even the same second. The suburban dealers, for instance, would drive to school (a "good" thing) while smoking weed (a "bad" thing). But there comes a point in peoples' lives when they make fateful identity choices. Who is it more important to be? Do I care more about being cool or about being a successful adult? It is possible to be both at the same time; but strengthening one identity, such as by dealing, may jeopardize another, such as by taking on additional risks. Drug dealing was at odds with the pursuit of conventional success. The suburban dealers always knew this, but with the accumulation of sometimes bitter experience, the point was driven home.

NOTES

INTRODUCTION

1. Burgess 1925. For studies of the history of suburbia, see Beauregard 2006; Binford 1985; Bruegmann 2005; Fishman 1987; Fogelson 2005; Hayden 2003; Jackson 1985; Kotkin 2005; Stilgoe 1988; Warner 1978.
2. For information regarding the challenges of transportation in metropolitan Atlanta, see Dunham-Jones 2005.
3. For studies and commentary on the lack of physical diversity in suburban communities, see Brueggman 2005; Duany, Plater-Zyberk, and Speck 2010; Fogelson 2005; Hayden 2003; B. M. Kelly 1993; Kushner 2009; Langdon 1994; Schwarzer 2005; Venturi, Brown, and Izenour 1977.
4. All names are pseudonyms.

CHAPTER 1

1. For studies of suburbanites as privacy-oriented individuals, see Fogelson 2005; B. M. Kelly 1993; Low 2004. For studies of suburbanites as lacking intimacy with fellow community members, see Brueggman 2005; Duany, Plater-Zyberk, and Speck 2010; Fishman 1987; Krieger 2005; Kunstler 1993; Langdon 1994; Marshall 2000; Oliver 2001.
2. For academic treatments of "cool" and "coolness," see Anderson 1976; Connor 1995; Danesi 1994; Frank 1997; Hooks 2004; Majors and Billson 1992; Milner 2006; Pountain and Robbins 2000; Stearns 1994.
3. See also Danesi 1994; Milner 2006.
4. See also Danesi 1994; Milner 2006.
5. See also Danesi 1994; Harrison and Morgan 2005; Milner 2006.
6. See also Danesi 1994; E. Goffman 1963b; Milner 2006.
7. See Wooden and Blazak 2001.
8. See also Milner 2006.
9. Danesi 1994; Milner 2006.
10. See Anderson 1999; Milner 2006.
11. Throughout this book we consider how our participants sought to present themselves as cool to their peers; see E. Goffman 1959.
12. See also Foster and Spencer 2013.
13. Moffitt (1993) proposes a similar theory. Our interpretation of her theory is that

"adolescent-limited offenders" (ALOs) are motivated to commit crime because it confers a sense of mature status, power, and privilege. For us, however, ALOs are motivated by the accrual of coolness (which is a form of status in itself), which earns respect and social desirability (which may be seen as aspects of power and privilege) and thereby produces feelings of self-worth.

14. For studies of the connection between offending and peer status, see Danesi 1994; Faris and Felmlee 2011; Gould 2003; Kreager 2007; Kreager, Rulison, and Moody 2011; Maggs and Hurrelmann 1998; Milner 2006; Moffitt 1993. For the effect of peer influence on substance use, see, e.g., Gallupe and Bouchard 2013; Parker, Aldridge, and Measham 1998.

15. See H. Becker 1963; Perrone 2009.

16. See B. C. Kelly 2006.

17. See also Milner 2006.

18. See Veblen (1899) 1994.

19. For additional studies of the motives associated with dealing drugs, see Adler 1993; Anderson 1999; Atkyns and Hanneman 1974; Carey 1968; Curcione 1997; Jacinto et al. 2008; Jacobs 1999; Levitt and Venkatesh 2000; Lieb and Olson 1976; Mohamed and Fritsvold 2009; Uggen and Thompson 2003; VanNostrand and Tewksbury 1999; Waldorf, Reinarman, and Murphy 1991. For other criminal ways to afford a drug habit, see, e.g., Goldstein 1985; Bennett and Holloway 2007.

20. See also Milner 2006.

21. See also Besen-Cassino 2013, 2014.

22. See also Danesi 1994; Milner 2006.

23. See Veblen (1899) 1994.

24. For further examples of drug dealers providing their friends with free drugs, see Aldridge, Measham, and Williams 2011; Coomber 2003; Jacobs 1999; Mouledoux 1972; Weisheit 1991; Williams 1989.

25. For a history of privacy in the home, see Bryson 2010.

26. For studies of housing in suburbia, see Archer 2005; Duany, Plater-Zyberk, and Speck 2010; Hayden 2002; Jackson 1985; B. M. Kelly 1993; Schwarzer 2005; Teaford 2008; G. Wright 1981.

27. For theories of altruism, see Batson 1991; Dugatkin 2006; Mauss (1950) 2002; Sober and Wilson 1998.

28. For discussions of suburbia as an uninspiring place in which to reside, see Gans 1967; Krieger 2005.

29. See Harrison and Morgan 2005.

CHAPTER 2

1. See also Hammersvik, Sandberg, and Pedersen 2012.

2. For information on the different levels of the drug-dealing hierarchy, see Sevigny and Caulkins 2004.

3. See also Thompson and Uggen 2012.

4. Cf. Hirschi 1969.

5. See Granovetter 1973; Milner 2006.

6. Baumgartner 1988.

7. Milner 2006.

8. Milner 2006.

9. Milner 2006.

10. For discussions of the importance of subcultural language in shaping perceptions of coolness, see Danesi 1994; Milner 2006.
11. See E. Goffman 1959, 1963b.
12. See also Wright, Cullen, and Williams 1997. Cf. Laub and Sampson 2003.
13. For studies and commentary on the lack of social diversity and integration in suburban communities, see Archer 2005; Brueggman 2005; Duany, Plater-Zyberk, and Speck 2010; Fogelson 2005; Gainsborough 2001; Gans 1967; Kirp, Dwyer, and Rosenthal 1997; Krieger 2005; Kruse 2005; Lamb 2005; McKenzie 1994; Oliver 2001; Pietila 2010; Self 2003; Teaford 2006; Wiese 2004; G. Wright 1981. On the history of community regulations as a means of segregation, see Fogelson 2005; Freund 2007. On "white flight" as a means of segregation, see Kruse 2005; Kushner 2009; Teaford 2006; G. Wright 1981.
14. Drug traders typically conduct business with persons demographically similar to themselves; see Alexander 2010.
15. See also Bourgois 2003, 32.
16. See also Coomber 2003; Jacobs 1999.
17. See Merry 1981.
18. For studies and commentary on the importance of automobiles in suburbia, see Archer 2005; Brueggman 2005; Duany, Plater-Zyberk, and Speck 2010; Dunham-Jones and Williamson 2011; Fishman 1987; Flint 2006; Jackson 1985; Kunstler 1993; Langdon 1994; Riesman 1957; Teaford 2006.

CHAPTER 3

1. For the role of rationality in criminal behavior, see Cornish and Clarke 2014; Leclerc and Wortley 2013.
2. See also Atkyns and Hanneman 1974; Belackova and Vaccaro 2013; Caulkins and Pacula 2006; Curcione 1997.
3. See also Moffitt 1993.
4. See also Milner 2006.
5. See also Tewksbury and Mustaine 1998.
6. For studies of female drug market participants, see, e.g., Boeri 2013; Carbone-Lopez and Miller 2012; Denton 2001; Maher 1997; Miller 2001.
7. See also Alexander 2010.
8. See Toby 1957.
9. Cf. Hirschi 1969.
10. See also Anderson 1990, 83; Graeber 2001.
11. See Sykes and Matza 1957.
12. Sykes and Matza 1957.

CHAPTER 4

1. Although dealing could result in other costs—namely, suspension from school or being fired from work—none of the dealers in our sample suffered such consequences.
2. In the current chapter we consider how the dealers sought to present themselves as "law-abiding, good kids" to police and parents; see E. Goffman 1959, 1963b, 1969, 1974; Katz 1988.
3. Absolute deterrence is when a person refrains from ever committing a specific offense for fear of the punishment associated with it. Restrictive deterrence is when an

offender restricts the frequency, magnitude, or seriousness of his offenses in order to avoid punishment. See Gibbs 1975.

4. See also Mohamed and Fritsvold 2009.
5. Cf. Alexander 2010.
6. For examples of techniques used by drug dealers to prevent law enforcement, see Adler and Adler 1980; Buerger 1992; Cross 2000; Jacobs 1993, 1996; Jacobs and Miller 1998; Johnson and Natarajan 1995; Knowles 1999.
7. See Jacobs 1993, 1996.
8. See also H. Becker 1963.
9. See Gibbs 1975.
10. See also Gambetta 2009; Sutherland 1937.
11. See E. Goffman 1963b.
12. Cf. J. Wilson and Kelling 1982. See also Duneier 1999.
13. See E. Goffman 1963b.
14. See E. Goffman 1963a; Morrill and Snow 2005.
15. For the role of neighbors as guardians against crime, see Reynald 2010.
16. For the role of social support, including parental support, in criminological theory, see especially Cullen 1994.
17. See also Baumgartner 1988; Luthar and Goldstein 2008.
18. See also Baumgartner 1988.
19. See also H. Becker 1963.
20. Cf. Hirschi 1969.

CHAPTER 5

1. Compared with someone who does not buy drugs, a pure buyer (i.e., nonseller) does have an increased risk of being defrauded on a day-to-day basis. But such victimizations are relatively trivial because the amounts involved are small. Two other kinds of victimization that could be experienced by pure buyers are unseen theft and robbery. Nevertheless, it does not seem as though being a pure buyer in and of itself substantially increases the risk of experiencing either, although correlated behaviors—such as being around intoxicated persons—may indirectly increase that possibility.
2. For studies exploring the perception that suburbs are safer than the cities they surround and thus a good place to live, see Blakely and Snyder 1999; Fogelson 2005; Hayden 2003; Jackson 1985; Kotkin 2005; Low 2004; Teaford 2008.
3. For prior research on why illicit drug sellers are attractive targets for predators, see, e.g., Jacobs 1999, 2000; R. Wright and Decker 1994, 1997.
4. For examples of techniques used by drug dealers to prevent victimization, see Belackova and Vaccaro 2013; Cross 2000; Topalli, Wright, and Fornango 2002.
5. For a discussion of routine precautions, see M. Felson and Clarke 2010.
6. See Moffitt 1993.
7. For racial stereotyping of Blacks as criminal or dangerous, see Bourgois and Schonberg 2009, 30–31; Chiricos, McEntire, and Gertz 2001; Pickett et al. 2012; Quillian and Pager 2001, 2010. Blacks also appear to be more afraid of Blacks than of Whites; see R. Felson and Painter-Davis 2012; R. Wright and Decker 1994, 1997.
8. See also Anderson 2011; Anderson et al. 2012.
9. See E. Goffman 1963a, 1971.
10. See Black 1983.
11. See E. Goffman 1963b, 1974.

12. See Sykes and Matza 1957.
13. But see Hawkins et al. 2002.
14. Cf. Anderson 1999; Jacobs and Wright 2006.
15. For examples of victimization suffered by drug dealers, see Goldstein 1985; Jacobs 1999, 2000; Jacobs and Wright 2006; Mohamed and Fritsvold 2009; Topalli, Wright, and Fornango 2002; Waldorf and Murphy 1995; R. Wright and Decker 1994, 1997.

CHAPTER 6

1. For examples from other studies of how drug dealers respond to victimization, see Adler 1993; Brownstein et al. 1995; Goldstein 1985; Hoffer 2006; Jacobs 1999; Jacobs and Wright 2006; Levitt and Venkatesh 2000; Meeson and Morselli 2012; Mohamed and Fritsvold 2009; Scott Phillips 2003; Reuter 2010; Taylor 2007; Topalli, Wright, and Fornango 2002.
2. Baumgartner 1988.
3. For cross-cultural, sociologically focused perspectives on conflict management, see Black 1998; Cooney 1998, 2009; Gould 2003; Horwitz 1990.
4. Parsons 1951. For a discussion about studying nonoccurring events, see Lewis and Lewis 1980.
5. Baumgartner 1988.
6. See Geertz 1983.
7. See Katz 1988.
8. Cf. Anderson 1999; Jacobs and Wright 2006.
9. See also Baumgartner 1988.
10. See Vaisey 2009.
11. Baumgartner 1988; see also Felstiner 1974.
12. E. Goffman 1971, 348.
13. See Katz 1988.
14. E. Goffman 1967, 15.
15. Gulliver 1979.
16. See also Jacobs and Wright 2006.
17. See Cohen and Felson 1979; M. Felson 2006.
18. See Katz 1988.
19. See Collins 2008.
20. A fourth instance of violent retaliation was not a response to victimization but rather evolved out of a dispute over drug prices and market share. Such disputes among suburban drug dealers occur from time to time, but this is the only one in our study to be managed with force. As recounted by Josh, one of the dealers involved in the conflict: "This guy from [another high school nearby] that I met at a party with my friends, he was slinging and he was selling to people at the party and he's like, 'If you find somebody that's selling it for more, then let me know, and I'll sell it for less.' And so I got pissed off 'cause I was there at the same time and I was slinging it at the same time and I got pissed and I was a little drunk and I kind of got in his face a little bit and told him that if he keeps doing it, he's gonna get his ass beat. And then I had another conflict with him [at a later date] and like told him again, and I hit him twice, and he hit me once. But I told him that if he keeps doing it, [then] it will be even worse. He got the hint and quit doing it."
21. For the role of group dynamics in facilitating or inhabiting violence, see Cooney 1998; Gould 2003; Scott Phillips and Cooney 2005.
22. See Cooney 1998.

23. See Collins 2012.
24. See Collins 2008.

CHAPTER 7

1. For examples of negative events leading to desistance, see Bennett 1986, 93; Cusson and Pinsonneault 1986, 73–75; Decker and Lauritsen 2002; Haggård, Gumpert, and Grann 2001, 1055–56; Laub and Sampson 2003, 139; Sampson and Laub 1993, 223–24, 230–31; Sutherland 1937, 183–91; Waldorf, Murphy, and Lauderback 1994.
2. See Braithwaite 1989; Kornhauser 1978; Sampson and Laub 1993.
3. See Katz 1999.
4. For a discussion of the importance of legal representation, see Black 1989.
5. See Mohamed and Fritsvold 2009.
6. See also Massoglia and Uggen 2010.

CONCLUSION

1. For other examples of nonstereotypical drug sellers, see Adler 1993; Blum and Associates 1972; Carey 1968; Coomber 2006; Coomber and Maher 2006; Curcione 1997; Dunlap, Johnson, and Manwar 1994; Jacinto et al. 2008; Lieb and Olson 1976; Secret and Zraick 2010; Waldorf, Reinarman, and Murphy 1991.
2. See, e.g., Anderson 1999; Decker and Van Winkle 1996; Jacobs 1999; St. Jean 2007; Venkatesh 2006, 2008; Young 2004. For studies of Hispanic, urban drug dealers in the United States, see Bourgois 2003; Williams 1989. For thoughtful discussions of the prevalence and impact of stereotypes, see Anderson 2012; Berreby 2008; Duneier 1992.
3. Anderson 1999.
4. Anderson 1999; Harding 2010; W. Wilson 1987, 1996; Young 2004.
5. See, e.g., Jacobs, Topalli, and Wright 2003; Jacobs and Wright 2006; Jacques, Allen, and Wright 2014; Jacques and Wright 2013; Topalli and Wright 2003; R. Wright and Decker 1994, 1997.
6. See, e.g., Chapman 2010; Dunham-Jones and Williamson 2011; Frey 2001, 2011; Gans 1962; Hanlon 2010; Hanlon, Short, and Vicino 2010; Holiday and Dwyer 2009; Kneebone and Garr 2010; Kruse and Surgue 2006; Lacy 2007; McGirr 2012; Nicolaides 2002; Patillo 2007; Patillo-McCoy 1999; Rubinowitz and Rosenbaum 2000; Whyte 1993; Wiese 2005; W. Wilson and Taub 2007.
7. Anderson 1999; Sampson, Sharkey, and Raudenbush 2008; Sampson and Wilson 1995; Sharkey 2008.
8. See also Danesi 1994.
9. Anderson 1999.
10. Anderson 1999; Jacobs 1999.
11. See also Baumgartner 1988.
12. For studies on the use of community regulations to create an orderly appearance, see Blakely and Snyder 1999; Fogelson 2005; Low 2004; McKenzie 1994; Russell 2005.
13. Anderson 1999; see also St. Jean 2007. For the role of race in creating perceptions of neighborhood disorder, see Sampson 2009, 2012a, 2012b; Sampson and Raudenbush 2004.
14. Anderson 1999; Pager 2007a.
15. See also Majors and Billson 1992; Milner 2006.

16. Anderson 1999; Decker and Van Winkle 1996; Jacobs 1999.

17. Jacobs 1999, 29.

18. Anderson 1999; Decker and Van Winkle 1996; Jacobs 1999.

19. Anderson 1999, 271; see also Anderson 1990.

20. Anderson 1999.

21. For discussions of the role of coolness in the lives of Black men, see Hooks 2004; Majors and Billson 1992.

22. Anderson 1999; Jacobs 1999.

23. Anderson 1999; Jacobs 1999.

24. Anderson 1999; Jacobs 1999.

25. Jacobs 1999, 35.

26. Jacobs 1999, 35.

27. Cf. Mauss (1950) 2002.

28. Anderson 1999; Floyd and Brown 2013.

29. Jacobs 1999, 30.

30. Anderson 1999, 122.

31. Anderson 1999. For the role of older peers as mentors in disadvantaged urban areas, see Harding 2009.

32. See Mauss (1950) 2002.

33. See, e.g., Beaver and Barnes 2012.

34. Cf. Whyte 1993.

35. See also Danesi 1994; Milner 2006; Majors and Billson 1992; Moffitt 1993.

36. See also Messner and Rosenfeld 2012; Milner 2006.

37. See Milner 2006.

38. See also Baumgartner 1988; Gans 1967; Wyden 1962.

39. Toby 1957.

40. Cf. Moffitt 1993; Merton 1996, chap. 11.

41. Cf. Agnew 1992; Merton 1938.

42. Anderson 1999; Liebow 1967; W. Wilson 1996. But see Newman 1999.

43. W. Wilson 2009, 145.

44. W. Wilson 2009.

45. W. Wilson 1996, 2009.

46. Darity and Mason 1998; Pager and Shepherd 2008. For the role of racial segregation in the creation and persistence of poverty-stricken neighborhoods, see Massey and Denton 1993.

47. Pager 2007c; Pager, Western, and Bonikowski 2009.

48. Grodsky and Pager 2001; Pager, Western, and Bonikowski 2009.

49. Grodsky and Pager 2001.

50. Holzer 2009.

51. Farkas and Vicknair 1996; Heckman 1998; Neal and Johnson 1996.

52. Sastry and Pebley 2010.

53. Sampson 2008; Sampson, Sharkey, and Raudenbush 2008.

54. Peterson 2012; Peterson, Krivo, and Hagan 2012; Sampson 2012a.

55. Sharkey 2010.

56. Wodtke, Harding, and Elwert 2011.

57. Anderson 1999; Drummond, Bolland, and Harris 2011; Harding 2010; Liebow 1967.

58. Jacobs 1999, 28.

59. Jacobs 1999, 29.

60. Jacobs 1999, 33. But see Levitt and Dubner 2005; Levitt and Venkatesh 2000.
61. See Katz 1999.
62. See also Baumgartner 1988; Siennick 2011.
63. Anderson 1999; Liebow 1967; W. Wilson 1987.
64. Anderson 1999; Liebow 1967.
65. Anderson 1999.
66. Anderson 1999.
67. Anderson 1999, 133.
68. Anderson 1999, 133.
69. Jacobs 1999, 29.
70. Jacobs 1999, 29. See also Anderson 1990; Decker and Van Winkle 1996.
71. Anderson 1996; Du Bois (1899) 1996, (1903) 2003; A. Goffman 2009, 2014; Skolnick 2007.
72. Anderson 1999; Brunson 2007; Duneier 1999.
73. Paradoxically, however, urbanites also often perceive the police as not doing enough about other people's crimes; see Anderson 1996, 1999; Brunson 2007; Du Bois (1899) 1996, (1903) 2003; Venkatesh 2006.
74. Jacobs and Wright 2006, 26.
75. Jacobs and Wright 2006, 26.
76. Brunson 2007; Decker and Van Winkle 1996; Duneier 1999; Jacobs 1999; Stewart 2007. For examples from the perspective of police officers, see Moskos 2008.
77. Jacobs and Wright 2006, 26.
78. Jacobs and Wright 2006, 27.
79. For examples, see Natapoff 2009.
80. Decker and Van Winkle 1996, 108.
81. Jacobson 1999; Mazerolle, Soole, and Rombouts 2007.
82. Natapoff 2009.
83. Natapoff 2009; Phillips 2012; Rosenfeld, Jacobs, and Wright 2003.
84. Alexander 2010.
85. See, e.g., Jacobs 1999; Young 2004.
86. Cf. Jacobs 1999.
87. See also Jacobs 1999.
88. See also Mohamed and Fritsvold 2009.
89. Alexander 2010; Snyder and Sickmund 2006; Western 2006.
90. Alexander 2010; Beckett 2012; Beckett, Nyrop, and Pfingst 2006; DeFleur 1975; Golub, Johnson, and Dunlap 2007; Human Rights Watch 2009; Snyder and Sickmund 2006; Western 2006. For the differential risk of legal trouble for drug use, possession, or both between Whites and Blacks, see, e.g., Beckett et al. 2005; Golub, Johnson, and Dunlap 2007; Nguyen and Reuter 2012. But see Engel, Smith, and Cullen 2012.
91. Blumstein and Nakamura 2009; Holzer, Raphael, and Stoll 2004, 2007; Pager 2007a.
92. Holzer, Raphael, and Stoll 2004; Pager 2003; Stoll and Bushway 2008.
93. Blumstein and Nakamura 2009; Freeman 2008; Pager 2003; Stoll and Bushway 2008.
94. Pettit and Lyons 2009; Wakefield and Uggen 2010. But see Kling 2006; Loeffler 2013.
95. See Granovetter 1974; G. Becker 1993; Lin, Cook, and Burt 2001.
96. Pager 2007a; Western 2007; Western, Kling, and Weiman 2001.

97. Pager 2007a.
98. Pettit and Western 2004; Pettit and Lyons 2009; Wakefield and Uggen 2010; Western 2002.
99. Holzer, Raphael, and Stoll 2007. But see Pager 2007b.
100. See Western and Beckett 1999; Pettit 2012; Wakefield and Uggen 2010; Western 2002.
101. Lyons and Pettit 2011; Pager 2003, 2007a; Pager, Western, and Sugie 2009; Pettit 2012; Wakefield and Uggen 2010; Western 2006.
102. Pager 2003, 2007a.
103. See Fogelson 2005; Jackson 1985.
104. Ellen and O'Regan 2009; FBI 2011; Kneebone and Raphael 2011.
105. Kneebone and Raphael 2011; Peterson, Krivo, and Hagan 2012; Sampson 2012a.
106. Topalli, Wright, and Fornango 2002, 347.
107. Contreras 2013; Jacobs 1999, 2000; R. Wright and Decker 1994, 1997.
108. R. Wright and Decker 1997, 62.
109. R. Wright and Decker 1997, 63.
110. R. Wright and Decker 1997, 64.
111. Copes, Forsyth, and Brunson 2007; Copes et al. 2011; Curtis and Wendel 2007; Jacques and Wright 2013; Mohamed and Fritsvold 2009; Moskos 2008; Rosenfeld, Jacobs, and Wright 2003; Topalli 2005.
112. See Black 1976; Klinger 1997; Moskos 2008.
113. R. Wright and Decker 1997, 66.
114. Levitt and Venkatesh 2000, 758.
115. Reuter, MacCoun, and Murphy 1990, 97.
116. Blumstein and Wallman 2000.
117. See Anderson 1999.
118. But see Jacques and Wright 2013.
119. Retaliation is another reason why urban dealers have such high victimization rates. They are attacked for offending against others (such as by "shorting" a customer), not paying down their debt to a supplier, or infringing on a competitor's turf and market share. See, e.g., Levitt and Venkatesh 2000.
120. Topalli, Wright, and Fornango 2002, 340.
121. Jacobs and Wright 2006, 36.
122. Jacobs and Wright 2006, 34.
123. Topalli, Wright, and Fornango 2002, 342–43.
124. Topalli, Wright, and Jacobs 2002, 344.
125. Anderson 1999; see also Allen and Lo 2012; Baumer et al. 2003; Brezina et al. 2004; Jacobs and Wright 2006; Kubrin and Weitzer 2003; Simons and Burt 2011; Stewart and Simons 2010.
126. Topalli, Wright, and Fornango 2002, 342.
127. Topalli, Wright, and Fornango 2002, 342–43.
128. Anderson 1999; Jacobs and Wright 2006; Kirk and Papachristos 2011; Kubrin and Weitzer 2003; Wilkinson, Beaty, and Lurry 2009.
129. Jacobs and Wright 2006, 29.
130. Jacobs and Wright 2006, 30.
131. Jacobs and Wright 2006, 30.
132. Jacobs and Wright 2006, 30.
133. Anderson 1999; Jacobs and Wright 2006.
134. See Anderson 1999; Sandberg 2008; Sandberg and Pedersen 2009.

135. See Beaver et al. 2012; Bingenheimer, Brennan, and Earls 2005; Wolfgang and Ferracuti 1967.
136. See Anderson 1999; Harding 2010; Jacobs and Wright 2006.
137. See also Majors and Billson 1992.
138. See Anderson 1999; Jacobs and Wright 2006.
139. See also Moffitt 1993, 689.
140. See Anderson 1999; Jacobs and Wright 2006. But see Stewart, Schreck, and Simons 2006.
141. Anderson 1999.
142. Anderson 1999.
143. See Decker and Van Winkle 1996; R. Wright and Decker 1997.
144. Anderson 1999.
145. Topalli, Wright, and Fornango 2002, 342.
146. See also Moffitt 1993.
147. See also Jackson-Jacobs 2013.
148. Zimring and Hawkins (1997) suggest that the amount of violence associated with an illicit drug market is contingent on the aggressive, or peaceful, propensities of its participants. "Where potential drug sellers have the habits and skills of violent predators, the overlap between hard narcotics and violence can be expected to be substantial because problems of credibility and nonenforceability would seem to call for violent measures. On the other hand, where lethal violence is not part of the background and predilection of those who organize and engage in illegal drug transactions, the rate of violence generated by the drug trade will be smaller" (152). For a test of this theory, see Ousey and Lee 2002.
149. Jacobs and Wright 2006, 56.
150. Jacobs and Wright 2006.
151. See also Baumgartner 1988.
152. Jacobs 1999; Jacques and Wright 2011; Topalli, Wright, and Fornango 2002.
153. But see Topalli 2005.
154. See also Moffitt 1993.
155. Cf. Maruna 2001.
156. Laub and Sampson 2003; Toby 1957.
157. Anderson 1999; Decker and Van Winkle 1996; Harding 2010.
158. Anderson 1999, 267.
159. Young 2004, 108–9. See also Corsaro, Brunson, and McGarrell 2013.
160. See Jacobs 2010.
161. Jacobs 1999; Young 2004.
162. Anderson 1999.
163. For an in-depth look at the persistence of social disadvantage, see Sharkey 2013.
164. For a discussion of this mind-set among poor urban residents, see Anderson 1999; Hannerz 1969; Liebow 1967.
165. Brezina, Tekin, and Topalli 2009, 1115.
166. Brezina, Tekin, and Topalli 2009, 1113.
167. Brezina, Tekin, and Topalli 2009, 1114.
168. Brezina, Tekin, and Topalli 2009, 1115.
169. Brezina, Tekin, and Topalli 2009, 1115.
170. Brezina, Tekin, and Topalli 2009, 1116.
171. Anderson 1999; Brezina, Tekin, and Topalli 2009.
172. E. Goffman 1959, 1963b, 1974.

REFERENCES

Adler, Patricia. 1993. *Wheeling and Dealing: An Ethnography of an Upper-Level Drug Dealing and Smuggling Community.* 2nd ed. New York: Columbia University Press.

Adler, Patricia A., and Peter Adler. 1980. "The Irony of Secrecy in the Drug World." *Journal of Contemporary Ethnography* 8:447–65.

Agnew, Robert. 1992. "Foundation for a General Theory of Crime and Delinquency." *Criminology* 30:47–87.

Aldridge, Judith, Fiona Measham, and Lisa Williams. 2011. *Illegal Leisure Revisited: Changing Patterns of Alcohol and Drug Use in Adolescents and Young Adults.* New York: Routledge.

Alexander, Michelle. 2010. *The New Jim Crow: Mass Incarceration in the Age of Colorblindness.* New York: New Press.

Allen, Andrea, and Celia C. Lo. 2012. "Drugs, Guns, and Disadvantaged Youths: Co-occurring Behavior and the Code of the Street." *Crime and Delinquency* 58:932–53.

Anderson, Elijah. 1976. *A Place on the Corner.* Chicago: University of Chicago Press.

———. 1990. *Streetwise: Race, Class, and Change in an Urban Community.* Chicago: University of Chicago Press.

———. 1996. Introduction to *The Philadelphia Negro: A Social Study,* by W. E. B. Du Bois. Philadelphia: University of Pennsylvania Press.

———. 1999. *Code of the Street: Decency, Violence, and the Moral Life of the Inner City.* New York: W. W. Norton.

———. 2011. *The Cosmopolitan Canopy: Race and Civility in Everyday Life.* New York: W. W. Norton.

———. 2012. "The Iconic Ghetto." *Annals of the American Academy of Political and Social Science* 642:8–24.

Anderson, Elijah, Duke W. Austin, Craig Lapriece Holloway, and Vani S. Kulkarni. 2012. "The Legacy of Racial Caste: An Exploratory Ethnography." *Annals of the American Academy of Political and Social Science* 642:25–42.

Archer, John. 2005. *Architecture and Suburbia: From English Villa to American Dream House.* Minneapolis: University of Minnesota Press.

Atkyns, Robert L., and Gerhard J. Hanneman. 1974. "Illicit Drug Distribution and Dealer Communication Behavior." *Journal of Health and Social Behavior* 15:36–43.

Batson, C. Daniel. 1991. *The Altruism Question: Toward a Social-Psychological Answer.* Hillsdale, NJ: Lawrence Erlbaum.

Baumer, Eric, Julie Horney, Richard Felson, and Janet L. Lauritsen. 2003. "Neighborhood Disadvantage and the Nature of Violence." *Criminology* 41:39–72.

Baumgartner, M. P. 1988. *The Moral Order of a Suburb*. New York: Oxford University Press.

Beauregard, Robert A. 2006. *When America Became Suburban*. Minneapolis: University of Minnesota Press.

Beaver, Kevin M., and J. C. Barnes. 2012. "Admission of Drug-Selling Behaviors Is Structured by Genetic and Nonshared Environmental Factors: Results from a Longitudinal Twin-Based Study." *Addictive Behaviors* 37:697–702.

Beaver, Kevin M., Chris L. Gibson, Matt DeLisi, Machel G. Vaughn, and John Paul Wright. 2012. "The Interaction between Neighborhood Disadvantage and Genetic Factors in the Prediction of Antisocial Outcomes." *Youth Violence and Juvenile Delinquency* 10:25–40.

Becker, Gary S. 1993. *Human Capital: A Theoretical and Empirical Analysis with Special Reference to Education*. 3rd ed. Chicago: University of Chicago Press.

Becker, Howard S. 1963. *Outsiders: Studies in the Sociology of Deviance*. New York: Free Press.

Beckett, Katherine. 2012. "Race, Drugs, and Law Enforcement: Toward Equitable Policing." *Criminology and Public Policy* 11:641–53.

Beckett, Katherine, Kris Nyrop, and Lori Pfingst. 2006. "Race, Drugs, and Policing: Understanding Disparities in Drug Delivery Arrests." *Criminology* 44:105–37.

Beckett, Katherine, Kris Nyrop, Lori Pfingst, and Melissa Bowen. 2005. "Drug Use, Drug Possession Arrests, and the Question of Race: Lessons from Seattle." *Social Problems* 52:419–41.

Belackova, Vendula, and Christian Alexander Vaccaro. 2013. "'A Friend with Weed Is a Friend Indeed': Understanding the Relationship between Friendship Identity and Market Relations among Marijuana Users." *Journal of Drug Issues* 43:289–313.

Bennett, Trevor. 1986. "A Decision-Making Approach to Opioid Addiction." In *The Reasoning Criminal: Rational Choice Perspectives on Offending*, edited by Derek B. Cornish and Ronald V. Clarke. New York: Springer-Verlag.

Bennett, Trevor, and Katy Holloway. 2007. *Drug-Crime Connections*. New York: Cambridge University Press.

Berreby, David. 2008. *Us and Them: The Science of Identity*. Chicago: University of Chicago Press.

Besen-Cassino, Yasemine. 2013. "Cool Stores, Bad Jobs." *Contexts* 12:42–47.

———. 2014. *Consuming Work: Youth Labor in America*. Philadelphia: Temple University Press.

Binford, Henry C. 1985. *The First Suburbs: Residential Communities on the Boston Periphery, 1815–1860*. Chicago: University of Chicago Press.

Bingenheimer, Jeffrey B., Robert T. Brennan, and Felton J. Earls. 2005. "Firearm Violence Exposure and Serious Violent Behavior." *Science* 308:1323–26.

Black, Donald. 1976. *The Behavior of Law*. New York: Academic Press.

———. 1983. "Crime as Social Control." *American Sociological Review* 48:34–45.

———. 1989. *Sociological Justice*. New York: Oxford University Press.

———. 1998. *The Social Structure of Right and Wrong*. Rev. ed. San Diego: Academic Press.

———. 2011. *Moral Time*. New York: Oxford University Press.

Blakely, Edward J., and Mary Gail Snyder. 1999. *Fortress America: Gated Communities in the United States*. Washington, DC: Brookings Institution Press.

Blum, Richard H., and Associates. 1972. *The Dream Sellers: Perspectives on Drug Dealers*. San Francisco: Jossey-Bass.

Blumstein, Alfred, and Kiminori Nakamura. 2009. "Redemption in the Presence of Widespread Criminal Background Checks." *Criminology* 47:327–59.

Blumstein, Alfred, and Joel Wallman, eds. 2000. *The Crime Drop in America.* New York: Cambridge University Press.

Boeri, Miriam. 2013. *Women on Ice: Methamphetamine Use among Suburban Women.* New Brunswick, NJ: Rutgers University Press.

Bourgois, Philippe. 2003. *In Search of Respect.* 2nd ed. New York: Cambridge University Press.

Bourgois, Philippe, and Jeff Schonberg. 2009. *Righteous Dopefiend.* Berkeley: University of California Press.

Braithwaite, John. 1989. *Crime, Shame and Reintegration.* New York: Cambridge University Press.

Brezina, Timothy, Robert Agnew, Francis T. Cullen, and John Paul Wright. 2004. "The Code of the Street: A Quantitative Assessment of Elijah Anderson's Subculture of Violence Thesis and Its Contribution to Youth Violence Research." *Youth Violence and Juvenile Justice* 2:303–28.

Brezina, Timothy, Erdal Tekin, and Volkan Topalli. 2009. "'Might Not Be a Tomorrow': A Multimethods Approach to Anticipated Early Death and Youth Crime." *Criminology* 47:1091–1129.

Brownstein, Henry H., Barry J. Spunt, Susan M. Crimmins, and Sandra C. Langley. 1995. "Women Who Kill in Drug Market Situations." *Justice Quarterly* 12:473–98.

Bruegmann, Robert. 2005. *Sprawl: A Compact History.* Chicago: University of Chicago Press.

Brunson, Rod K. 2007. "'Police Don't Like Black People': African-American Young Men's Accumulated Police Experiences." *Criminology and Public Policy* 6:71–102.

Bryson, Bill. 2010. *At Home: A Short History of Private Life.* New York: Doubleday.

Buerger, Michael E. 1992. "Defensive Strategies of the Street-Level Drug Trade." *Journal of Crime and Justice* 15:32–51.

Burgess, Ernest W. 1925. "The Growth of the City: An Introduction to a Research Project." In *The City: Suggestions for Investigation of Human Behavior in the Urban Environment,* edited by Robert E. Park and Ernest W. Burgess. Chicago: University of Chicago Press.

Carbone-Lopez, Kristin, and Jody Miller. 2012. "Precocious Role Entry as a Mediating Factor in Women's Methamphetamine Use: Implications for Life-Course and Pathways Research." *Criminology* 50:187–220.

Carey, James T. 1968. *The College Drug Scene.* Englewood Cliffs, NJ: Prentice-Hall.

Caulkins, Jonathan P., and Rosalie Liccardo Pacula. 2006. "Marijuana Markets: Inferences from Reports by the Household Population." *Journal of Drug Issues* 36:173–200.

Chapman, Dan. 2010. "Poverty Moves Fast to Suburbs." *Atlanta Journal-Constitution.* Accessed March 26, 2013. http://www.ajc.com/news/news/local/poverty-moves-fast-to -suburbs/nQb8B/.

Chiricos, Ted, Ranee McEntire, and Marc Gertz. 2001. "Perceived Racial and Ethnic Composition of Neighborhood and Perceived Risk of Crime." *Social Problems* 48:322–40.

Cohen, Lawrence, and Marcus Felson. 1979. "Social Change and Crime Rate Trends: A Routine Activity Approach." *American Sociological Review* 44:588–608.

Collins, Randall. 2008. *Violence: A Micro-sociological Theory.* Princeton, NJ: Princeton University Press.

———. 2012. "C-Escalation and D-Escalation: A Theory of the Time-Dynamics of Conflict." *American Sociological Review* 77:1–20.

Connor, Marlene Kim. 1995. *What Is Cool: Understanding Black Manhood in America.* New York: Crown.

Contreras, Randol. 2013. *The Stickup Kids: Race, Drugs, Violence, and the American Dream.* Berkeley: University of California Press.

Coomber, Ross. 2003. "There's No Such Thing as a Free Lunch: How 'Freebies' and 'Credit' Operate as Part of Rational Drug Market Activity." *Journal of Drug Issues* 33:939–62.

———. 2006. *Pusher Myths: Re-situating the Drug Dealer.* London: Free Association Books.

Coomber, Ross, and Lisa Maher. 2006. "Street-Level Drug Market Activity in Sydney's Primary Heroin Markets: Organization, Adulteration Practices, Pricing, Marketing and Violence." *Journal of Drug Issues* 36:719–53.

Cooney, Mark. 1998. *Warriors and Peacemakers: How Third Parties Shape Violence.* New York: New York University Press.

———. 2009. *Is Killing Wrong? A Study in Pure Sociology.* Charlottesville: University of Virginia Press.

Copes, Heith, Rod K. Brunson, Craig J. Forsyth, and Heather White. 2011. "Leaving No Stone Unturned: Exploring Responses to and Consequences of Failed Crack-for-Car Transactions." *Journal of Drug Issues* 41:151–74.

Copes, Heith, Craig J. Forsyth, and Rod K. Brunson. 2007. "Rock Rentals: The Social Organization and Interpersonal Dynamics of Crack-for-Cars Transactions in Louisiana, USA." *British Journal of Criminology* 47:885–99.

Cornish, Derek B., and Ronald V. Clarke, eds. 2014. *The Reasoning Criminal: Rational Choice Perspectives on Offending.* New Brunswick, NJ: Transaction.

Corsaro, Nicholas, Rod K. Brunson, and Edmund F. McGarrell. 2013. "Problem-Oriented Policing and Open-Air Drug Markets: Examining the Rockford Pulling Levers Deterrence Strategy." *Crime and Delinquency* 59:1085–1107.

Cross, John C. 2000. "Passing the Buck: Risk Avoidance and Risk Management in the Illegal/Informal Drug Trade." *International Journal of Sociology and Social Policy* 20:68–94.

Cullen, Francis T. 1994. "Social Support as an Organizing Concept for Criminology: Presidential Address to the Academy of Criminal Justice Sciences." *Justice Quarterly* 11:527–59.

Curcione, N. 1997. "Suburban Snowmen: Facilitating Factors in the Careers of Middle-Class Coke Dealers." *Deviant Behavior* 18:233–53.

Curtis, Ric, and Travis Wendel. 2007. "'You're Always Training the Dog': Strategic Interventions to Reconfigure Drug Markets." *Journal of Drug Issues* 37:867–90.

Cusson, Maurice, and Pierre Pinsonneault. 1986. "The Decision to Give Up Crime." In *The Reasoning Criminal: Rational Choice Perspectives on Offending,* edited by Derek B. Cornish and Ronald V. Clarke. New York: Springer-Verlag.

Danesi, Marcel. 1994. *Cool: The Signs and Meanings of Adolescence.* Toronto: University of Toronto Press.

Darity, William A., and Patrick L. Mason. 1998. "Evidence of Discrimination in Employment: Codes of Color, Codes of Gender." *Journal of Economic Perspectives* 12:63–90.

Decker, Scott H., and Janet L. Lauritsen. 2002. "Leaving the Gang." In *Gangs in America III,* edited by C. Ronald Huff. Thousand Oaks, CA: Sage.

Decker, Scott H., and Barrik Van Winkle. 1996. *Life in the Gang: Family, Friends, and Violence.* New York: Cambridge University Press.

DeFleur, Lois B. 1975. "Biasing Influences on Drug Arrest Records: Implications for Deviance Research." *American Sociological Review* 40:88–103.

Denton, Barbara. 2001. *Dealing: Women in the Drug Economy.* Sydney: University of New South Wales Press.

Drummond, Holli, John M. Bolland, and Waverly Ann Harris. 2011. "Becoming Violent: Evaluating the Mediating Effect of Hopelessness on the Code of the Street Thesis." *Deviant Behavior* 32:191–223.

Duany, Andres, Elizabeth Plater-Zyberk, and Jeff Speck. 2010. *Suburban Nation: The Rise of Sprawl and the Decline of the American Dream.* 10th anniversary ed. New York: North Point Press.

Du Bois, W. E. B. (1899) 1996. *The Philadelphia Negro: A Social Study.* Philadelphia: University of Pennsylvania Press.

———. (1903) 2003. *The Souls of Black Folk.* New York: Modern Library.

Dugatkin, Lee Alan. 2006. *The Altruism Equation: Seven Scientists Search for the Origins of Goodness.* Princeton, NJ: Princeton University Press.

Duneier, Mitchell. 1992. *Slim's Table: Race, Respectability, and Masculinity.* Chicago: University of Chicago Press.

———. 1999. *Sidewalk.* New York: Farrar, Straus, and Giroux.

Dunham-Jones, Ellen. 2005. "Smart Growth in Atlanta: A Response to Krieger and Kiefer." In *Sprawl and Suburbia,* edited by William S. Saunders. Minneapolis: University of Minnesota Press.

Dunham-Jones, Ellen, and June Williamson. 2011. *Retrofitting Suburbia: Urban Design Solutions for Redesigning Suburbs.* Hoboken, NJ: John Wiley and Sons.

Dunlap, Eloise, Bruce D. Johnson, and Ali Manwar. 1994. "A Successful Female Crack Dealer: Case Study of a Deviant Career." *Deviant Behavior* 15:1–25.

Ellen, Ingrid Gould, and Katherine O'Regan. 2009. "Crime and U.S. Cities: Recent Patterns and Implications." *Annals of the American Academy of Political and Social Science* 626:22–38.

Engel, Robin S., Michael R. Smith, and Francis T. Cullen. 2012. "Race, Place, and Drug Enforcement: Reconsidering the Impact of Citizen Complaints and Crime Rates on Drug Arrests." *Criminology and Public Policy* 11:603–35.

Faris, Robert, and Diane Felmlee. 2011. "Status Struggles: Network Centrality and Gender Segregation in Same- and Cross-Gender Aggression." *American Sociological Review* 76:48–73.

Farkas, George, and Keven Vicknair. 1996. "Appropriate Tests of Racial Wage Discrimination Require Controls for Cognitive Skills: Comment on Cancio, Evans, and Maume." *American Sociological Review* 61:557–60.

Federal Bureau of Investigation (FBI). 2011. *Crime in the United States.* Washington, DC: US Department of Justice.

Felson, Marcus. 2006. *Crime and Nature.* Thousand Oaks, CA: Sage.

Felson, Marcus, and Ronald V. Clarke. 2010. "Routine Precautions, Criminology, and Crime Prevention." In *Criminology and Public Policy: Putting Theory to Work,* edited by Hugh Barlow and Scott H. Decker. Philadelphia: Temple University Press.

Felson, Richard B., and Noah Painter-Davis. 2012. "Another Cost of Being a Young Black Male: Race, Weaponry, and Lethal Outcomes in Assaults." *Social Science Research* 41:1241–53.

Felstiner, William L. F. 1974. "Influences of Social Organization on Dispute Processing." *Law and Society Review* 9:63–94.

Fishman, Robert. 1987. *Bourgeois Utopias: The Rise and Fall of Suburbia.* New York: Basic Books.

Flint, Anthony. 2006. *This Land: The Battle over Sprawl and the Future of America.* Baltimore: Johns Hopkins University Press.

Floyd, Leah J., and Qiana Brown. 2013. "Attitudes toward and Sexual Partnerships with

Drug Dealers among Young Adult African American Females in Socially Disorganized Communities." *Journal of Drug Issues* 43:154–63.

Fogelson, Robert M. 2005. *Bourgeois Nightmares: Suburbia, 1870–1930*. New Haven, CT: Yale University Press.

Foster, Karen, and Dale Spencer. 2013. "'It's Just a Social Thing': Drug Use, Friendship, and Borderwork among Marginalized Young People." *International Journal of Drug Policy*. doi: 10.1016/j.drugpo.2012.12.005.

Frank, Thomas. 1997. *The Conquest of Cool: Business Culture, Counterculture, and the Rise of Hip Consumerism*. Chicago: University of Chicago Press.

Freeman, Richard. 2008. "Incarceration, Criminal Background Checks, and Employment in a Low(er) Crime Society." *Criminology and Public Policy* 7:405–12.

Freund, David M. P. 2007. *Colored Property: State Policy and White Racial Politics in Suburban America*. Chicago: University of Chicago Press.

Frey, William H. 2001. *Melting Pot Suburbs: A Census 2000 Study of Suburban Diversity*. Washington, DC: Brookings Institution.

———. 2011. *Melting Pot Cities and Suburbs: Racial and Ethnic Changes in Metro America in the 2000s*. Washington, DC: Brookings Institution.

Gainsborough, Juliet F. 2001. *Fenced Off: The Suburbanization of American Politics*. Washington, DC: Georgetown University Press.

Gallupe, Owen, and Martin Bouchard. 2013. "Adolescent Parties and Substance Use: A Situational Approach to Peer Influence." *Journal of Criminal Justice* 41:162–71.

Gambetta, Diego. 2009. *Codes of the Underworld: How Criminals Communicate*. Princeton, NJ: Princeton University Press.

Gans, Herbert J. 1962. *The Urban Villagers: Group and Class in the Life of Italian-Americans*. New York: Free Press.

———. 1967. *The Levittowners: Ways of Life and Politics in a New Suburban Community*. New York: Vintage Books.

Geertz, Clifford. 1983. *Local Knowledge: Further Essays in Interpretative Anthropology*. New York: Basic Books.

Gibbs, Jack P. 1975. *Crime, Punishment, and Deterrence*. New York: Elsevier.

Goffman, Alice. 2009. "On the Run: Wanted Men in a Philadelphia Ghetto." *American Sociological Review* 74:339–57.

———. 2014. *On the Run: Fugitive Life in an American City*. Chicago: University of Chicago Press.

Goffman, Erving. 1959. *The Presentation of Self in Everyday Life*. New York: Anchor Books.

———. 1963a. *Behavior in Public Places: Notes on the Social Organization of Gatherings*. New York: Free Press.

———. 1963b. *Stigma: Notes on the Management of Spoiled Identity*. New York: Simon and Schuster.

———. 1967. *Interaction Ritual: Essays on Face-to-Face Behavior*. New York: Pantheon Books.

———. 1969. *Strategic Interaction*. Philadelphia: University of Pennsylvania Press.

———. 1971. *Relations in Public: Microstudies of the Public Order*. New Brunswick, NJ: Transaction.

———. 1974. *Frame Analysis: An Essay on the Organization of Experience*. Boston: Northeastern University Press.

Goldstein, Paul J. 1985. "The Drugs/Violence Nexus: A Tripartite Conceptual Framework." *Journal of Drug Issues* 15:493–506.

Golub, Andrew, Bruce D. Johnson, and Eloise Dunlap. 2007. "The Race/Ethnicity Disparity in Misdemeanor Marijuana Arrests in New York City." *Criminology and Public Policy* 6:131–64.

Gould, Roger V. 2003. *Collision of Wills: How Ambiguity about Social Rank Breeds Conflict.* Chicago: University of Chicago Press.

Graeber, David. 2001. *Toward an Anthropological Theory of Value.* New York: Palgrave.

Granovetter, Mark S. 1973. "The Strength of Weak Ties." *American Journal of Sociology* 78:1360–80.

———. 1974. *Getting a Job: A Study of Careers and Contacts.* Cambridge, MA: Harvard University Press.

Grodsky, Eric, and Devah Pager. 2001. "The Structure of Disadvantage: Individual and Occupational Determinants of the Black-White Wage Gap." *American Sociological Review* 66:542–67.

Gulliver, P. H. 1979. *Disputes and Negotiations: A Cross-Cultural Perspective.* New York: Academic Press.

Haggård, Ulrika, Clara H. Gumpert, and Martin Grann. 2001. "Against All Odds: A Qualitative Follow-Up of High-Risk Violent Offenders Who Were Not Reconvicted." *Journal of Interpersonal Violence* 16:1048–65.

Hammersvik, Eirik, Sveinung Sandberg, and Willy Pedersen. 2012. "Why Small-Scale Cannabis Growers Stay Small: Five Mechanisms That Prevent Small-Scale Growers from Going Large Scale." *International Journal of Drug Policy* 23:458–64.

Hanlon, Bernadette. 2010. *Once the American Dream: Inner-Ring Suburbs of the Metropolitan United States.* Philadelphia: Temple University Press.

Hanlon, Bernadette, John Rennie Short, and Thomas J. Vicino. 2010. *Cities and Suburbs: New Metropolitan Realities in the US.* New York: Routledge.

Hannerz, Ulf. 1969. *Soulside: Inquiries into Ghetto Culture and Community.* Chicago: University of Chicago Press.

Harding, David J. 2009. "Violence, Older Peers, and the Socialization of Adolescent Boys in Disadvantaged Neighborhoods." *American Sociological Review* 74:445–64.

———. 2010. *Living the Drama: Community, Conflict, and Culture among Inner-City Boys.* Chicago: University of Chicago Press.

Harrison, Tyler R., and Susan E. Morgan. 2005. "Hanging Out among Teenagers: Resistance, Gender, and Personal Relationships." In *Together Alone: Personal Relationships in Public Places,* edited by Calvin Morrill, Cindy H. White, and David A. Snow. Berkeley: University of California Press.

Hawkins, Stephanie R., Amy Campanaro, Traci Bice Pitts, and Hans Steiner. 2002. "Weapons in an Affluent Suburban School." *Journal of School Violence* 1:53–65.

Hayden, Dolores. 2002. *Redesigning the American Dream.* Rev., exp. ed. New York: W. W. Norton.

———. 2003. *Building Suburbia: Green Fields and Urban Growth, 1820–2000.* New York: Vintage Books.

Heckman, James J. 1998. "Detecting Discrimination." *Journal of Economic Perspectives* 12:101–16.

Hirschi, Travis. 1969. *Causes of Delinquency.* Berkeley: University of California Press.

Hoffer, Lee D. 2006. *Junkie Business: The Evolution and Operation of a Heroin Dealing Network.* Belmont, CA: Wadsworth.

Holiday, Amy L., and Rachel E. Dwyer. 2009. "Suburban Neighborhood Poverty in U.S. Metropolitan Areas in 2000." *City and Community* 8:155–76.

Holzer, Harry J. 2009. "The Labor Market and Young Black Men: Updating Moynihan's Perspective." *Annals of the American Academy of Political and Social Science* 621:47–69.

Holzer, Harry J., Steven Raphael, and Michael J. Stoll. 2004. "Will Employers Hire Former Offenders? Employer Preferences, Background Checks, and Their Determinants." In *Imprisoning America: The Social Effects of Mass Incarceration*, edited by Mary Patillo, David Weiman, and Bruce Western. New York: Russell Sage Foundation.

———. 2007. "The Effect of an Applicant's Criminal History on Employer Hiring Decisions and Screening Practices: Evidence from Los Angeles." In *Barriers to Reentry? The Labor Market for Released Prisoners in Post-industrial America*, edited by Shawn Bushway, Michael A. Stoll, and David F. Weiman. New York: Russell Sage Foundation.

hooks, bell. 2004. *We Real Cool: Black Men and Masculinity*. New York: Routledge.

Horwitz, Allan V. 1990. *The Logic of Social Control*. New York: Plenum Press.

Human Rights Watch. 2009. *Decades of Disparity: Drug Arrests and Race in the United States*. New York: Human Rights Watch.

Jacinto, Camille, Micheline Duterte, Paloma Sales, and Sheigla Murphy. 2008. "'I'm Not a Real Dealer': The Identity Process of Ecstasy Sellers." *Journal of Drug Issues* 38:419–44.

Jackson, Kenneth T. 1985. *Crabgrass Frontiers: The Suburbanization of the United States*. New York: Oxford University Press.

Jackson-Jacobs, Curtis. 2013. "Constructing Physical Fights: An Interactionist Analysis of Violence among Affluent, Suburban Youth." *Qualitative Sociology* 36:23–52.

Jacobs, Bruce A. 1993. "Undercover Deception Clues: A Case of Restrictive Deterrence." *Criminology* 31:281–99.

———. 1996. "Crack Dealers and Restrictive Deterrence: Identifying Narcs." *Criminology* 34:409–31.

———. 1999. *Dealing Crack: The Social World of Streetcorner Selling*. Boston: Northeastern University Press.

———. 2000. *Robbing Drug Dealers: Violence beyond the Law*. New York: Aldine de Gruyter.

———. 2010. "Deterrence and Deterrability." *Criminology* 48:417–41.

Jacobs, Bruce A., and Jody Miller. 1998. "Crack Dealing, Gender, and Arrest Avoidance." *Social Problems* 45:550–69.

Jacobs, Bruce A., Volkan Topalli, and Richard Wright. 2003. "Carjacking, Streetlife, Offender Motivation." *British Journal of Criminology* 43:19–34.

Jacobs, Bruce A., and Richard Wright. 2006. *Street Justice: Retaliation in the Criminal Underworld*. New York: Cambridge University Press.

Jacobson, Jessica. 1999. *Policing Drug Hot-Spots*. London: Home Office.

Jacques, Scott, Andrea Allen, and Richard Wright. 2014. "Drug Dealers' Rational Choices on Which Customers to Rip-Off." *International Journal of Drug Policy* 25:251–56.

Jacques, Scott, and Richard Wright. 2011. "Informal Control and Illicit Drug Trade." *Criminology* 49:726–65.

———. 2013. "How Victimized Drug Traders Mobilize Police." *Journal of Contemporary Ethnography* 42:545–75.

Johnson, Bruce D., and Mangai Natarajan. 1995. "Strategies to Avoid Arrest: Crack Sellers' Responses to Intensified Policing." *American Journal of Police* 14:49–69.

Katz, Jack. 1988. *Seductions of Crime: Moral and Sensual Attractions in Doing Evil*. New York: Basic Books.

———. 1999. *How Emotions Work*. Chicago: University of Chicago Press.

Kelly, Barbara M. 1993. *Expanding the American Dream: Building and Rebuilding Levittown*. Albany: State University of New York Press.

Kelly, Brian C. 2006. "Bongs and Blunts." *Journal of Ethnicity in Substance Abuse* 4: 81–97.

Kirk, David S., and Andrew V. Papachristos. 2011. "Cultural Mechanisms and the Persistence of Neighborhood Violence." *American Journal of Sociology* 116:1190–1233.

Kirp, David L., John P. Dwyer, and Larry A. Rosenthal. 1997. *Our Town: Race, Housing, and the Soul of Suburbia.* New Brunswick, NJ: Rutgers University Press.

Kling, Jeffrey R. 2006. "Incarceration Length, Employment, and Earnings." *American Economic Review* 96:863–76.

Klinger, David A. 1997. "Negotiating Order in Patrol Work: An Ecological Theory of Police Response to Deviance." *Criminology* 35:277–306.

Kneebone, Elizabeth, and Emily Garr. 2010. *The Suburbanization of Poverty: Trends in Metropolitan America, 2000 to 2008.* Washington, DC: Brookings Institute.

Kneebone, Elizabeth, and Steven Raphael. 2011. *City and Suburban Crime Trends in Metropolitan America.* Washington, DC: Brookings Institute.

Knowles, Gordon J. 1999. "Deception, Detection, and Evasion: A Trade Craft Analysis of Honolulu, Hawaii's Street Crack-Cocaine Traffickers." *Journal of Criminal Justice* 27:443–55.

Kornhauser, Ruth Rosner. 1978. *Social Sources of Delinquency.* Chicago: University of Chicago Press.

Kotkin, Joel. 2005. *The City: A Global History.* New York: Modern Library.

Kreager, Derek A. 2007. "When It's Good to Be 'Bad': Violence and Adolescent Peer Acceptance." *Criminology* 45:893–923.

Kreager, Derek A., Kelly Rulison, and James Moody. 2011. "Delinquency and the Structure of Adolescent Peer Groups." *Criminology* 49:95–127.

Krieger, Alex. 2005. "The Costs—and Benefits?—of Sprawl." In *Sprawl and Suburbia,* edited by William S. Saunders. Minneapolis: University of Minnesota Press.

Kruse, Kevin M. 2005. *White Flight: Atlanta and the Making of Modern Conservatism.* Princeton, NJ: Princeton University Press.

Kruse, Kevin M., and Thomas J. Surgue, eds. 2006. *The New Suburban History.* Chicago: University of Chicago Press.

Kubrin, Charis E., and Ronald Weitzer. 2003. "Retaliatory Homicide: Concentrated Disadvantage and Neighborhood Culture." *Social Problems* 50:157–80.

Kunstler, James Howard. 1993. *The Geography of Nowhere: The Rise and Decline of America's Man Made Landscape.* New York: Touchstone.

Kushner, David. 2009. *Levittown: Two Families, One Tycoon, and the Fight for Civil Rights in America's Legendary Suburb.* New York: Walker.

Lacy, Karyn R. 2007. *Blue-Chip Black: Race, Class, and Status in the New Black Middle Class.* Berkeley: University of California Press.

Lamb, Charles M. 2005. *Housing Segregation in Suburban America since 1960.* New York: Cambridge University Press.

Langdon, Phillip. 1994. *A Better Place to Live: Reshaping the American Suburb.* Amherst: University of Massachusetts Press.

Laub, John H., and Robert J. Sampson. 2003. *Shared Beginnings, Divergent Lives: Delinquent Boys to Age 70.* Cambridge, MA: Harvard University Press.

Leclerc, Benoit, and Richard Wortley, eds. 2013. *Cognition and Crime: Offender Decision-Making and Script Analyses.* New York: Routledge.

Levitt, Steven D., and Stephen J. Dubner. 2005. *Freakonomics: A Rogue Economist Explores the Hidden Side of Everything.* New York: Penguin Books.

Levitt, Steven D., and Sudhir A. Venkatesh. 2000. "An Economic Analysis of a Drug-Selling Gang's Finances." *Quarterly Journal of Economics* 115:755–89.

Lewis, George H., and Jonathan F. Lewis. 1980. "The Dog in the Night-time: Negative Evidence in Social Research." *British Journal of Sociology* 31:544–58.

Lieb, John, and Sheldon Olson. 1976. "Prestige, Paranoia, and Profit: On Becoming a Dealer of Illicit Drugs in a University Community." *Journal of Drug Issues* 6:356–67.

Liebow, Elliot. 1967. *Tally's Corner: A Study of Negro Streetcorner Men.* New York: Little, Brown.

Lin, Nan, Karen Cook, and Ronald S. Burt, eds. 2001. *Social Capital: Theory and Research.* New Brunswick, NJ: Aldine Transaction.

Loeffler, Charles E. 2013. "Does Imprisonment Alter the Life Course? Evidence on Crime and Employment from a Natural Experiment." *Criminology* 51:137–66.

Low, Setha. 2004. *Behind the Gates: Life, Security, and the Pursuit of Happiness in Fortress America.* New York: Routledge.

Luthar, Suniya S., and Adam S. Goldstein. 2008. "Substance Use and Related Behaviors among Suburban Late Adolescents: The Importance of Perceived Parent Containment." *Development and Psychopathology* 20:591–614.

Lyons, Christopher J., and Becky Pettit. 2011. "Compounded Disadvantage: Race, Incarceration, and Wage Growth." *Social Problems* 58:257–80.

Maggs, Jennifer L., and Klaus Hurrelmann. 1998. "Do Substance Use and Delinquency have Differential Associations with Adolescents' Peer Relations?" *International Journal of Behavioral Development* 22:367–88.

Maher, Lisa. 1997. *Sexed Work: Gender, Race and Resistance in a Brooklyn Drug Market.* New York: Oxford University Press.

Majors, Richard, and Janet Mancini Billson. 1992. *Cool Pose: The Dilemmas of Black Manhood in America.* New York: Touchstone.

Marshall, Alex. 2000. *How Cities Work: Suburbs, Sprawl, and the Roads Not Taken.* Austin: University of Texas Press.

Maruna, Shadd. 2001. *Making Good: How Ex-Convicts Reform and Rebuild Their Lives.* Washington, DC: American Psychological Association.

Massey, Douglas S., and Nancy A. Denton. 1993. *American Apartheid: Segregation and the Making of the Underclass.* Cambridge, MA: Harvard University Press.

Massoglia, Michael, and Christopher Uggen. 2010. "Settling Down and Aging Out: Toward an Interactionist Theory of Desistance and the Transition to Adulthood." *American Journal of Sociology* 116:543–82.

Mauss, Marcel. (1950) 2002. *The Gift: The Form and Reason for Exchange in Archaic Societies.* New York: Routledge Classics.

Mazerolle, Lorraine, David Soole, and Sacha Rombouts. 2007. "Drug Law Enforcement: A Review of the Evaluation Literature." *Police Quarterly* 10:115–53.

McGirr, Lisa. 2012. "The New Suburban Poverty." *New York Times.* Accessed March 26, 2013. http://campaignstops.blogs.nytimes.com/2012/03/19/the-new-suburban-poverty.

McKenzie, Evan. 1994. *Privatopia: Homeowner Associations and the Rise of Residential Private Governments.* New Haven, CT: Yale University Press.

Meeson, Julie-Soleil, and Carlo Morselli. 2012. "La violence et la résolution de conflits chez des trafiquants de cocaïne." *Criminologie* 45:213–41.

Merry, Sally Engel. 1981. *Urban Danger: Life in a Neighborhood of Strangers.* Philadelphia: Temple University Press.

Merton, Robert K. 1938. "Social Structure and Anomie." *American Sociological Review* 3:672–82.

———. 1996. *On Social Structure and Science.* Chicago: University of Chicago Press.

Messner, Steven F., and Richard Rosenfeld. 2012. *Crime and the American Dream*. 5th ed. Belmont, CA: Wadsworth.

Miller, Jody. 2001. *One of the Guys: Girls, Gangs, and Gender*. New York: Oxford University Press.

Milner, Murray, Jr. 2006. *Freaks, Geeks, and Cool Kids: American Teenagers, Schools, and the Culture of Consumption*. New York: Routledge.

Moffitt, Terrie E. 1993. "Adolescence-Limited and Life-Course-Persistent Antisocial Behavior: A Developmental Taxonomy." *Psychological Review* 100:674–701.

Mohamed, A. Rafik, and Erik D. Fritsvold. 2009. *Dorm Room Dealers: Drugs and the Privileges of Race and Class*. Boulder, CO: Lynne Rienner.

Morrill, Calvin, and David A. Snow. 2005. "The Study of Personal Relationships in Public Places." In *Together Alone: Personal Relationships in Public Places*, edited by Calvin Morrill, Cindy H. White, and David A. Snow. Berkeley: University of California Press.

Moskos, Peter. 2008. *Cop in the Hood: My Year Policing Baltimore's Eastern District*. Princeton, NJ: Princeton University Press.

Mouledoux, Joseph. 1972. "Ideological Aspects of Drug Dealership." In *Society's Shadows: Studies in the Sociology of Countercultures*, edited by K. Wethues. New York: McGraw-Hill.

Natapoff, Alexandra. 2009. *Snitching: Criminal Informants and the Erosion of American Justice*. New York: New York University Press.

Neal, Derek A., and William R. Johnson. 1996. "The Role of Premarket Factors in Black-White Wage Differences." *Journal of Political Economy* 104:869–95.

Newman, Katherine S. 1999. *No Shame in My Game: The Working Poor in the Inner City*. New York: Vintage Books.

Nguyen, Holly, and Peter Reuter. 2012. "How Risky Is Marijuana Possession? Considering the Role of Age, Race, and Gender." *Crime and Delinquency* 58:879–910.

Nicolaides, Becky M. 2002. *My Blue Heaven: Life and Politics in the Working-Class Suburbs of Los Angeles, 1920–1965*. Chicago: University of Chicago Press.

Oliver, J. Eric 2001. *Democracy in Suburbia*. Princeton, NJ: Princeton University Press.

Ousey, Graham C., and Matthew R. Lee. 2002. "Examining the Conditional Nature of the Illicit Drug Market–Homicide Relationship: A Partial Test of the Theory of Contingent Causation." *Criminology* 40:73–102.

Pager, Devah. 2003. "The Mark of a Criminal Record." *American Journal of Sociology* 108:937–75.

———. 2007a. *Marked: Race, Crime, and Finding Work in an Era of Mass Incarceration*. Chicago: University of Chicago Press.

———. 2007b. "Two Strikes and You're Out: The Intensification of Racial and Criminal Stigma." In *Barriers to Reentry? The Labor Market for Released Prisoners in Post-industrial America*, edited by Shawn Bushway, Michael A. Stoll, and David F. Weiman. New York: Russell Sage Foundation.

———. 2007c. "The Use of Field Experiments for Studies of Employment Discrimination: Contributions, Critiques, and Directions for the Future." *Annals of the American Academy of Political and Social Sciences* 609:104–33.

Pager, Devah, and Hana Shepherd. 2008. "The Sociology of Discrimination: Racial Discrimination in Employment, Housing, Credit, and Consumer Markets." *Annual Review of Sociology* 34:181–209.

Pager, Devah, Bruce Western, and Bart Bonikowski. 2009. "Discrimination in a Low-Wage Labor Market: A Field Experiment." *American Sociological Review* 74:777–99.

Pager, Devah, Bruce Western, and Naomi Sugie. 2009. "Sequencing Disadvantage: Barriers to Employment Facing Young Black and White Men with Criminal Records." *Annals of the American Academy of Political and Social Sciences* 623:195–213.

Parker, Howard, Judith Aldridge, and Fiona Measham. 1998. *Illegal Leisure: The Normalization of Adolescent Recreational Drug Use.* New York: Routledge.

Parsons, Talcott. 1951. *The Social System.* New York: Free Press.

Patillo, Mary. 2007. *Black on the Block: The Politics of Race and Class in the City.* Chicago: University of Chicago Press.

Patillo-McCoy, Mary. 1999. *Black Picket Fences: Privilege and Peril among the Black Middle Class.* Chicago: University of Chicago Press.

Perrone, Dina. 2009. *The High Life: Club Kids, Harm and Drug Policy.* Monsey, NY: Criminal Justice Press.

Peterson, Ruth D. 2012. "The Central Place of Race in Crime and Justice—the American Society of Criminology's 2011 Sutherland Address." *Criminology* 50:303–28.

Peterson, Ruth D., Lauren J. Krivo, and John Hagan. 2012. *Divergent Social Worlds: Neighborhood Crime and the Racial-Spatial Divide.* New York: Russell Sage Foundation.

Pettit, Becky. 2012. *Invisible Men: Mass Incarceration and the Myth of Black Progress.* New York: Russell Sage Foundation.

———. 2009. "Incarceration and the Legitimate Labor Market: Examining Age-Graded Effects on Employment and Wages." *Law and Society Review* 43:725–56.

Pettit, Becky, and Bruce Western. 2004. "Mass Imprisonment and the Life Course: Race and Class Inequality in U.S. Incarceration." *American Sociological Review* 69:151–69.

Phillips, Scott. 2003. "The Social Structure of Vengeance: A Test of Black's Model." *Criminology* 41:673–708.

Phillips, Scott, and Mark Cooney. 2005. "Aiding Peace, Abetting Violence: Third Parties and the Management of Conflict." *American Sociological Review* 70:334–54.

Phillips, Susan A. 2012. *Operation Fly Trap: L.A. Gangs, Drugs, and the Law.* Chicago: University of Chicago Press.

Pickett, Justin T., Ted Chiricos, Kristin M. Golden, and Marc Gertz. 2012. "Reconsidering the Relationship between Perceived Neighborhood Racial Composition and Whites' Perceptions of Victimization Risk: Do Racial Stereotypes Matter?" *Criminology* 50:145–86.

Pietila, Antero. 2010. *Not in My Neighborhood: How Bigotry Shaped a Great American City.* Chicago: Ivan R. Dee.

Pountain, Dick, and David Robbins. 2000. *Cool Rules: Anatomy of an Attitude.* London: Reaktion Books.

Quillian, Lincoln, and Devah Pager. 2001. "Black Neighbors, Higher Crime? The Role of Racial Stereotypes in Evaluations of Neighborhood Crime." *American Journal of Sociology* 107:717–67.

———. 2010. "Estimating Risk: Stereotype Amplification and the Perceived Risk of Criminal Victimization." *Social Psychological Quarterly* 73:79–104.

Reuter, Peter. 2010. "Systemic Violence in Drug Markets." *Crime, Law and Social Change* 52:275–89.

Reuter, Peter, Robert MacCoun, and Patrick Murphy. 1990. *Money from Crime: A Study of the Economics of Drug Dealing in Washington, D.C.* Santa Monica, CA: Rand Corp.

Reynald, Danielle M. 2010. "Guardians on Guardianship: Factors Affecting the Willingness to Supervise, the Ability to Detect Potential Offenders, and the Willingness to Intervene." *Journal of Research in Crime and Delinquency* 47:358–90.

Riesman, David. 1957. "The Suburban Dislocation." *Annals of the American Academy of Political and Social Science* 314:123–46.

Rosenfeld, Richard, Bruce Jacobs, and Richard Wright. 2003. "Snitching and the Code of the Street." *British Journal of Criminology* 43:291–309.

Rubinowitz, Leonard S., and James E. Rosenbaum. 2000. *Crossing the Color Lines: From Public Housing to White Suburbia.* Chicago: University of Chicago Press.

Russell, James S. 2005. "Privatized Lives: On the Embattled 'Burbs." In *Sprawl and Suburbia,* edited by William S. Saunders. Minneapolis: University of Minnesota Press.

Sampson, Robert J. 2008. "Moving to Inequality: Neighborhood Effects and Experiments Meet Social Structure." *American Journal of Sociology* 114:189–231.

———. 2009. "Disparity and Diversity in the Contemporary City: Social (Dis)Order Revisited." *British Journal of Sociology* 60:1–31.

———. 2012a. *Great American City: Chicago and the Enduring Neighborhood Effect.* Chicago: University of Chicago Press.

———. 2012b. "When Things Aren't What They Seem: Context and Cognition in Appearance-Based Regulation." *Harvard Law Review Forum* 125:97–107.

Sampson, Robert J., and John H. Laub. 1993. *Crime in the Making: Pathways and Turning Points through Life.* Cambridge, MA: Harvard University Press.

Sampson, Robert J., and Stephen W. Raudenbush. 2004. "Seeing Disorder: Neighborhood Stigma and the Social Construction of Broken Windows." *Social Psychology Quarterly* 67:319–42.

Sampson, Robert J., Patrick Sharkey, and Stephen W. Raudenbush. 2008. "Durable Effects of Concentrated Disadvantage on Verbal Ability among African-American Children." *Proceedings of the National Academy of Sciences* 105:845–52.

Sampson, Robert J., and William Julius Wilson. 1995. "Toward a Theory of Race, Crime, and Urban Inequality." In *Crime and Inequality,* edited by John Hagan and Ruth D. Peterson. Stanford, CA: Stanford University Press.

Sandberg, Sveinung. 2008. "Street Capital: Ethnicity and Violence on the Streets of Oslo." *Theoretical Criminology* 12:153–71.

Sandberg, Sveinung, and Willy Pedersen. 2009. *Street Capital: Black Cannabis Dealers in a White Welfare State.* Portland, OR: Policy Press.

Sastry, Narayan, and Anne R. Pebley. 2010. "Family and Neighborhood Sources of Socioeconomic Inequality in Children's Achievement." *Demography* 47:777–800.

Schwarzer, Mitchell. 2005. "The Spectacle of Ordinary Building." In *Sprawl and Suburbia,* edited by William S. Saunders. Minneapolis: University of Minnesota Press.

Secret, Mosi, and Karen Zraick. 2010. "5 at Columbia Are Charged in Drug Sales." *New York Times,* December 8, A27.

Self, Robert O. 2003. *American Babylon: Race and the Struggle for Postwar Oakland.* Princeton, NJ: Princeton University Press.

Sevigny, Eric, and Jonathan P. Caulkins. 2004. "Kingpins or Mules: An Analysis of Drug Offenders Incarcerated in Federal and State Prisons." *Criminology and Public Policy* 3:101–35.

Sharkey, Patrick. 2008. "The Intergenerational Transmission of Context." *American Journal of Sociology* 113:931–69.

———. 2010. "The Acute Effect of Local Homicides on Children's Cognitive Performance." *Proceedings of the National Academy of Sciences* 107:11733–38.

———. 2013. *Stuck in Place: Urban Neighborhoods and the End of Progress toward Racial Equality.* Chicago: University of Chicago Press.

Siennick, Sonja E. 2011. "Tough Love? Crime and Parental Assistance in Young Adulthood." *Criminology* 49:163–95.

Simons, Ronald L., and Callie Harbin Burt. 2011. "Learning to Be Bad: Adverse Social Conditions, Social Schemas, and Crime." *Criminology* 49:553–98.

Skolnick, Jerome H. 2007. "Racial Profiling—Then and Now." *Criminology and Public Policy* 6:65–70.

Snyder, Howard N., and Melissa Sickmund. 2006. *Juvenile Offenders and Victims: 2006 National Report*. Washington, DC: National Institute of Justice. Accessed March 3, 2013. http://www.ojjdp.gov/ojstatbb/nr2006/downloads/NR2006.pdf.

Sober, Elliot, and David Sloan Wilson. 1998. *Unto Others: The Evolution and Psychology of Unselfish Behavior*. Cambridge, MA: Harvard University Press.

Stearns, Peter N. 1994. *American Cool: Constructing a Twentieth-Century Emotional Style*. New York: New York University Press.

Stewart, Eric A. 2007. "Either They Don't Know or They Don't Care: Black Males and Negative Police Experiences." *Criminology and Public Policy* 7:123–30.

Stewart, Eric A., Christopher J. Schreck, and Ronald L. Simons. 2006. "'I Ain't Gonna Let No One Disrespect Me': Does the Code of the Street Reduce or Increase Violent Victimization among African American Adolescents?" *Journal of Research in Crime and Delinquency* 43:427–58.

Stewart, Eric A., and Ronald L. Simons. 2010. "Race, Code of the Street, and Violent Delinquency: A Multilevel Investigation of Neighborhood Street Culture and Individual Norms of Violence." *Criminology* 48:569–605.

Stilgoe, John R. 1988. *Borderland: Origins of the American Suburb, 1820–1939*. New Haven, CT: Yale University Press.

St. Jean, Peter K. B. 2007. *Pockets of Crime: Broken Windows, Collective Efficacy, and the Criminal Point of View*. Chicago: University of Chicago Press.

Stoll, Michael A., and Shawn D. Bushway. 2008. "The Effect of Criminal Background Checks on Hiring Ex-Offenders." *Criminology and Public Policy* 7:371–404.

Sutherland, Edwin Hardin. 1937. *The Professional Thief*. Chicago: University of Chicago Press.

Sykes, Gresham M., and David Matza. 1957. "Techniques of Neutralization: A Theory of Delinquency." *American Sociological Review* 22:664–70.

Taylor, Angela P. 2007. *How Drug Dealers Settle Disputes: Violent and Nonviolent Outcomes*. Monsey, NY: Criminal Justice Press.

Teaford, John. 2006. *The Metropolitan Revolution: The Rise of Post-urban America*. New York: Columbia University Press.

———. 2008. *The American Suburb: The Basics*. New York: Routledge.

Tewksbury, Richard, and Elizabeth Ehrhardt Mustaine. 1998. "Lifestyle of the Wheelers and Dealers: Drug Dealing among American College Students." *Journal of Crime and Justice* 21:37–56.

Thompson, Melissa, and Christopher Uggen. 2012. "Dealers, Thieves, and the Common Determinants of Drug and Nondrug Illegal Earnings." *Criminology* 50:1057–87.

Toby, Jackson. 1957. "Social Disorganization and Stake in Conformity: Complementary Factors in the Predatory Behavior of Hoodlums." *Journal of Criminal Law, Criminology, and Police Science* 48:12–17.

Topalli, Volkan. 2005. "When Being Good Is Bad: An Expansion of Neutralization Theory." *Criminology* 43:797–836.

Topalli, Volkan, and Richard Wright. 2003. "Dubs and Dees, Beats and Rims: Carjackers and Urban Violence." In *Crime Types: A Text Reader,* edited by Dean Dabney. Belmont, CA: Wadsworth.

Topalli, Volkan, Richard Wright, and Robert Fornango. 2002. "Drug Dealers, Robbery and Retaliation: Vulnerability, Deterrence, and the Contagion of Violence." *British Journal of Criminology* 42:337–51.

Uggen, Christopher, and Melissa Thompson. 2003. "The Socioeconomic Determinants of Ill-Gotten Gains: Within-Person Changes in Drug Use and Illegal Earnings." *American Journal of Sociology* 109:146–85.

Vaisey, Stephen. 2009. "Motivation and Justification: A Dual-Process Model of Culture in Action." *American Journal of Sociology* 114:1675–1715.

VanNostrand, Lisa-Marie, and Richard Tewksbury. 1999. "The Motives and Mechanics of Operating an Illegal Drug Enterprise." *Deviant Behavior* 20:57–83.

Veblen, Thorstein. (1899) 1994. *The Theory of the Leisure Class.* New York: Dover.

Venkatesh, Sudhir. 2006. *Off the Books: The Underground Economy of the Urban Poor.* Cambridge, MA: Harvard University Press.

———. 2008. *Gang Leader for a Day: A Rogue Sociologist Takes to the Streets.* New York: Penguin Press.

Venturi, Robert, Denise Scott Brown, and Steven Izenour. 1977. *Learning from Las Vegas.* Boston: MIT Press.

Wakefield, Sara, and Christopher Uggen. 2010. "Incarceration and Stratification." *Annual Review of Sociology* 36:387–406.

Waldorf, Dan, and Sheigla Murphy. 1995. "Perceived Risks and Criminal Justice Pressures on Middle Class Cocaine Sellers." *Journal of Drug Issues* 25:11–32.

Waldorf, Dan, Sheigla Murphy, and David Lauderback. 1994. "Middle-Class Cocaine Sellers: Self-Reported Reasons for Stopping Sales." *Addiction Research* 2:109–26.

Waldorf, Dan, Craig Reinarman, and Sheigla Murphy. 1991. *Cocaine Changes: The Experience of Using and Quitting.* Philadelphia: Temple University Press.

Warner, Sam Bass, Jr. 1978. *Streetcar Suburbs: The Process of Growth in Boston, 1870–1900.* 2nd ed. Cambridge, MA: Harvard University Press.

Weisheit, Ralph A. 1991. "The Intangible Rewards from Crime: The Case of Domestic Marijuana Cultivation." *Crime and Delinquency* 37:506–27.

Western, Bruce. 2002. "The Impact of Incarceration on Wage Mobility and Inequality." *American Sociological Review* 67:526–46.

———. 2006. *Punishment and Inequality in America.* New York: Russell Sage Foundation.

———. 2007. "The Penal System and the Labor Market." In *Barriers to Reentry? The Labor Market for Released Prisoners in Post-industrial America,* edited by Shawn Bushway, Michael A. Stoll, and David F. Weiman. New York: Russell Sage Foundation.

Western, Bruce, and Katherine Beckett. 1999. "How Unregulated Is the U.S. Labor Market? The Penal System as a Labor Market Institution." *American Journal of Sociology* 104:1030–60.

Western, Bruce, Jeffrey R. Kling, and David F. Weiman. 2001. "The Labor Market Consequences of Incarceration." *Crime and Delinquency* 47:410–27.

Whyte, William Foote. 1993. *Street Corner Society: The Social Structure of an Italian Slum.* 4th ed. Chicago: University of Chicago Press.

Wiese, Andrew. 2004. *Places of Their Own: African American Suburbanization in the Twentieth Century.* Chicago: University of Chicago Press.

Wilkinson, Deanna L., Chauncey C. Beaty, and Regina M. Lurry. 2009. "Youth Violence— Crime or Self-Help? Marginalized Urban Males' Perspectives on the Limited Efficacy of the Criminal Justice System to Stop Youth Violence." *Annals of the American Academy of Political and Social Sciences* 623:25–38.

Williams, Terry. 1989. *The Cocaine Kids: The Inside Story of a Teenage Drug Ring.* New York: Perseus Books.

Wilson, James Q., and George L. Kelling. 1982. "Broken Windows: The Police and Neighborhood Safety." *Atlantic Monthly* 249:29–38.

Wilson, William Julius. 1987. *The Truly Disadvantaged: The Inner City, the Underclass, and Public Policy.* Chicago: University of Chicago Press.

———. 1996. *When Work Disappears: The World of the New Urban Poor.* New York: Alfred A. Knopf.

———. 2009. *More Than Just Race: Being Black and Poor in the Inner City.* New York: W. W. Norton.

Wilson, William Julius, and Richard P. Taub. 2007. *There Goes the Neighborhood: Racial, Ethnic, and Class Tensions in Four Chicago Neighborhoods and Their Meaning for America.* New York: Vintage Books.

Wodtke, Geoffrey T., David J. Harding, and Felix Elwert. 2011. "Neighborhood Effects in Temporal Perspective: The Impact of Long-Term Exposure to Concentrated Disadvantage on High School Graduation." *American Sociological Review* 76:713–36.

Wolfgang, Marvin E., and Franco Ferracuti. 1967. *The Subculture of Violence: Towards an Integrated Theory in Criminology.* New York: Tavistock.

Wooden, Wayne S., and Randy Blazak. 2001. *Renegade Kids, Suburban Outlaws: From Youth Culture to Delinquency.* 2nd ed. Belmont, CA: Wadsworth.

Wright, Gwendolyn. 1981. *Building the Dream: A Social History of Housing in America.* Cambridge, MA: MIT Press.

Wright, John Paul, Francis T. Cullen, and Nicolas Williams. 1997. "Working While in School and Delinquent Involvement: Implications for Social Policy." *Crime and Delinquency* 43:203–21.

Wright, Richard, and Scott Decker. 1994. *Burglars on the Job: Streetlife and Residential Break-Ins.* Boston: Northeastern University Press.

———. 1997. *Armed Robbers in Action: Stickups and Street Culture.* Boston: Northeastern University Press.

Wyden, Peter. 1962. *Suburbia's Coddled Kids.* Garden City, NJ: Doubleday.

Young, Alford A. 2004. *The Minds of Marginalized Black Men: Making Sense of Mobility, Opportunity, and Future Life Chances.* Princeton, NJ: Princeton University Press.

Zimring, Franklin E., and Gordon Hawkins. 1997. *Crime Is Not the Problem: Lethal Violence in America.* New York: Oxford University Press.

INDEX

Page numbers in italics refer to figures.

"adolescent-limited offenders" (ALOs),
165–66n13
Anderson, Elijah, 147–48
avoidance, as conflict management tactic
used by suburban drug dealers, 100–
106, 108–9, 159

Black urban youth: and greater impact of
criminal record on employment opportunities than for White youth, 152;
limited educational opportunities for
and job skills of, 144–45; as more likely
than White youth to be arrested and
imprisoned for drug dealing, 150–52.
See also urban drug dealers

cell phones, as means of establishing deals,
47–48, 79–80
"chilling," 39–40
class. *See* social class
"code of the street," 155, 156
"code of the suburb," 99–100, 103–4, 113,
114, 118, 123, 158
conflict management, of suburban drug
dealers: through avoidance, 100–106,
108–9, 159; choice of less confrontational response, 113; "code of the
suburb" in, 100, 103–4; led dealers
to reevaluate chances of trouble with
parents or the law, 123–25; as most
common problem leading dealers to

stop selling drugs, 122–27; through
negotiation, 106–10, 159; through
sneaky retaliation, 110–14, 159; through
toleration, 98–100, 109, 159
conventionality, and suburban drug dealers, 122–36; and coolness as countermeasure to lack of conventional success,
5–7, 142–46; value of victimization in
maintaining, 122–27
coolness: versus conventionality, 142–46;
as countermeasure to lack of conventional success, 5–7, 142–46; derived
from attractiveness and likableness,
6, 140; enhancement of for suburban
drug dealers, 21–23, 44, 133, 140–41,
145–46; enhancement of for urban
drug dealers, 145–46; equation with
friendship, 43; equation with number
of friends, 43; establishing, 27–28; and
"hooking up," 58; importance of in
lives of teens, 21, 76; psychological and
social benefits of, 6
customers, acquiring in suburbs: friends of
dealers, 42–44; "friends-of-friends," 43–
44, 69; limited number of females, 46–
47; primarily White suburban males,
45–47; workplace colleagues, 44–45
customers, dealing with in suburbs, 47–63;
customer filtering, 48, 68–71, 84–87;
dealers' illusion of busyness when drugs
are not available, 51–52; dealers' illu-

34897578R00123

Made in the USA
Middletown, DE
30 January 2019